Excel® Power Pivot & Power Query

FOR

DUMMIES®

A Wiley Brand

Excel® Power Pivot & Power Query

FOR DUMMIES®

A Wiley Brand

by Michael Alexander

FOR DUMMIES®

A Wiley Brand

Excel® Power Pivot & Power Query For Dummies®

Published by: **John Wiley & Sons, Inc.,** 111 River Street, Hoboken, NJ 07030-5774, www.wiley.com

Copyright © 2016 by John Wiley & Sons, Inc., Hoboken, New Jersey

Published simultaneously in Canada

For general information on our other products and services, please contact our Customer Care Department within the U.S. at 877-762-2974, outside the U.S. at 317-572-3993, or fax 317-572-4002. For technical support, please visit www.wiley.com/techsupport.

Wiley publishes in a variety of print and electronic formats and by print-on-demand. Some material included with standard print versions of this book may not be included in e-books or in print-on-demand. If this book refers to media such as a CD or DVD that is not included in the version you purchased, you may download this material at http://booksupport.wiley.com. For more information about Wiley products, visit www.wiley.com.

Library of Congress Control Number: 2016933854

ISBN 978-1-119-21064-1 (pbk); ISBN 978-1-119-21066-5 (ebk); ISBN 978-1-119-21065-8 (ebk)

Manufactured in the United States of America

10 9 8 7 6 5 4 3 2 1

Contents at a Glance

Table of Contents

Introduction

Over the past few years, the concept of self-service business intelligence (BI) has taken over the corporate world. Self-service BI is a form of business intelligence in which end users can independently generate their own reports, run their own queries, and conduct their own analyses, without the need to engage the IT department.

The demand for self-service BI is a direct result of several factors:

- ✔ **More power users:** Organizations are realizing that no single enterprise reporting system or BI tool can accommodate all of their users. Predefined reports and high-level dashboards may be sufficient for casual users, but a large portion of today's users are savvy enough to be considered power users. Power users have a greater understanding of data analysis and prefer to perform their own analysis, often within Excel.

- ✔ **Changing analytical needs:** In the past, business intelligence primarily consisted of IT-managed dashboards showing historic data on an agreed-upon set of key performance metrics. Managers now demand more dynamic predictive analysis, the ability to perform data discovery iteratively, and the freedom to take the hard left and right turns on data presentation. These managers often turn to Excel to provide the needed analytics and visualization tools.

- ✔ **Speed of BI:** Users are increasingly dissatisfied with the inability of IT to quickly deliver new reporting and metrics. Most traditional BI implementations fail specifically because the need for changes and answers to new questions overwhelmingly outpaces the IT department's ability to deliver them. As a result, users often find ways to work around the perceived IT bottleneck and ultimately build their own shadow BI (under the radar) solutions in Excel.

Recognizing the importance of the self-service BI revolution and the role Excel plays in it, Microsoft has made substantial investments in making Excel the cornerstone of its self-service BI offering. These investments have appeared starting with Excel 2007. Here are a few of note: the ability to handle over a million rows, tighter integration to SQL Server, pivot table slicers, and not least of all, the introduction of the Power Pivot and Power Query add-ins.

With the release of Excel 2016, Microsoft has aggressively moved to make Excel a player in the self-service BI arena by embedding both Power Pivot and Power Query directly into Excel.

For the first time, Excel is an integral part of the Microsoft BI stack. You can integrate multiple data sources, define relationships between data sources, process analysis services cubes, and develop interactive dashboards that can be shared on the web. Indeed, the new Microsoft BI tools blur the line between Excel analysis and what is traditionally IT enterprise-level data management and reporting capabilities.

With these new tools in the Excel wheelhouse, it's becoming important for business analysts to expand their skill sets to new territory, including database management, query design, data integration, multidimensional reporting, and a host of other skills. Excel analysts have to expand their skill set knowledge base from the one-dimensional spreadsheets to relational databases, data integration, and multidimensional reporting,

That's where this book comes in. Here, you're introduced to the mysterious world of Power Pivot and Power Query. You find out how to leverage the rich set of tools and reporting capabilities to save time, automate data clean-up, and substantially enhance your data analysis and reporting capabilities.

About This Book

The goal of this book is to give you a solid overview of the self-service BI functionality offered by Power Pivot and Power Query. Each chapter guides you through practical techniques that enable you to

- Extract data from databases and external files for use in Excel reporting
- Scrape and import data from the web
- Build automated processes to clean and transform data
- Easily slice data into various views on the fly, gaining visibility from different perspectives
- Analyze large amounts of data and report them in a meaningful way
- Create powerful, interactive reporting mechanisms and dashboards

Foolish Assumptions

Over the past few years, Microsoft has adopted an agile release cycle, allowing the company to release updates to Microsoft Office and the power BI tools practically monthly. This is great news for those who love seeing new features added to Power Pivot and Power Query. (It's not-so-great news if you're trying to document the features of these tools in a book.)

My assumption is that Microsoft will continue to add new bells and whistles to Power Pivot and Power Query at a rapid pace after publication of this book. So you may encounter new functionality not covered here.

The good news is that both Power Pivot and Power Query have stabilized and already have a broad feature set. So I'm also assuming that although changes will be made to these tools, they won't be so drastic as to turn this book into a doorstop. The core functionality covered in these chapters will remain relevant — even if the mechanics change a bit.

How This Book Is Organized

The chapters in this book are organized into three parts. Part I focuses on Power Pivot. Part II explores Power Query. Part III wraps up the book with the classic Part of Tens.

Part I: Supercharged Reporting with Power Pivot

Part I is all about getting you started with Power Pivot. Chapters 1 and 2 start you off with basic Power Query functionality and the fundamentals of data management. Chapter 3 provides an overview of pivot tables — the cornerstone of Microsoft BI analysis and presentation. In Chapters 4 and 5, you discover how to develop powerful reporting with external data and the Power Pivot data model. Chapter 6 focuses on creating and managing calculations and formulas in Power Pivot. Chapter 7 rounds out Part I with a look at publishing your Power Pivot reports.

Part II: Wrangling Data with Power Query

In Part II, you take an in-depth look at the functionality found in Power Query. Chapters 8 and 9 present the fundamentals of creating queries and connecting to various data sources, respectively. Chapter 10 shows you how you can leverage Power Query to automate and simply the steps for cleaning and transforming data. In Chapter 11, you see some options for making queries work together. Chapter 12 wraps up this look at Power Query with an exploration of custom functions and a description of how to leverage recorded steps to create your own amazing functions.

Part III: The Part of Tens

Part III is the classic Part of Tens section found in titles in the *For Dummies* series. The chapters in this part present ten or more pearls of wisdom, delivered in bite-size pieces. In Chapter 13, I share with you ten ways to improve the performance of your Power Pivot reports. Chapter 14 offers a rundown of ten tips for getting the most out of Power Query.

Icons Used In This Book

As you look in various places in this book, you see icons in the margins that indicate material of interest (or not, as the case may be). This section briefly describes each icon in this book.

Tips are beneficial because they help you save time or perform a task without having to do a lot of extra work. The tips in this book are time-saving techniques or pointers to resources that you should check out to get the maximum benefit from Excel.

Try to avoid doing anything marked with a Warning icon, which (as you might expect) represents a danger of one sort or another.

Whenever you see this icon, think *advanced* tip or technique. You might find these tidbits of useful information just too boring for words, or they could contain the solution you need to get a program running. Skip these bits of information whenever you like.

If you get nothing else out of a particular chapter or section, remember the material marked by this icon. This text usually contains an essential process or a bit of information you ought to remember.

Paragraphs marked with this icon reference the sample files for the book. If you want to follow along with the examples, you can download the sample files at www.dummies.com/go/powerpivotpowerqueryfd. The files are organized by chapter.

Beyond the Book

A lot of extra content that you won't find in this book is available at www.dummies.com. Go online to find the following:

- ✔ **Excel files used in the examples in this book can be found at**

  www.dummies.com/go/excelpowerpivotpowerqueryfd

- ✔ **Online articles covering additional topics are at**

  www.dummies.com/extras/excelpowerpivotpowerquery

  On this page, you can see how to integrate Power Pivot and Power Query to create a dynamic reporting duo. You can also uncover a list of resources to aid you in your Power BI journey.

- ✔ **The Cheat Sheet for this book is at**

  www.dummies.com/cheatsheet/excelpowerpivotpowerquery

  On this page, you find a list of useful Power Query functions that can be used to enhance the data clean-up and transformation process.

- ✔ **Updates to this book, if we have any, are also available at**

  www.dummies.com/extras/excelpowerpivotpowerquery

Where to Go from Here

It's time to start your self-service BI adventure! If you're primarily interested in Power Pivot, start with Chapter 1. If you want to dive right into Power Query, jump to Part II, which begins at Chapter 8.

Part I

Supercharged Reporting with Power Pivot

In this part . . .

- ✔ Discover how to think about data like a relational database.
- ✔ Get a solid understanding of the fundamentals of Power Pivot and pivot table reporting.
- ✔ Uncover the best practices for creating calculated columns and fields using Power Pivot formulas.
- ✔ Explore a few options for publishing your Power Pivot report.

Chapter 1

Thinking Like a Database

In This Chapter

▶ Examining traditional Excel limitations

▶ Keeping up with database terminology

▶ Looking into relationships

With the introduction of business intelligence (BI) tools such as Power Pivot and Power Query, it's becoming increasingly important for Excel analysts to understand core database principles. Unlike traditional Excel concepts, where the approach to developing solutions is relatively intuitive, you need to have a basic understanding of database terminology and architecture in order to get the most benefit from Power Pivot and Power Query. This chapter introduces you to a handful of fundamental concepts that you should know before taking on the rest of this book.

Exploring the Limits of Excel and How Databases Help

Years of consulting experience have brought this humble author face to face with managers, accountants, and analysts who all have had to accept this simple fact: Their analytical needs had outgrown Excel. They all faced fundamental challenges that stemmed from one or more of Excel's three problem areas: scalability, transparency of analytical processes, and separation of data and presentation.

Scalability

Scalability is the ability of an application to develop flexibly to meet growth and complexity requirements. In the context of this chapter, scalability refers to Excel's ability to handle ever-increasing volumes of data. Most Excel aficionados are quick to point out that as of Excel 2007, you can place 1,048,576 rows of data into a single Excel worksheet — an overwhelming increase from the limitation of 65,536 rows imposed by previous versions of Excel. However, this increase in capacity does not solve all the scalability issues that inundate Excel.

Imagine that you're working in a small company and using Excel to analyze its daily transactions. As time goes on, you build a robust process complete with all the formulas, pivot tables, and macros you need in order to analyze the data that is stored in your neatly maintained worksheet.

As the amount of data grows, you will first notice performance issues. The spreadsheet will become slow to load and then slow to calculate. Why does this happen? It has to do with the way Excel handles memory. When an Excel file is loaded, the entire file is loaded into RAM. Excel does this to allow for quick data processing and access. The drawback to this behavior is that every time the data in your spreadsheet changes, Excel has to reload the entire document into RAM. The net result in a large spreadsheet is that it takes a great deal of RAM to process even the smallest change. Eventually, every action you take in the gigantic worksheet is preceded by an excruciating wait.

Your pivot tables will require bigger pivot caches, almost doubling the Excel workbook's file size. Eventually, the workbook will become too big to distribute easily. You may even consider breaking down the workbook into smaller workbooks (possibly one for each region). This causes you to duplicate your work.

In time, you may eventually reach the 1,048,576-row limit of the worksheet. What happens then? Do you start a new worksheet? How do you analyze two datasets on two different worksheets as one entity? Are your formulas still good? Will you have to write new macros?

These are all issues that need to be addressed.

Of course, you will also encounter the Excel power customers, who will find various clever ways to work around these limitations. In the end, though, these methods will always be simply workarounds. Eventually, even these power-customers will begin to think less about the most effective way to perform and present analysis of their data and more about how to make data "fit" into Excel without breaking their formulas and functions. Excel is flexible enough that a proficient customer can make most things fit just fine. However, when customers think only in terms of Excel, they're undoubtedly limiting themselves, albeit in an incredibly functional way.

In addition, these capacity limitations often force Excel customers to have the data prepared for them. That is, someone else extracts large chunks of data from a large database and then aggregates and shapes the data for use in Excel. Should the serious analyst always be dependent on someone else for her data needs? What if an analyst could be given the tools to access vast quantities of data without being reliant on others to provide data? Could that analyst be more valuable to the organization? Could that analyst focus on the accuracy of the analysis and the quality of the presentation instead of routing Excel data maintenance?

A relational database system (such as Access or SQL Server) is a logical next step for the analyst who faces an ever-increasing data pool. Database systems don't usually have performance implications with large amounts of stored data, and are built to address large volumes of data. An analyst can then handle larger datasets without requiring the data to be summarized or prepared to fit into Excel. Also, if a process ever becomes more crucial to the organization and needs to be tracked in a more enterprise-acceptable environment, it will be easier to upgrade and scale up if that process is already in a relational database system.

Transparency of analytical processes

One of Excel's most attractive features is its flexibility. Each individual cell can contain text, a number, a formula, or practically anything else the customer defines. Indeed, this is one of the fundamental reasons that Excel is an effective tool for data analysis. Customers can use named ranges, formulas, and macros to create an intricate system of interlocking calculations, linked cells, and formatted summaries that work together to create a final analysis.

So what is the problem? The problem is that there is no transparency of analytical processes. It is extremely difficult to determine what is actually going on in a spreadsheet. Anyone who has had to work with a spreadsheet created by someone else knows all too well the frustration that comes with deciphering the various gyrations of calculations and links being used to perform analysis. Small spreadsheets that are performing modest analysis are painful to decipher, and large, elaborate, multi-worksheet workbooks are virtually impossible to decode, often leaving you to start from scratch.

Compared to Excel, database systems might seem rigid, strict, and unwavering in their rules. However, all this rigidity comes with a benefit.

Because only certain actions are allowable, you can more easily come to understand what is being done within structured database objects such as queries or stored procedures. If a dataset is being edited, a number is being calculated, or any portion of the dataset is being affected as part of an analytical process, you can readily see that action by reviewing the query syntax or the stored procedure code. Indeed, in a relational database system, you never encounter hidden formulas, hidden cells, or dead named ranges.

Separation of data and presentation

Data should be separate from presentation; you don't want the data to become too tied into any particular way of presenting it. For example, when you receive an invoice from a company, you don't assume that the financial data on that invoice is the true source of your data. It is *a presentation of* your data. It can be presented to you in other manners and styles on charts or on websites, but such representations are never the actual source of the data.

What exactly does this concept have to do with Excel? People who perform data analysis with Excel tend, more often than not, to fuse the data, the analysis, and the presentation. For example, you often see an Excel workbook that has 12 worksheets, each representing a month. On each worksheet, data for that month is listed along with formulas, pivot tables, and summaries. What happens when you're asked to provide a summary by quarter? Do you add more formulas and worksheets to consolidate the data on each of the month worksheets? The fundamental problem in this scenario is that the worksheets actually represent data values that are fused into the presentation of the analysis.

The point being made here is that data should not be tied to a particular presentation, no matter how apparently logical or useful it may be. However, in Excel, it happens all the time.

In addition, as discussed earlier in this chapter, because all manners and phases of analysis can be done directly within a spreadsheet, Excel cannot effectively provide adequate transparency to the analysis. Each cell has the potential to hold formulas, be hidden, and contain links to other cells. In Excel, this blurs the line between analysis and data, which makes it difficult to determine exactly what is going on in a spreadsheet. Moreover, it takes a great deal of effort in the way of manual maintenance to ensure that edits and unforeseen changes don't affect previous analyses.

Relational database systems inherently separate analytical components into tables, queries, and reports. By separating these elements, databases make data less sensitive to changes and create a data analysis environment in which you can easily respond to new requests for analysis without destroying previous analyses.

You may find that you manipulate Excel's functionalities to approximate this database behavior. If so, you must consider that if you're using Excel's functionality to make it behave like a database application, perhaps the real thing just might have something to offer. Utilizing databases for data storage and analytical needs would enhance overall data analysis and would allow Excel power-customers to focus on the presentation in their spreadsheets.

In these days of big data, customers demand more, not less, complex data analysis. Excel analysts will need to add tools to their repertoires to avoid being simply "spreadsheet mechanics." Excel can be stretched to do just about anything, but maintaining such creative solutions can be a tedious manual task. You can be sure that the sexy aspect of data analysis does not lie in the routine data management within Excel; rather, it lies in leveraging BI Tools such as providing clients with the best solution for any situation.

Getting to Know Database Terminology

The terms *database, table, record, field,* and *value* indicate a hierarchy from largest to smallest. These same terms are used with virtually all database systems, so you should learn them well.

Databases

Generally, the word *database* is a computer term for a collection of information concerning a certain topic or business application. A database helps you organize this related information in a logical fashion for easy access and retrieval. Certain older database systems used the term *database* to describe individual tables. The current use of *database* applies to all elements of a database system.

Databases aren't only for computers. Manual databases are sometimes referred to as manual filing systems or manual database systems. These filing systems usually consist of people, papers, folders, and filing cabinets — paper is the key to a manual database system. In a real-life manual database system, you probably have in-baskets and out-baskets and some type of formal filing method. You access information manually by opening a file cabinet, removing a file folder, and finding the correct piece of paper. Customers fill out paper forms for input, perhaps by using a keyboard to input information that is printed on forms. You find information by manually sorting the papers or by copying information from many papers to another piece of paper (or even into an Excel spreadsheet). You may use a spreadsheet or calculator to analyze the data or display it in new and interesting ways.

Tables

A database stores information in a carefully defined structure known as a table. A *table* is just a container for raw information (called *data*), similar to a folder in a manual filing system. Each table in a database contains information about a single entity, such as a person or product, and the data in the table is organized into rows and columns. A relational database system stores data in related tables. For example, a table containing employee data (names and addresses) may be related to a table containing payroll information (pay date, pay amount, and check number).

To use database wording, a table is an object. As you design and work with databases, it's important to see each table as a unique entity and to see how each table relates to the other objects in the database.

In most database systems, you can view the contents of a table in a spreadsheet-like form called a *datasheet,* composed of rows and columns (known as *records* and *fields,* respectively — see the following section). Although a datasheet and a spreadsheet are superficially similar, a datasheet is quite a different type of object. You typically cannot make changes or add calculations directly within a table. Your interaction with tables will primarily come in the form of queries or views — see the later section "Queries").

Records, fields, and values

A database table is divided into rows (called *records*) and columns (called *fields*), with the first row (the heading on top of each column) containing the names of the fields in the database.

Each row is a single record containing fields that are related to that record. In a manual system, the rows are individual forms (sheets of paper), and the fields are equivalent to the blank areas on a printed form that you fill in.

Each column is a field that includes many properties specifying the type of data contained within the field and how the database should handle the field's data. These properties include the name of the field (Company) and the type of data in the field (Text). A field may include other properties as well. For example, the Address field's Size property tells the database the maximum number of characters allowed for the address.

At the intersection of a record and a field is a *value* — the actual data element. For example, in a field named Company, a company name entered into that field would represent one data value.

When working with Microsoft Access, the term *field* is used to refer to an attribute stored in a record. In many other database systems, including SQL Server, *column* is the expression you hear most often in place of *field* — field and column mean the same thing. The exact terminology that's used relies somewhat on the context of the database system underlying the table containing the record.

Queries

Most relational database systems allow the creation of queries (sometimes called views). A query extracts information from the tables in the database; a query selects and defines a group of records that fulfill a certain condition. Most database outputs are based on queries that combine, filter, or sort data before it's displayed. Queries are often called from other database objects, such as stored procedures, macros, or code modules. In addition to extracting data from tables, queries can be used to change, add, or delete database records.

An example of a query is when a person at the sales office tells the database, "Show me all customers, in alphabetical order by name, who are located in Massachusetts and who made a purchase over the past six months." Or "Show me all customers who bought Chevrolet car models within the past six months, and display them sorted by customer name and then by sale date."

Rather than ask the question using English words, a person uses a special syntax, such as Structured Query Language (or SQL), to communicate to the database what the query will need to do.

Understanding Relationships

After you understand the basic terminology of databases, it's time to focus on one of their more useful features: A *relationship* is the mechanism by which separate tables are related to each other. You can think of a relationship as a VLOOKUP, in which you relate the data in one data range to the data in another data range using an index or a unique identifier. In databases, relationships do the same thing, but without the hassle of writing formulas.

Relationships are important because most of the data you work with fits into a multidimensional hierarchy of sorts. For example, you may have a table showing customers who buy products. These customers require invoices that have invoice numbers. Those invoices have multiple lines of transactions listing what they bought. A hierarchy exists there.

Now, in the one-dimensional spreadsheet world, this data typically would be stored in a flat table, like the one shown in Figure 1-1.

	A	B	C	D	E	F
1	CustomerID	CustomerName	InvoiceNumber	InvoiceDate	Quantity	UnitPrice
2	BAKERSEM0001	Baker's Emporium Inc.	ORDST1025	5/8/2005	1	19.95
3	BAKERSEM0001	Baker's Emporium Inc.	ORDST1025	5/8/2005	5	1759.95
4	BAKERSEM0001	Baker's Emporium Inc.	ORDST1025	5/8/2005	4	9.95
5	BAKERSEM0001	Baker's Emporium Inc.	STDINV2251	4/12/2007	4	9.95
6	AARONFIT0001	Aaron Fitz Electrical	ORDST1026	5/8/2005	5	9.95
7	AARONFIT0001	Aaron Fitz Electrical	ORDST1026	5/8/2005	3	1759.95
8	AARONFIT0001	Aaron Fitz Electrical	ORDST1026	5/8/2005	2	79.95
9	AARONFIT0001	Aaron Fitz Electrical	STDINV2252	4/12/2007	3	1759.95
10	AARONFIT0001	Aaron Fitz Electrical	STDINV2252	4/12/2007	5	9.95
11	METROPOL0001	Metropolitan Fiber Systems	ORD1002	5/7/2004	1	9.95
12	AARONFIT0001	Aaron Fitz Electrical	INV1024	2/10/2004	1	119.95
13	AARONFIT0001	Aaron Fitz Electrical	INV1025	2/15/2004	1	109.95
14	LECLERC0001	LeClerc & Associates	ORDPH1005	5/10/2004	2	189.95
15	MAGNIFIC0001	Magnificent Office Images	ORD1000	5/8/2004	1	359.95
16	HOLLINGC0001	Holling Communications Inc.	ORD1001	5/10/2004	2	59.95
17	MAHLERST0001	Mahler State University	ORDST1008	5/10/2004	1	5999.95

Figure 1-1:
Data is stored in an Excel spreadsheet using a flat-table format.

Because customers have more than one invoice, the customer information (in this example, CustomerID and CustomerName) has to be repeated. This causes a problem when that data needs to be updated.

For example, imagine that the name of the company Aaron Fitz Electrical changes to Fitz and Sons Electrical. Looking at Figure 1-1, you see that multiple rows contain the old name. You would have to ensure that every row containing the old company name is updated to reflect the change. Any rows you miss will not correctly map back to the right customer.

Wouldn't it be more logical and efficient to record the name and information of the customer only one time? Then, rather than have to write the same customer information repeatedly, you could simply have some form of customer reference number.

This is the idea behind relationships. You can separate customers from invoices, placing each in their own tables. Then you can use a unique identifier (such as CustomerID) to relate them together.

Figure 1-2 illustrates how this data would look in a relational database. The data would be split into three separate tables: Customers, InvoiceHeader, and InvoiceDetails. Each table would then be related using unique identifiers (CustomerID and InvoiceNumber, in this case).

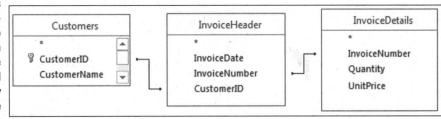

The Customers table would contain a unique record for each customer. That way, if you need to change a customer's name, you would need to make the change in only that record. Of course, in real life, the Customers table would include other attributes, such as customer address, customer phone number, and customer start date. Any of these other attributes could also be easily stored and managed in the Customers table.

The most common relationship type is a *one-to-many* relationship. That is, for each record in one table, one record can be matched to many records in a separate table. For example, an invoice header table is related to an invoice detail table. The invoice header table has a unique identifier: Invoice Number. The invoice detail will use the Invoice Number for every record representing a detail of that particular invoice.

Another kind of relationship type is the *one-to-one* relationship: For each record in one table, one and only one matching record is in a different table. Data from different tables in a one-to-one relationship can technically be combined into a single table.

Finally, in a *many-to-many* relationship, records in both tables can have any number of matching records in the other table. For instance, a database at a bank may have a table of the various types of loans (home loan, car loan, and so on) and a table of customers. A customer can have many types of loans. Meanwhile, each type of loan can be granted to many customers.

If your head is spinning from all this database talk, don't worry. You don't need to be an expert database modeler to use Power Pivot. But it's important to understand these concepts. The better you understand how data is stored and managed in databases, the more effectively you'll leverage Power Pivot for reporting.

Chapter 2

Introducing Power Pivot

● ●

● ●

*O*ver the past decade or so, corporate managers, eager to turn impossible amounts of data into useful information, drove the business intelligence (BI) industry to innovate new ways of synthesizing data into meaningful insights. During this period, organizations spent lots of time and money implementing big enterprise reporting systems to help keep up with the hunger for data analytics and dashboards.

Recognizing the importance of the BI revolution and the place that Excel holds within it, Microsoft proceeded to make substantial investments in improving Excel's BI capabilities. It specifically focused on Excel's *self-service* BI capabilities and its ability to better manage and analyze information from the increasing number of available data sources.

The key product of that endeavor was essentially Power Pivot (introduced in Excel 2010 as an add-In). With Power Pivot came the ability to set up relationships between large, disparate data sources. For the first time, Excel analysts were able to add a relational view to their reporting without the use of problematic functions such as VLOOKUPS. The ability to merge data sources with hundreds of thousands of rows into one analytical engine within Excel was groundbreaking.

With the release of Excel 2016, Microsoft incorporated Power Pivot directly into Excel. The powerful capabilities of Power Pivot are available out of the box!

In this chapter, you get an overview of those capabilities by exploring the key features, benefits, and capabilities of Power Pivot.

Understanding the Power Pivot Internal Data Model

At its core, Power Pivot is essentially a SQL Server Analysis Services engine made available by way of an in-memory process that runs directly within Excel. Its technical name is the xVelocity analytics engine. However, in Excel, it's referred to as the Internal Data Model.

Every Excel workbook contains an *Internal Data Model,* a single instance of the Power Pivot in-memory engine. The most effective way to interact with the Internal Data Model is to use the Power Pivot Ribbon interface, which becomes available when you activate the Power Pivot Add-In.

The Power Pivot Ribbon interface exposes the full set of functionality you don't get with the standard Excel Data tab. Here are a few examples of functionality available with the Power Pivot interface:

- ✔ You can browse, edit, filter, and apply custom sorting to data.
- ✔ You can create custom calculated columns that apply to all rows in the data import.
- ✔ You can define a default number format to use when the field appears in a pivot table.
- ✔ You can easily configure relationships via the handy Graphical Diagram view.
- ✔ You can choose to prevent certain fields from appearing in the Pivot Table Field List.

As with everything else in Excel, the Internal Data Model does have limitations. Most Excel users will not likely hit these limitations, because Power Pivot's compression algorithm is typically able to shrink imported data to about one-tenth its original size. For example, a 100MB text file would take up only approximately 10MB in the Internal Data Model.

Nevertheless, it's important to understand the maximum and configurable limits for Power Pivot Data Models. Table 2-1 highlights them.

Table 2-1	Limitations of the Internal Data Model
Object	**Specification**
Data model size	In 32-bit environments, Excel workbooks are subject to a 2GB limit. This includes the in-memory space shared by Excel, the Internal Data Model, and add-ins that run in the same process. In 64-bit environments, there are no hard limits on file size. Workbook size is limited only by available memory and system resources.
Number of tables in the data model	No hard limits exist on the count of tables. However, all tables in the data model cannot exceed 2,147,483,647 bytes.
Number of rows in each table in the data model	1,999,999,997
Number of columns and calculated columns in each table in the data model	The number cannot exceed 2,147,483,647 bytes.
Number of distinct values in a column	1,999,999,997
Characters in a column name	100 characters
String length in each field	It's limited to 536,870,912 bytes (512MB), equivalent to 268,435,456 Unicode characters (256 mega-characters).
Data model size	In 32-bit environments, Excel workbooks are subject to a 2GB limit. This includes the in-memory space shared by Excel, the Internal Data Model, and add-ins that run in the same process. In 64-bit environments, no hard limits on file size exist. Workbook size is limited only by available memory and system resources.
Number of tables in the data model	No hard limits exist on the count of tables. However, all tables in the data model cannot exceed 2,147,483,647 bytes.
Number of rows in each table in the data model	1,999,999,997
Number of columns and calculated columns in each table in the data model	The number cannot exceed 2,147,483,647 bytes.
Number of distinct values in a column	1,999,999,997

(continued)

Table 2-1 *(continued)*

Object	Specification
Characters in a column name	100 characters
String length in each field	It's limited to 536,870,912 bytes (512MB), equivalent to 268,435,456 Unicode characters (256 mega-characters).
Data model size	In 32-bit environments, Excel workbooks are subject to a 2GB limit. This includes the in-memory space shared by Excel, the Internal Data Model, and add-ins that run in the same process.

Activating the Power Pivot Add-In

As mentioned earlier in this chapter, the Power Pivot Ribbon interface is available only when you activate the Power Pivot Add-In. The Power Pivot Add-In does not install with every edition of Office. For example, if you have Office Home Edition, you cannot see or activate the Power Pivot Add-In and therefore cannot have access to the Power Pivot Ribbon interface.

As of this writing, the Power Pivot Add-In is available to you only if you have one of these editions of Office or Excel:

- ✔ **Office 2013 or 2016 Professional Plus:** Available only through volume licensing
- ✔ **Office 365 Pro Plus:** Available with an ongoing subscription to Office365.com
- ✔ **Excel 2013 or Excel 2016 Stand-alone Edition:** Available for purchase via any retailer

If you have any of these editions, you can activate the Power Pivot add-in by following these steps:

1. **Open Excel and look for the Power Pivot tab on the Ribbon.**

   If you see the tab, the Power Pivot add-in is already activated. You can skip the remaining steps.

2. **Go to the Excel Ribbon and choose File ➪ Options.**

3. **Choose the Add-Ins option on the left, and then look at the bottom of the dialog box for the Manage drop-down list. Select COM Add-Ins from that list, and then click Go.**

4. **Look for Microsoft Office Power Pivot for Excel in the list of available COM add-ins, and select the check box next to this option. Click OK.**

5. **If the Power Pivot tab does not appear in the Ribbon, close Excel and restart.**

After installing the add-in, you should see the Power Pivot tab on the Excel Ribbon, as shown in Figure 2-1.

Figure 2-1:
When the add-in has been activated, you see a new Power Pivot tab on the Ribbon.

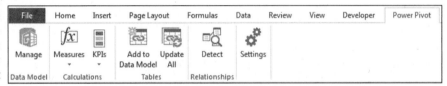

A word on compatibility

Since Excel 2010 was released, Microsoft has made several versions of the Power Pivot add-in available for download. Starting with Excel 2013, the add-in has been included out of the box with Excel. The bottom line is that different versions of Power Pivot are now being used, each designed to work with different versions of Excel. This situation obviously leads to some compatibility considerations you should be aware of.

You have to be careful when sharing Power Pivot workbooks in environments where some members of your audience are using earlier versions of Excel (Excel 2010, for example)

and others are using later versions of Excel. Opening and refreshing a workbook that contains a Power Pivot model created with an older version of the Power Pivot add-in triggers an automatic upgrade of the underlying model. After this happens, users with older versions of the add-in can no longer use the workbook.

As a general rule, Power Pivot workbooks created in a version of Excel that is equal to or less than your version should give you no problems. However, you cannot use Power Pivot workbooks created in a version of Excel greater than your version.

Linking Excel Tables to Power Pivot

The first step in using Power Pivot is to fill it with data. You can either import data from external data sources or link to Excel tables in your current workbook. I cover importing data from external data sources in Chapter 3. For now, let me start this walkthrough by showing you how to link three Excel tables to Power Pivot.

You can find the sample file for this chapter on this book's companion website at www.dummies.com/go/excelpowerpivotpowerqueryfd in the workbook named Chapter 2 Samples.xlsx.

In this scenario, you have three data sets in three different worksheets: Customers, InvoiceHeader, and InvoiceDetails (see Figure 2-2).

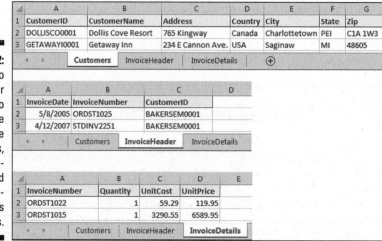

Figure 2-2: You want to use Power Pivot to analyze the data in the Customers, Invoice-Header, and Invoice-Details worksheets.

	A	B	C	D	E	F	G
1	CustomerID	CustomerName	Address	Country	City	State	Zip
2	DOLLISCO0001	Dollis Cove Resort	765 Kingway	Canada	Charlottetown	PEI	C1A 1W3
3	GETAWAYI0001	Getaway Inn	234 E Cannon Ave.	USA	Saginaw	MI	48605

Customers | InvoiceHeader | InvoiceDetails

	A	B	C	D
1	InvoiceDate	InvoiceNumber	CustomerID	
2	5/8/2005	ORDST1025	BAKERSEM0001	
3	4/12/2007	STDINV2251	BAKERSEM0001	

Customers | InvoiceHeader | InvoiceDetails

	A	B	C	D	E
1	InvoiceNumber	Quantity	UnitCost	UnitPrice	
2	ORDST1022	1	59.29	119.95	
3	ORDST1015	1	3290.55	6589.95	

Customers | InvoiceHeader | InvoiceDetails

The Customers data set contains basic information, such as CustomerID, Customer Name, and Address. The InvoiceHeader data set contains data that points specific invoices to specific customers. The InvoiceDetails data set contains the specifics of each invoice.

To analyze revenue by customer and month, it's clear that you first need to somehow join these three tables together. In the past, you would have to go through a series of gyrations involving VLOOKUP or other clever formulas. But with Power Pivot, you can build these relationships in just a few clicks.

Preparing Excel tables

When linking Excel data to Power Pivot, best practice is to first convert the Excel data to explicitly named tables. Although not technically necessary, giving tables friendly names helps track and manage your data in the Power Pivot data model. If you don't convert your data to tables first, Excel does it for you and gives your tables useless names like Table1, Table2, and so on.

Follow these steps to convert each data set into an Excel table:

1. **Go to the Customers tab and click anywhere inside the data range.**

2. **Press Ctrl+T on the keyboard.**

    This step opens the Create Table dialog box, shown in Figure 2-3.

Figure 2-3: Convert the data range into an Excel table.

3. **In the Create Table dialog box, ensure that the range for the table is correct and that the My Table Has Headers check box is selected. Click the OK button.**

    You should now see the Table Tools Design tab on the Ribbon.

4. **Click the Table Tools Design tab, and use the Table Name input to give your table a friendly name, as shown in Figure 2-4.**

    This step ensures that you can recognize the table when adding it to the Internal Data Model.

5. **Repeat Steps 1 through 4 for the Invoice Header and Invoice Details data sets.**

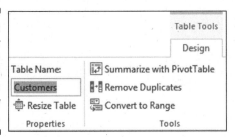

Figure 2-4: Give your newly created Excel table a friendly name.

Adding Excel Tables to the data model

After you convert your data to Excel tables, you're ready to add them to the Power Pivot data model. Follow these steps to add the newly created Excel tables to the data model using the Power Pivot tab:

1. **Place the cursor anywhere inside the Customers Excel table.**

2. **Go to the Power Pivot tab on the Ribbon and click the Add to Data Model command.**

Power Pivot creates a copy of the table and opens the Power Pivot window, shown in Figure 2-5.

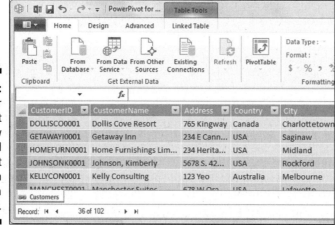

Figure 2-5:
The Power Pivot window shows all the data that exists in your data model.

Although the Power Pivot window looks like Excel, it's a separate program altogether. Notice that the grid for the Customers table has no row or column references. Also notice that you cannot edit the data within the table. This data is simply a snapshot of the Excel table you imported.

Additionally, if you look at the Windows taskbar at the bottom of the screen, you can see that Power Pivot has a separate window from Excel. You can switch between Excel and the Power Pivot window by clicking each respective program on the taskbar.

Repeat Steps 1 and 2 in the preceding list for your other Excel tables: Invoice Header, Invoice Details. After you've imported all your Excel tables into the data model, the Power Pivot window will show each dataset on its own tab, as shown in Figure 2-6.

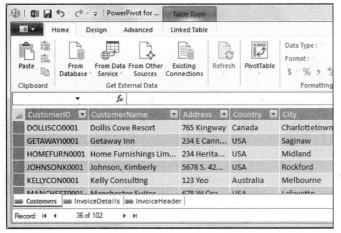

Figure 2-6:
Each table
you add to
the data
model is
placed on
its own tab
in Power
Pivot.

The tabs in the Power Pivot window shown in Figure 2-6 have a Hyperlink icon next to the tab names, indicating that the data contained in the tab is a linked Excel table. Even though the data is a snapshot of the data at the time you added it, the data automatically updates whenever you edit the source table in Excel.

Creating relationships between Power Pivot tables

At this point, Power Pivot knows that you have three tables in the data model but has no idea how the tables relate to one another. You connect these tables by defining relationships between the Customers, Invoice Details, and Invoice Header tables. You can do so directly within the Power Pivot window.

If you've inadvertently closed the Power Pivot window, you can easily reopen it by clicking the Manage command button on the Power Pivot Ribbon tab.

Follow these steps to create relationships between your tables:

1. **Activate the Power Pivot window and click the Diagram View command button on the Home tab.**

   The Power Pivot screen you see shows a visual representation of all tables in the data model, as shown in Figure 2-7.

   You can move the tables in Diagram view by simply clicking and dragging them.

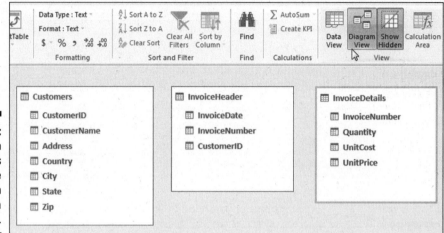

Figure 2-7:
Diagram
view allows
you to see
all tables in
the data
model.

The idea is to identify the primary index keys in each table and connect them. In this scenario, the Customers table and the Invoice Header table can be connected using the CustomerID field. The Invoice Header and Invoice Details tables can be connected using the InvoiceNumber field.

2. **Click and drag a line from the CustomerID field in the Customers table to the CustomerID field in the Invoice Header table, as demonstrated in Figure 2-8.**

3. **Click and drag a line from the InvoiceNumber field in the Invoice Header table to the InvoiceNumber field in the Invoice Details table.**

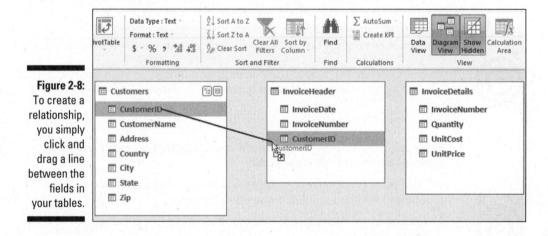

Figure 2-8:
To create a
relationship,
you simply
click and
drag a line
between the
fields in
your tables.

At this point, your diagram will look similar to Figure 2-9. Notice that Power Pivot shows a line between the tables you just connected. In database terms, these are referred to as *joins*.

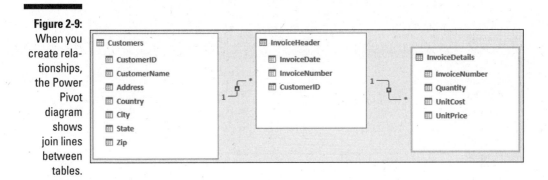

The joins in Power Pivot are always one-to-many joins. This means that when a table is joined to another, one of the tables has unique records with unique index numbers, while the other can have many records where index numbers are duplicated.

A common example, illustrated in Figure 2-9, is the relationship between the Customers table and the Invoice Header table. In the Customers table, you have a unique list of customers, each with its own, unique identifier. No CustomerID in that table is duplicated. The Invoice header table has many rows for each CustomerID; each customer can have many invoices.

Notice that the join lines have arrows pointing from a table to another table. The arrow in these join lines always points to the table that has the dupli-cated unique index.

To close the diagram and return to seeing the data tables, click the Data View command in the Power Pivot window.

Managing existing relationships

If you need to edit or delete a relationship between two tables in your data model, you can do so by following these steps:

1. **Open the Power Pivot window, select the Design tab, and then select the Manage Relationships command.**

2. In the Manage Relationships dialog box, shown in Figure 2-10, click the relationship you want to work with and click Edit or Delete.

Figure 2-10:
Use the
Manage
Relation-
ships dialog
box to edit
or delete
existing
relation-
ships.

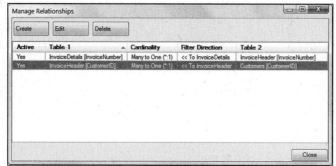

3. If you clicked Edit, the Edit Relationship dialog box appears, as shown in Figure 2-11. Use the drop-down and list box controls on this form to select the appropriate table and field names to redefine the relationship.

Figure 2-11:
Use the Edit
Relationship
dialog box
to adjust the
tables and
field names
that define
the selected
relationship.

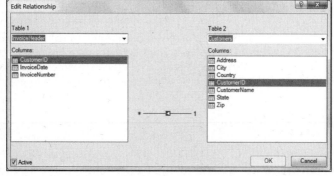

In Figure 2-11, you see a graphic of an arrow between the list boxes. The graphic has an asterisk next to the list box on the left, and a number 1 next to the list box on the right. The number 1 basically indicates that the model will use the table listed on the right as the source for a unique primary key.

Every relationship must have a field that you designate as the primary key. Primary key fields are necessary in the data model to prevent aggregation errors and duplications. In that light, the Excel data model must impose some strict rules around the primary key.

You cannot have any duplicates or null values in a field being used as the primary key. So the Customers table (refer to Figure 2-11) must have all unique values in the CustomerID field, with no blanks or null values. This is the only way that Excel can ensure data integrity when joining multiple tables.

At least one of your tables must contain a field that serves as a primary key — that is, a field that contains only unique values and no blanks.

Using the Power Pivot data model in reporting

After you define the relationships in your Power Pivot data model, it's essentially ready for action. In terms of Power Pivot, *action* means analysis with a pivot table. In fact, all Power Pivot data is presented through the framework of pivot tables.

In Chapter 3, you dive deep into the workings of pivot tables. For now, dip just a toe in and create a simple pivot table from your new Power Pivot data model:

1. **Activate the Power Pivot window, select the Home tab, and then click the Pivot Table command button.**

2. **Specify whether you want the pivot table placed on a new worksheet or an existing sheet.**

3. **Build out the needed analysis just as you would build out any other standard pivot table, using the Pivot Field List.**

The pivot table shown in Figure 2-12 contains all tables in the Power Pivot data model. In this configuration, you essentially have a powerful cross-table analytical engine in the form of a familiar pivot table. Here, you can see that you're calculating the average unit price by customer.

Row Labels	Average of UnitPrice
Aaron Fitz Electrical	$272
Adam Park Resort	$640
Advanced Paper Co.	$192
Advanced Tech Satellite System	$63
American Science Museum	$157
Associated Insurance Company	$325
Astor Suites	$1,583
Atmore Retirement Center	$40
Baker's Emporium Inc.	$601
Blue Yonder Airlines	$856
Boyle's Country Inn's	$610
Breakthrough Telemarketing	$864
Castle Inn Resort	$120
Central Communications LTD	$769
Central Distributing	$125
Central Illinois Hospital	$1,705
Communication Connections	$127
Computerized Phone Systems	$120
Contoso, Ltd.	$8,912
Country View Estates	$129
Dollis Cove Resort	$120

PivotTable Fields

ACTIVE | ALL

Choose fields to add to report:

Search

▷ ▦ Customers

▷ ▦ **InvoiceDetails**

▷ ▦ InvoiceHeader

Drag fields between areas below:

▼ FILTERS | ▥ COLUMNS

▦ ROWS | Σ VALUES

CustomerName ▼ | Average of UnitPrice ▼

☐ Defer Layout Update | UPDATE

Figure 2-12: You now have a Power Pivot-driven pivot table that aggregates across multiple tables.

In the days before Power Pivot, this analysis would have been a bear to create. You would have had to build VLOOKUP formulas to get from Customer Number to Invoice Number, and then another set of VLOOKUP formulas to get from Invoice Numbers to Invoice Details. And after all that formula building, you still would have had to find a way to aggregate the data to the average unit price per customer.

Chapter 3

The Pivotal Pivot Table

When creating Power Pivot data models, you will have to use some form of pivot table structure to expose the data in those models available to your audience.

Pivot tables have a reputation for being complicated, but if you're new to pivot tables, rest easy. This chapter gives you the fundamental understanding you need in order to analyze and report on the data in your Power Pivot data model. After completing this introduction, you'll be pleasantly surprised at how easy it is to create and use pivot tables.

You can find the sample files for this chapter on this book's companion website at www.dummies.com/go/excelpowerpivotpowerqueryfd in the workbooks named Chapter 3 Samples.xlsx and Chapter 3 Slicers.xlsx.

Introducing the Pivot Table

A *pivot table* is a robust tool that allows you to create an interactive view of your dataset, commonly referred to as a *pivot table report*. With a pivot table report, you can quickly and easily categorize your data into groups, summarize large amounts of data into meaningful analyses, and interactively perform a wide variety of calculations.

Pivot tables get their name from the way they allow you to drag and drop fields within the pivot table report to dynamically change (or *pivot*) perspective and give you an entirely new analysis using the same data source.

Think of a pivot table as an object you can point at your dataset. When you look at your dataset through a pivot table, you can see your data from different perspectives. The dataset itself doesn't change, and it's not connected to the pivot table. The pivot table is simply a tool you're using to dynamically change analyses, apply varying calculations, and interactively drill down to the detail records.

The reason a pivot table is so well suited for reporting is that you can refresh the analyses shown through the pivot table by simply updating the dataset that it points to. You can set up the analysis and presentation layers only one time; then, to refresh the reporting mechanism, all you have to do is click a button.

Let's start this exploration of pivot tables with a lesson on the anatomy of a pivot table.

Defining the Four Areas of a Pivot Table

A pivot table is composed of four areas. The data you place in these areas defines both the utility and appearance of the pivot table. Take a moment to understand the function of each of these four areas.

Values area

The *values area,* as shown in Figure 3-1, is the large, rectangular area below and to the right of the column and row headings. In the example in Figure 3-1, the values area contains a sum of the values in the Sales Amount field.

The values area calculates and counts data. The data fields that you drag and drop there are typically those that you want to measure — fields, such as Sum of Revenue, Count of Units, or Average of Price.

Region	(All) ▼			
Sales Amount	Segment ▼			
Market ▼	Accessories	Bikes	Clothing	Components
Australia	23,974	1,351,873	43,232	203,791
Canada	119,303	11,714,700	383,022	2,246,255
Central	46,551	6,782,978	155,874	947,448
France	48,942	3,597,879	129,508	871,125
Germany	35,681	1,602,487	75,593	337,787
Northeast	51,246	5,690,285	163,442	1,051,702
Northwest	53,308	10,484,495	201,052	1,784,207
Southeast	45,736	6,737,556	165,689	959,337
Southwest	110,080	15,430,281	364,099	2,693,568
United Kingdom	43,180	3,435,134	120,225	712,588

Figure 3-1: The values area of a pivot table calculates and counts data.

Values area

Row area

The *row area* is shown in Figure 3-2. Placing a data field into the row area displays the unique values from that field down the rows of the left side of the pivot table. The row area typically has at least one field, although it's possible to have no fields.

Region	(All) ▼			
Sales Amount	Segment ▼			
Market ▼	Accessories	Bikes	Clothing	Components
Australia	23,974	1,351,873	43,232	203,791
Canada	119,303	11,714,700	383,022	2,246,255
Central	46,551	6,782,978	155,874	947,448
France	48,942	3,597,879	129,508	871,125
Germany	35,681	1,602,487	75,593	337,787
Northeast	51,246	5,690,285	163,442	1,051,702
Northwest	53,308	10,484,495	201,052	1,784,207
Southeast	45,736	6,737,556	165,689	959,337
Southwest	110,080	15,430,281	364,099	2,693,568
United Kingdom	43,180	3,435,134	120,225	712,588

Figure 3-2: The row area of a pivot table gives you a row-oriented perspective.

Row area

The types of data fields that you would drop here include those that you want to group and categorize, such as Products, Names, and Locations.

Column area

The *column area* is composed of headings that stretch across the top of columns in the pivot table.

As you can see in Figure 3-3, the column area stretches across the top of the columns. In this example, it contains the unique list of business segments.

Placing a data field into the column area displays the unique values from that field in a column-oriented perspective. The column area is ideal for creating a data matrix or showing trends over time.

Column area

Region	(All)		

Sales Amount	Segment		
Market	Accessories	Bikes	Clothing	Components
Australia	23,974	1,351,873	43,232	203,791
Canada	119,303	11,714,700	383,022	2,246,255
Central	46,551	6,782,978	155,874	947,448
France	48,942	3,597,879	129,508	871,125
Germany	35,681	1,602,487	75,593	337,787
Northeast	51,246	5,690,285	163,442	1,051,702
Northwest	53,308	10,484,495	201,052	1,784,207
Southeast	45,736	6,737,556	165,689	959,337
Southwest	110,080	15,430,281	364,099	2,693,568
United Kingdom	43,180	3,435,134	120,225	712,588

Figure 3-3: The column area of a pivot table gives you a column-oriented perspective.

Filter area

The *filter area* is an optional set of one or more drop-down lists at the top of the pivot table. In Figure 3-4, the filter area contains the Region field, and the pivot table is set to show all regions.

Placing data fields into the filter area allows you to filter the entire pivot table based on your selections. The types of data fields that you might drop here include those that you want to isolate and focus on; for example, Region, Line of Business, and Employees.

Filter area

Region	(All) ▾			
Sales Amount	Segment ▾			
Market ▾	Accessories	Bikes	Clothing	Components
Australia	23,974	1,351,873	43,232	203,791
Canada	119,303	11,714,700	383,022	2,246,255
Central	46,551	6,782,978	155,874	947,448
France	48,942	3,597,879	129,508	871,125
Germany	35,681	1,602,487	75,593	337,787
Northeast	51,246	5,690,285	163,442	1,051,702
Northwest	53,308	10,484,495	201,052	1,784,207
Southeast	45,736	6,737,556	165,689	959,337
Southwest	110,080	15,430,281	364,099	2,693,568
United Kingdom	43,180	3,435,134	120,225	712,588

Figure 3-4:
The filter area allows you to easily apply filters to the pivot table report.

Creating Your First Pivot Table

Now that you have a good understanding of the basic structure of a pivot table, it's time to try your hand at creating your first pivot table.

You can find the sample file for this chapter on this book's companion website.

Follow these steps:

1. **Click any single cell inside the *data source;* it's the table you use to feed the pivot table.**

   If you're following along, the data source would be the table found on the Sample Data tab.

2. **Select the Insert tab on the Ribbon. Here, find the PivotTable icon, as shown in Figure 3-5. Choose PivotTable from the drop-down list beneath the icon.**

File	Home	Insert	Page Layout	Formulas

PivotTable Recommended Table   Pictures Online   Shape
            PivotTables   Pictures   Smart
                                                        Scree
Tables   Illustrations

D13

	A	B	C	
1	Region	SubRegion	Market	Cus
2	North America	United States	Southeast	Trus
3	North America	United States	Southeast	Trus
4	North America	United States	Southeast	Trus
5	North America	United States	Southeast	Trus
6	North America	United States	Southeast	Tru

Figure 3-5:
Start a pivot table via the Insert tab.

This step opens the Create PivotTable dialog box, as shown in Figure 3-6. As you can see, this dialog box asks you to specify the location of the source data and the place where you want to put the pivot table.

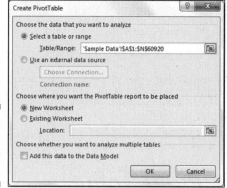

Figure 3-6:
The Create
PivotTable
dialog box.

Notice that in the Create PivotTable dialog box, Excel makes an attempt to fill in the range of your data for you. In most cases, Excel gets this right. However, always make sure that the correct range is selected.

Also note in Figure 3-6 that the default location for a new pivot table is New Worksheet. This means your pivot table is placed in a new work-sheet within the current workbook. You can change this by selecting the Existing Worksheet option and specifying the worksheet where you want the pivot table placed.

3. Click OK.

At this point, you have an empty pivot table report on a new worksheet. Next to the empty pivot table, you see the PivotTable Fields dialog box, shown in Figure 3-7.

The idea here is to add the fields you need into the pivot table by using the four *drop zones* found in the PivotTable Field List: Filters, Columns, Rows, and Values. Pleasantly enough, these drop zones cor-respond to the four areas of the pivot table described at the beginning of this chapter.

If clicking the pivot table doesn't open the PivotTable Fields dialog box, you can manually open it by right-clicking anywhere inside the pivot table and selecting Show Field List.

Now, before you go wild and start dropping fields into the various drop zones, you should ask yourself two questions: "What am I measuring?" and "How do I want to see it?" The answers to these questions give you some guidance when determining which fields go where.

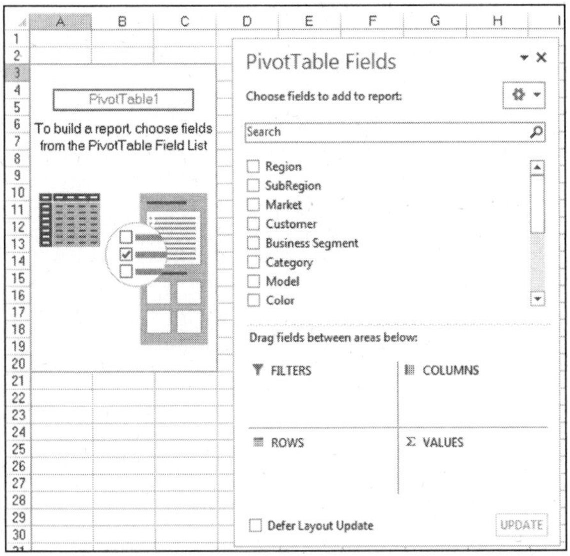

PivotTable Fields ▾ ✕

Choose fields to add to report: ⚙ ▾

Search 🔎

☐ Region
☐ SubRegion
☐ Market
☐ Customer
☐ Business Segment
☐ Category
☐ Model
☐ Color

Drag fields between areas below:

▼ FILTERS   ▥ COLUMNS

▥ ROWS   Σ VALUES

☐ Defer Layout Update   UPDATE

PivotTable1

To build a report, choose fields from the PivotTable Field List

Figure 3-7:
The Pivot-
Table Fields
dialog box.

For your first pivot table report, measure the dollar sales by market. This automatically tells you that you need to work with the Sales Amount field and the Market field.

How do you want to see that? You want markets to be listed down the left side of the report and the sales amount to be calculated next to each market. Remembering the four areas of the pivot table, you need to add the Market field to the Rows drop zone and add the Sales Amount field to the Values drop zone.

4. Select the Market check box in the list, as shown in Figure 3-8.

Now that you have regions in the pivot table, it's time to add the dollar sales.

5. Select the Sales Amount check box in the list, as shown in Figure 3-9.

Selecting a check box that is *non-numeric* (text or date) automatically places that field into the row area of the pivot table. Selecting a check box that is *numeric* automatically places that field in the values area of the pivot table.

What happens if you need fields in the other areas of the pivot table? Well, rather than select the field's check box, you can drag any field directly to the different drop zones.

One more thing: When you add fields to the drop zones, you may find it difficult to see all the fields in each drop zone. You can expand the PivotTable Fields dialog box by clicking and dragging the borders of the dialog box.

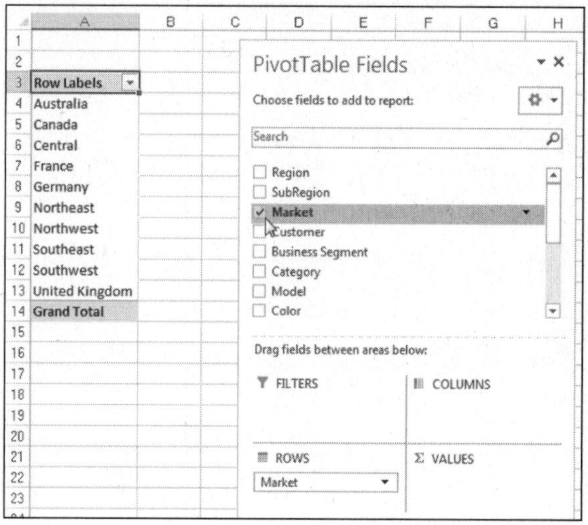

Figure 3-8:
Select the
Market
check box.

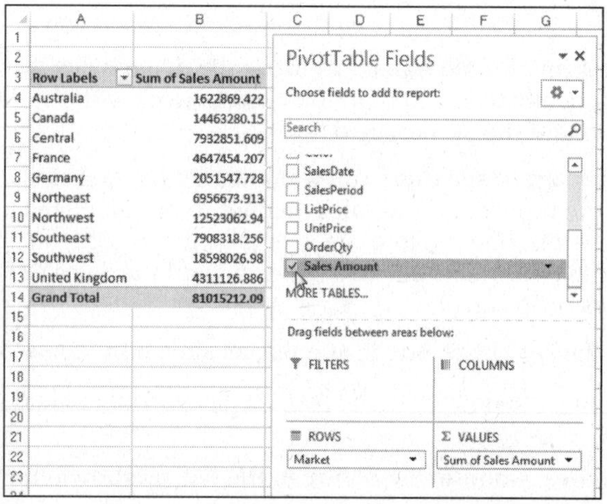

Figure 3-9:
Add the
Sales
Amount field
by selecting
its check
box.

As you can see, you have just analyzed the sales for each market in just five steps! That's an amazing feat, considering that you start with more than 60,000 rows of data. With a little formatting, this modest pivot table can become the starting point for a management report.

Changing and rearranging a pivot table

Now, here's the wonderful thing about pivot tables: You can add as many layers of analysis as made possible by the fields in the source data table.

Say that you want to show the dollar sales that each market earned by business segment. Because the pivot table already contains the Market and Sales Amount fields, all you have to add is the Business Segment field.

So, simply click anywhere on the pivot table to reopen the PivotTable Fields dialog box, and then select the Business Segment check box. Figure 3-10 illustrates what the pivot table should look like now.

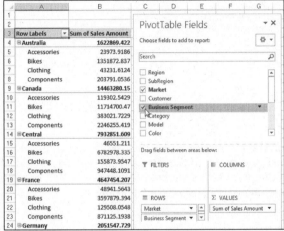

Figure 3-10:
Adding a layer of analysis is as easy as bringing in another field.

If clicking the pivot table doesn't open the PivotTable Fields dialog box, you can manually open it by right-clicking anywhere inside the pivot table and selecting Show Field List.

Imagine that your manager says that this layout doesn't work for him. He wants to see business segments displayed across the top of the pivot table report. No problem: Simply drag the Business Segment field from the Rows drop zone to the Columns drop zone. As you can see in Figure 3-11, this instantly restructures the pivot table to his specifications.

Adding a report filter

Often, you're asked to produce reports for one particular region, market, or product. Rather than work hours and hours building separate reports for every possible analysis scenario, you can leverage pivot tables to help create multiple views of the same data. For example, you can do so by creating a region filter in the pivot table.

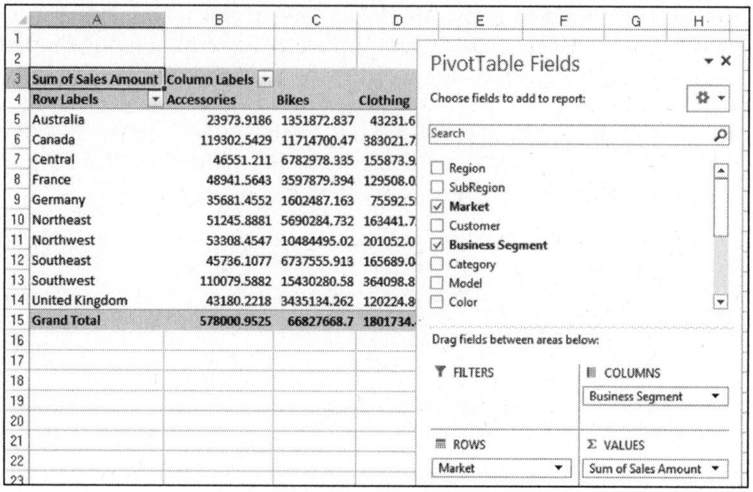

Figure 3-11:
Your
business
segments
are now
column
oriented.

Click anywhere on the pivot table to reopen the PivotTable Fields dialog box, and then drag the Region field to the Filters drop zone. This adds a drop-down selector to the pivot table, shown in Figure 3-12. You can then use this selector to analyze one particular region at a time.

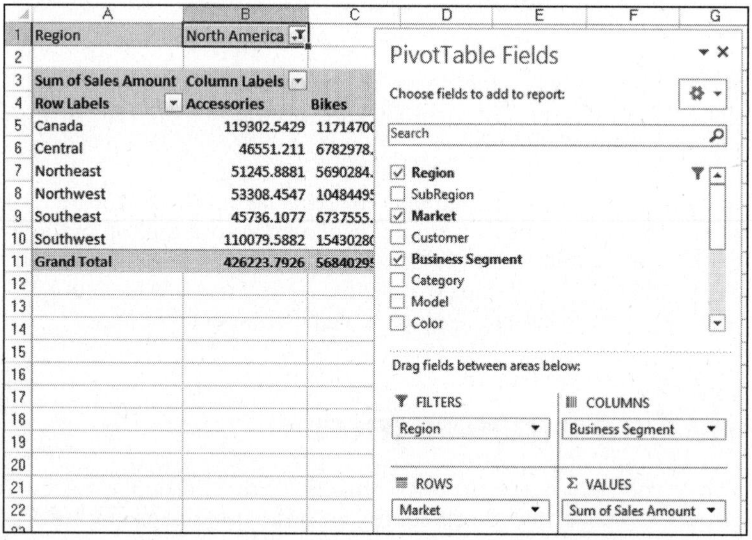

Figure 3-12:
Using pivot
tables to
analyze
regions.

Keeping the pivot table fresh

In Hollywood, it's important to stay fresh and relevant. As boring as the pivot tables may seem, they'll eventually become the stars of your reports. So it's just as important to keep your pivot tables fresh and relevant.

As time goes by, your data may change and grow with newly added rows and columns. The action of updating your pivot table with these changes is *refreshing* your data.

The pivot table report can be refreshed by simply right-clicking inside the pivot table report and selecting Refresh, as shown in Figure 3-13.

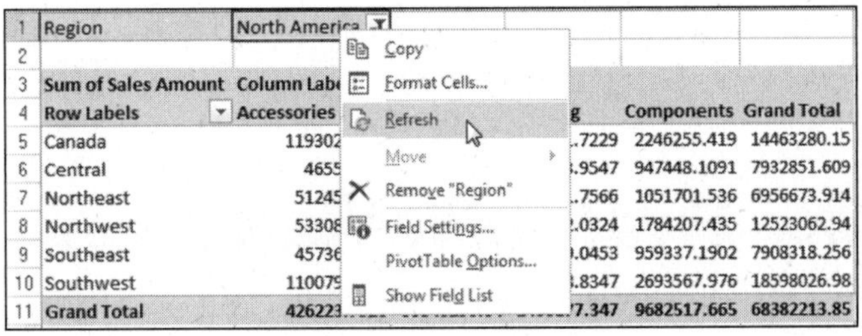

Figure 3-13:
Refreshing
the pivot
table
captures
changes
made to
your data.

	Region	North America					Components	Grand Total
1			Copy					
2			Format Cells...					
3	Sum of Sales Amount	Column Lab	Refresh					
4	Row Labels	Accessories	Move			Components	Grand Total	
5	Canada	119302	Remove "Region"	.7229	2246255.419	14463280.15		
6	Central	4655	Field Settings...	.9547	947448.1091	7932851.609		
7	Northeast	51245	PivotTable Options...	.7566	1051701.536	6956673.914		
8	Northwest	53308	Show Field List	.0324	1784207.435	12523062.94		
9	Southeast	45736		.0453	959337.1902	7908318.256		
10	Southwest	110079		.8347	2693567.976	18598026.98		
11	Grand Total	426223		7.347	9682517.665	68382213.85		

Sometimes, *you're* the data source that feeds your pivot table changes in structure. For example, you may have added or deleted rows or columns from the data table. These types of changes affect the range of the data source, not just a few data items in the table.

In these cases, performing a simple Refresh of the pivot table won't do. You have to update the range being captured by the pivot table. Here's how:

1. **Click anywhere inside the pivot table to select the PivotTable Tools context tab on the Ribbon.**

2. **Select the Analyze tab on the Ribbon.**

3. **Click Change Data Source, as shown in Figure 3-14.**

   The Change PivotTable Data Source dialog box appears.

4. **Change the range selection to include any new rows or columns (see Figure 3-15).**

5. **Click OK to apply the change.**

Figure 3-14:
Changing
the range
that feeds
the pivot
table.

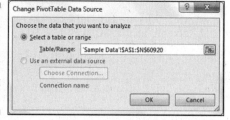

Figure 3-15:
Select the
new range
that feeds
the pivot
table.

Customizing Pivot Table Reports

The pivot tables you create often need to be tweaked to get the look and feel you're looking for. In this section, I cover some of the options you can adjust to customize your pivot tables to suit your reporting needs.

Changing the pivot table layout

Excel gives you a choice in the layout of the data in a pivot table. The three layouts, shown side by side in Figure 3-16, are the Compact Form, Outline Form, and Tabular Form. Although no layout stands out as better than the others, I prefer using the Tabular Form layout because it seems easiest to read and it's the layout that most people who have seen pivot tables are used to.

The layout you choose affects not only the look and feel of your reporting mechanisms but also, possibly, the way you build and interact with any reporting models based on your pivot tables.

Compact Form Layout			Outline Form Layout				Tabular Form Layout		
Row Labels	Sales		Market	Segment	Sales		Market	Segment	Sales
⊟Australia	1622869.422		⊟Australia		1622869.422		⊟Australia	Accessories	23973.9186
	Accessories	23973.9186		Accessories	23973.9186			Bikes	1351872.837
	Bikes	1351872.837		Bikes	1351872.837			Clothing	43231.6124
	Clothing	43231.6124		Clothing	43231.6124			Components	203791.0536
	Components	203791.0536		Components	203791.0536		Australia Total		1622869.422
⊟Canada	14463280.15		⊟Canada		14463280.15		⊟Canada	Accessories	119302.5429
	Accessories	119302.5429		Accessories	119302.5429			Bikes	11714700.47
	Bikes	11714700.47		Bikes	11714700.47			Clothing	383021.7229
	Clothing	383021.7229		Clothing	383021.7229			Components	2246255.419
	Components	2246255.419		Components	2246255.419		Canada Total		14463280.15
⊟Central	7932851.609		⊟Central		7932851.609		⊟Central	Accessories	46551.211
	Accessories	46551.211		Accessories	46551.211			Bikes	6782978.335
	Bikes	6782978.335		Bikes	6782978.335			Clothing	155873.9547
	Clothing	155873.9547		Clothing	155873.9547			Components	947448.1091
	Components	947448.1091		Components	947448.1091		Central Total		7932851.609
⊟France	4647454.207		⊟France		4647454.207		⊟France	Accessories	48941.5643
	Accessories	48941.5643		Accessories	48941.5643			Bikes	3597879.394
	Bikes	3597879.394		Bikes	3597879.394			Clothing	129508.0548
	Clothing	129508.0548		Clothing	129508.0548			Components	871125.1938
	Components	871125.1938		Components	871125.1938		France Total		4647454.207
⊟Germany	2051547.729		⊟Germany		2051547.729		⊟Germany	Accessories	35681.4552
	Accessories	35681.4552		Accessories	35681.4552			Bikes	1602487.163
	Bikes	1602487.163		Bikes	1602487.163			Clothing	75592.5945
	Clothing	75592.5945		Clothing	75592.5945			Components	337786.516
	Components	337786.516		Components	337786.516		Germany Total		2051547.729

Figure 3-16: The three layouts for a pivot table report.

Changing the layout of a pivot table is easy. Follow these steps:

1. **Click anywhere inside the pivot table to select the PivotTable Tools context tab on the Ribbon.**

2. **Select the Design tab on the Ribbon.**

3. **Click the Report Layout icon and choose the layout you like. See Figure 3-17.**

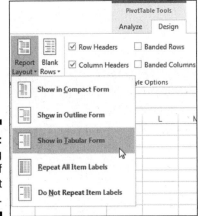

Figure 3-17: Changing the layout of the pivot table.

Customizing field names

Notice that every field in the pivot table has a name. The fields in the row, column, and filter areas inherit their names from the data labels in the source table. The fields in the values area are given a name, such as Sum of Sales Amount.

Sometimes you might prefer the name Total Sales instead of the unattractive default name, such as Sum of Sales Amount. In these situations, the ability to change your field names is handy. To change a field name, follow these steps:

1. **Right-click any value within the target field.**

   For example, if you want to change the name of the field Sum of Sales Amount, right-click any value under that field.

2. **Select Value Field Settings, as shown in Figure 3-18.**

Figure 3-18: Right-click any value in the target field to select the Value Field Settings option.

3	Row Labels	Sum of Sales Amount		
4	⊟ Australia	1622869.4		Copy
5	Accessories	23973.91		Format Cells...
6	Bikes	1351872.8		Number Format...
7	Clothing	43231.61		Refresh
8	Components	203791.05		
9	⊟ Canada	14463280		Sort
10	Accessories	119302.54	✕	Remove "Sum of Sales Amount"
11	Bikes	11714700		Summarize Values By
12	Clothing	383021.72		Show Values As
13	Components	2246255.4		
14	⊟ Central	7932851.6		Value Field Settings...
15	Accessories	46551.2		PivotTable Options...
16	Bikes	6782978.3		Show Field List
17	Clothing	155873.95		

The Value Field Settings dialog box appears.

Note that if you were changing the name of a field in the row area or column area, this selection is Field Settings.

3. **Enter the new name in the Custom Name input box, shown in Figure 3-19.**

4. **Click OK to apply the change.**

If you use the name of the data label used in the source table, you receive an error. For example, if you rename Sum of Sales Amount as Sales Amount, you see an error message because there's already a Sales Amount field in the source data table. Well, this is kind of lame, especially if Sales Amount is exactly what you want to name the field in your pivot table.

Figure 3-19:
Use the
Custom
Name input
box to
change the
name of
the field.

To get around this, you can name the field and add a space to the end of the name. Excel considers Sales Amount (followed by a space) to be different from Sales Amount. This way, you can use the name you want and no one will notice that it's any different.

Applying numeric formats to data fields

Numbers in pivot tables can be formatted to fit your needs; that is, formatted as currency, percentage, or number. You can easily control the numeric formatting of a field using the Value Field Settings dialog box. Here's how:

1. **Right-click any value within the target field.**

   For example, if you want to change the format of the values in the Sales Amount field, right-click any value under that field.

2. **Select Value Field Settings.**

   The Value Field Settings dialog box appears.

3. **Click the Number Format button.**

   The Format Cells dialog box opens.

4. **Apply the number format you desire, just as you typically would on your spreadsheet.**

5. **Click OK to apply the changes.**

   After you set the formatting for a field, the applied formatting persists, even if you refresh or rearrange the pivot table.

Changing summary calculations

When creating the pivot table report, Excel, by default, summarizes your data by either counting or summing the items. Rather than choose Sum or Count, you might want to choose functions, such as Average, Min, Max, for example. In all, 11 options are available, including

- ✔ Sum: Adds all numeric data.

- ✔ Count: Counts all data items within a given field, including numeric-, text-, and date-formatted cells.

- ✔ Average: Calculates an average for the target data items.

- ✔ Max: Displays the largest value in the target data items.

- ✔ Min: Displays the smallest value in the target data items.

- ✔ Product: Multiplies all target data items together.

- ✔ Count Nums: Counts only the numeric cells in the target data items.

- ✔ StdDevP and StdDev: Calculates the standard deviation for the target data items. Use StdDevP if your dataset contains the complete population. Use StdDev if your dataset contains a sample of the population.

- ✔ VarP and Var: Calculates the statistical variance for the target data items. Use VarP if your data contains a complete population. If your data contains only a sampling of the complete population, use Var to estimate the variance.

You can easily change the summary calculation for any given field by taking the following actions:

1. **Right-click any value within the target field.**

2. **Select Value Field Settings.**

   The Value Field Settings dialog box appears.

3. **Choose the type of calculation you want to use from the list of calculations. See Figure 3-20.**

4. **Click OK to apply the changes.**

Did you know that a single blank cell causes Excel to count instead of sum? That's right: If all cells in a column contain numeric data, Excel chooses Sum. If only one cell is either blank or contains text, Excel chooses Count.

Figure 3-20:
Changing
the type of
summary
calculation
used in
a field.

Be sure to pay attention to the fields that you place into the values area of the pivot table. If the field name starts with *Count Of,* Excel is counting the items in the field instead of summing the values.

Suppressing subtotals

Notice that every time you add a field to the pivot table, Excel adds a subtotal for that field. At times, however, the inclusion of subtotals either doesn't make sense or simply hinders a clear view of the pivot table report. For example, Figure 3-21 shows a pivot table in which the subtotals inundate the report with totals that hide the real data you're trying to report.

Figure 3-21:
Subtotals
sometimes
muddle the
data you're
trying
to show.

	A	B	C	D	E
1	Region	SubRegion	Market	Business Segment	Sum of Sales Amount
2	North America	United States	Central	Accessories	46,551
3				Bikes	6,782,978
4				Clothing	155,874
5				Components	947,448
6			Central Total		7,932,852
7			Northeast	Accessories	51,246
8				Bikes	5,690,285
9				Clothing	163,442
10				Components	1,051,702
11			Northeast Total		6,956,674
12			Northwest	Accessories	53,308
13				Bikes	10,484,495
14				Clothing	201,052
15				Components	1,784,207
16			Northwest Total		12,523,063
17			Southeast	Accessories	45,736
18				Bikes	6,737,556
19				Clothing	165,689
20				Components	959,337
21			Southeast Total		7,908,318
22			Southwest	Accessories	110,080
23				Bikes	15,430,281
24				Clothing	364,099
25				Components	2,693,568
26			Southwest Total		18,598,027
27		United States Total			53,918,934
28	North America Total				53,918,934

Removing all subtotals at one time

You can remove all subtotals at one time by taking these actions:

1. **Click anywhere inside the pivot table to select the PivotTable Tools context tab on the Ribbon.**

2. **Select the Design tab on the Ribbon.**

3. **Click the Subtotals icon and select Do Not Show Subtotals, as shown in Figure 3-22.**

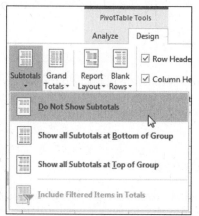

Figure 3-22: Use the Do Not Show Subtotals option to remove all subtotals at one time.

As you can see in Figure 3-23, the same report without subtotals is much more pleasant to review.

	A	B	C	D	E
1	Region	SubRegion	Market	Business Segment	Sum of Sales Amount
2	North America	United States	Central	Accessories	46,551
3				Bikes	6,782,978
4				Clothing	155,874
5				Components	947,448
6			Northeast	Accessories	51,246
7				Bikes	5,690,285
8				Clothing	163,442
9				Components	1,051,702
10			Northwest	Accessories	53,308
11				Bikes	10,484,495
12				Clothing	201,052
13				Components	1,784,207
14			Southeast	Accessories	45,736
15				Bikes	6,737,556
16				Clothing	165,689
17				Components	959,337
18			Southwest	Accessories	110,080
19				Bikes	15,430,281
20				Clothing	364,099
21				Components	2,693,568
22	Grand Total				53,918,934

Figure 3-23: The report shown in Figure 3-21, without subtotals.

Removing the subtotals for only one field

Maybe you want to remove the subtotals for only one field? In such a case, you can take the following actions:

1. **Right-click any value within the target field.**

2. **Select Field Settings.**

   The Field Settings dialog box appears.

3. **Choose the None option under Subtotals, as shown in Figure 3-24.**

4. **Click OK to apply the changes.**

Figure 3-24:
Choose the
None option
to remove
subtotals for
one field.

Removing grand totals

In certain instances, you may want to remove the grand totals from the pivot table. Follow these steps:

1. **Right-click anywhere on the pivot table.**

2. **Select PivotTable Options.**

   The PivotTable Options dialog box appears.

3. **Click the Totals & Filters tab.**

4. **Click the Show Grand Totals for Rows check box to deselect it.**

5. **Click the Show Grand Totals for Columns check box to deselect it.**

Showing and hiding data items

A pivot table summarizes and displays all records in a source data table. In certain situations, however, you may want to inhibit certain data items from being included in the pivot table summary. In these situations, you can choose to hide a data item.

In terms of pivot tables, hiding doesn't mean simply preventing the data item from being shown on the report. Hiding a data item also prevents it from being factored into the summary calculations.

In the pivot table illustrated in Figure 3-25, I show sales amounts for all business segments by market. In this example, I want to show totals without taking sales from the Bikes segment into consideration. In other words, I want to hide the Bikes segment.

	A	B	C
1	Market	Business Segment	Sum of Sales Amount
2	Australia	Accessories	$23,974
3		Bikes	$1,351,873
4		Clothing	$43,232
5		Components	$203,791
6	Australia Total		$1,622,869
7	Canada	Accessories	$119,303
8		Bikes	$11,714,700
9		Clothing	$383,022
10		Components	$2,246,255
11	Canada Total		$14,463,280
12	Central	Accessories	$46,551
13		Bikes	$6,782,978
14		Clothing	$155,874
15		Components	$947,448
16	Central Total		$7,932,852
17	France	Accessories	$48,942

Figure 3-25: To remove Bikes from this analysis . . .

You can hide the Bikes Business Segment by clicking the Business Segment drop-down arrow and deselecting the Bikes check box, as shown in Figure 3-26.

After you click OK to close the selection box, the pivot table instantly recalculates, leaving out the Bikes segment. As you can see in Figure 3-27, the Market total sales now reflect the sales without Bikes.

You can just as quickly reinstate all hidden data items for the field. You simply click the Business Segment drop-down arrow and click the Select All check box, as shown in Figure 3-28.

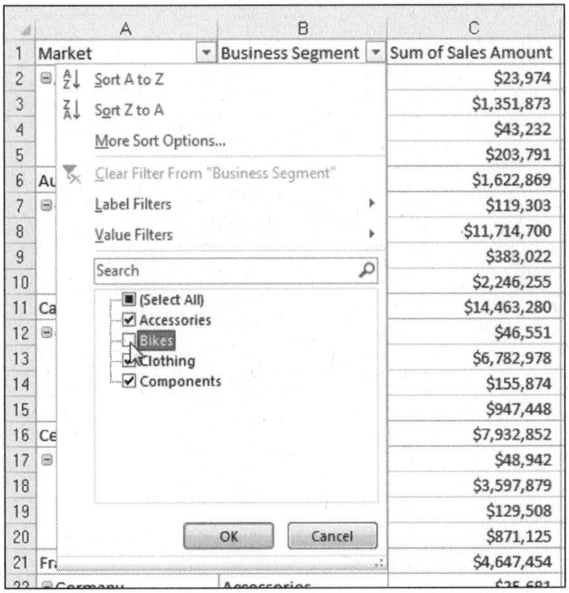

Figure 3-26: . . . deselect the Bikes check box.

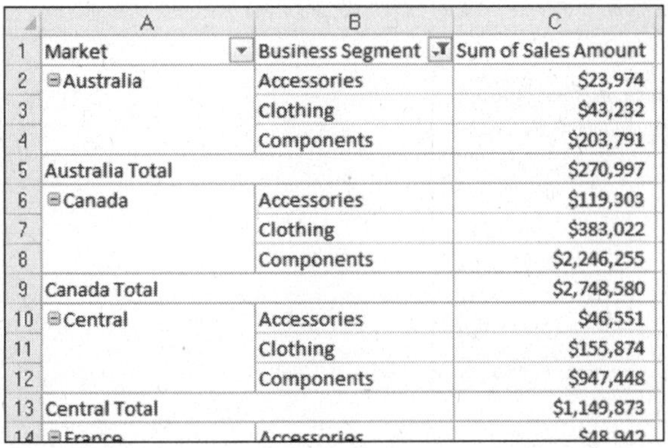

	A	B	C
1	Market	Business Segment	Sum of Sales Amount
2	Australia	Accessories	$23,974
3		Clothing	$43,232
4		Components	$203,791
5	Australia Total		$270,997
6	Canada	Accessories	$119,303
7		Clothing	$383,022
8		Components	$2,246,255
9	Canada Total		$2,748,580
10	Central	Accessories	$46,551
11		Clothing	$155,874
12		Components	$947,448
13	Central Total		$1,149,873

Figure 3-27: The analysis from Figure 3-25, without the Bikes segment.

Hiding or showing items without data

By default, the pivot table shows only data items that have data. This inherent behavior may cause unintended problems for your data analysis.

Look at Figure 3-29, which shows a pivot table with the SalesPeriod field in the row area and the Region field in the filter area. Note that the Region field is set to (All) and that every sales period appears in the report.

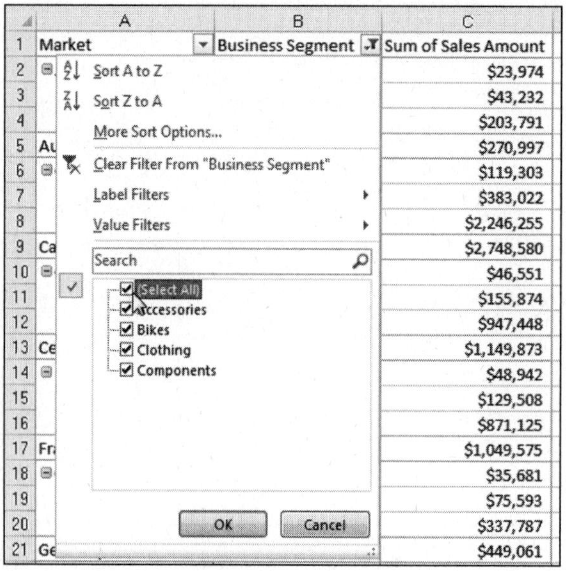

Figure 3-28: Clicking the Select All check box forces all data items in that field to become unhidden.

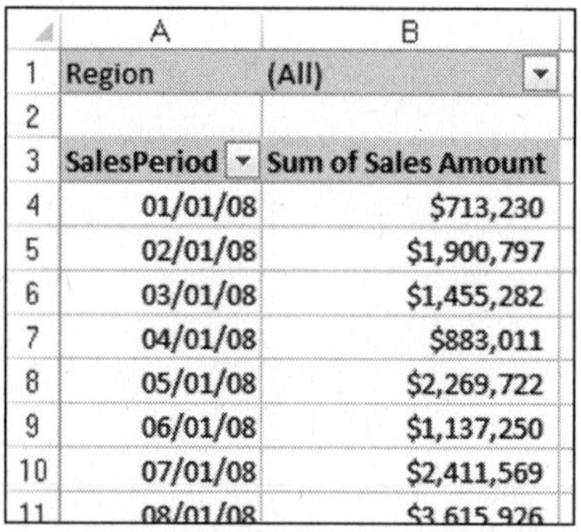

	A	B
1	Region	(All)
2		
3	SalesPeriod	Sum of Sales Amount
4	01/01/08	$713,230
5	02/01/08	$1,900,797
6	03/01/08	$1,455,282
7	04/01/08	$883,011
8	05/01/08	$2,269,722
9	06/01/08	$1,137,250
10	07/01/08	$2,411,569
11	08/01/08	$3,615,926

Figure 3-29: All sales periods are showing.

If you choose Europe in the filter area, only a portion of all the sales periods is shown (see Figure 3-30). The pivot table shows only those sales periods that apply to the Europe region.

From a reporting perspective, it isn't ideal if half the year's data disappears every time customers select Europe.

Here's how you can prevent Excel from hiding pivot items without data:

1. **Right-click any value within the target field.**

   In this example, the target field is the SalesPeriod field.

Figure 3-30:
Filtering for
the Europe
region
causes cer-
tain sales
periods to
disappear.

	A	B
1	Region	Europe ⊤
2		
3	SalesPeriod ▼	Sum of Sales Amount
4	07/01/08	$180,241
5	08/01/08	$448,373
6	09/01/08	$373,122
7	10/01/08	$119,384
8	11/01/08	$330,026
9	12/01/08	$254,011
10	01/01/09	$71,313
11	02/01/09	$264,487

2. **Select Field Settings.**

   The Field Settings dialog box appears.

3. **Select the Layout & Print tab in the Field Settings dialog box.**

4. **Select the Show Items with No Data option, as shown in Figure 3-31.**

5. **Click OK to apply the change.**

Figure 3-31:
Click the
Show Items
with No
Data option
to force
Excel to
display all
data items.

As you can see in Figure 3-32, after you choose the Show Items with No Data option, all sales periods appear whether the selected region had sales that period or not.

Now that you're confident that the structure of the pivot table is locked, you can use it to feed charts and other components on your report.

Figure 3-32: All sales periods are now displayed, even if there is no data to be shown.

	A	B
1	Region	Europe
2		
3	SalesPeriod ▾	Sum of Sales Amount
4	01/01/08	
5	02/01/08	
6	03/01/08	
7	04/01/08	
8	05/01/08	
9	06/01/08	
10	07/01/08	$180,241
11	08/01/08	$448,373
12	09/01/08	$373,122

Sorting the pivot table

By default, items in each pivot field are sorted in ascending sequence based on the item name. Excel gives you the freedom to change the sort order of the items in the pivot table.

Like many actions you can perform in Excel, you have lots of different ways to sort data within a pivot table. The easiest way is to apply the sort directly in the pivot table. Here's how:

1. **Right-click any value within the *target field* — the field you need to sort.**

   In the example shown in Figure 3-33, you want to sort by Sales Amount.

2. **Select Sort and then select the sort direction.**

   The changes take effect immediately and persist while you work with the pivot table.

4	Bib-Shorts	$168,003
5	Bike Racks	$200,077
6	Bottles and Cages	$7,555
7	Bottom Brackets	$51,826
8	Brakes	$66,062
9	Caps	$31,824
10	Chains	$9,386
11	Cleaners	$11,300
12	Cranksets	$204,065
13	Derailleurs	$70,263
14	Forks	$77,969
15	Gloves	$211,942
16	Handlebars	$170,657

Context menu:
- Copy
- Format Cells...
- Number Format...
- Refresh
- Sort ▸
  - Sort Smallest to Largest
  - Sort Largest to Smallest
  - More Sort Options...
- Remove "Sum of Sales Amount"
- Summarize Values By ▸
- Show Values As ▸
- Show Details
- Value Field Settings...

Figure 3-33: Applying a sort to a pivot table field.

Understanding Slicers

Slicers allow you to filter your pivot table in a way that's similar to the way Filter fields filter a pivot table. The difference is that slicers offer a user-friendly interface, enabling you to better manage the filter state of your pivot table reports.

As useful as Filter fields are, they have always had a couple of drawbacks.

First of all, Filter fields are not cascading filters — the filters don't work together to limit selections when needed. For example, in Figure 3-34, you can see that the Region filter is set to the North region. However, the Market filter still allows you to select markets that are clearly not in the North region (California, for example). Because the Market filter is not in any way limited based on the Region Filter field, you have the annoying possibility of selecting a market that could yield no data because it's not in the North region.

Figure 3-34: Default pivot table Filter fields do not work together to limit filter selections.

Another drawback is that Filter fields don't provide an easy way to tell what exactly is being filtered when you select multiple items. In Figure 3-35, you can see an example. The Region filter has been limited to three regions: Midwest, North, and Northeast. However, notice that the Region filter value shows (Multiple Items). By default, Filter fields show (Multiple Items) when you select more than one item. The only way to tell what has been selected is to click the drop-down menu. You can imagine the confusion on a printed version of this report, in which you can't click down to see which data items make up the numbers on the page.

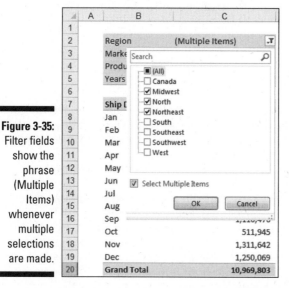

Figure 3-35:
Filter fields
show the
phrase
(Multiple
Items)
whenever
multiple
selections
are made.

By contrast, slicers don't have these issues. Slicers respond to one another. As you can see in Figure 3-36, the Market slicer visibly highlights the relevant markets when the North region is selected. The rest of the markets are muted, signaling that they are not part of the North region.

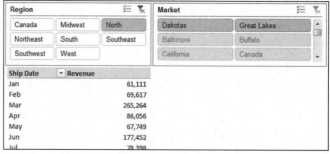

Figure 3-36:
Slicers work
together to
show you
relevant
data items
based on
your
selection.

When selecting multiple items in a slicer, you can easily see that multiple items have been chosen. In Figure 3-37, you can see that the pivot table is being filtered by the Midwest, North, and Northeast regions. No more (Multiple Items).

Figure 3-37: Slicers do a better job at displaying multiple item selections.

Region						
Canada	Midwest	North				
Northeast	South	Southeast				
Southwest	West					

Market			
Baltimore	Buffalo		
Chicago	Dakotas		
Great Lakes	Kansas City		

Ship Date	Revenue
Jan	431,794
Feb	1,142,718
Mar	697,451
Apr	510,333
May	1,405,497
Jun	586,846
Jul	477,691

Creating a Standard Slicer

Enough talk. It's time to create your first slicer. Just follow these steps:

1. **Place the cursor anywhere inside the pivot table, and then go up to the Ribbon and click the Analyze tab. There, click the Insert Slicer icon, shown in Figure 3-38.**

Figure 3-38: Inserting a slicer.

This step opens the Insert Slicers dialog box, shown in Figure 3-39. Select the dimensions you want to filter. In this example, the Region and Market slicers are created.

2. **After the slicers are created, simply click the filter values to filter the pivot table.**

As you can see in Figure 3-40, clicking Midwest in the Region slicer not only filters the pivot table, but the Market slicer also responds by highlighting the markets that belong to the Midwest region.

Figure 3-39:
Select the
dimensions
for which
you want
slicers
created.

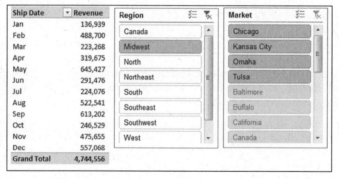

Figure 3-40:
Select the
dimensions
you want fil-
tered using
slicers.

You can also select multiple values by holding down the Ctrl key on the keyboard while selecting the needed filters. In Figure 3-41, I held down the Ctrl key while selecting Baltimore, California, Charlotte, and Chicago. This highlights not only the selected markets in the Market slicer but also their associated regions in the Region slicer.

To clear the filtering on a slicer, simply click the Clear Filter icon on the target slicer, as shown in Figure 3-42.

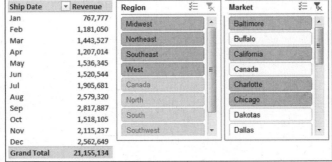

Getting Fancy with Slicer Customizations

The following sections cover a few formatting adjustments you can make to your slicers.

Size and placement

A slicer behaves like a standard Excel shape object in that you can move it around and adjust its size by clicking it and dragging its position points; see Figure 3-43.

You can also right-click the slicer and select Size and Properties. This brings up the Format Slicer pane (see Figure 3-44), allowing you to adjust the size of the slicer, how the slicer should behave when cells are shifted, and whether the slicer should appear on a printed copy of your report.

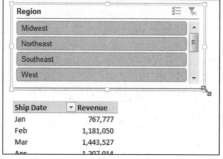

Figure 3-43:
Adjust the slicer size and placement by dragging its position points.

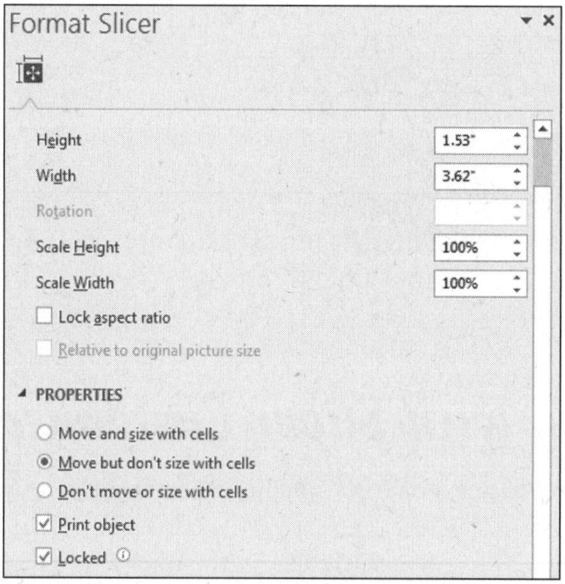

Figure 3-44:
The Format Slicer pane offers more control over how the slicer behaves in relation to the worksheet it's on.

Data item columns

By default, all slicers are created with one column of data items. You can change this number by right-clicking the slicer and selecting Size and Properties. This opens the Format Slicer pane. Under the Position and Layout section, you can specify the number of columns in the slicer. Adjusting the number to 2, as shown in Figure 3-45, forces the data items to be displayed in two columns, adjusting the number to 3 forces the data items to be displayed in three columns, and so on.

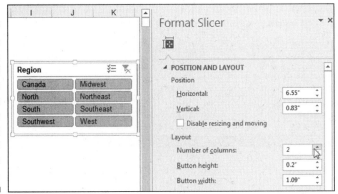

Figure 3-45:
Adjust the
Number of
Columns
property to
display the
slicer data
items in
more than
one column.

Miscellaneous slicer settings

Right-clicking the slicer and selecting Slicer Settings opens the Slicer Settings
dialog box, shown in Figure 3-46. Using this dialog box, you can control the
look of the slicer's header, how the slicer is sorted, and how filtered items
are handled.

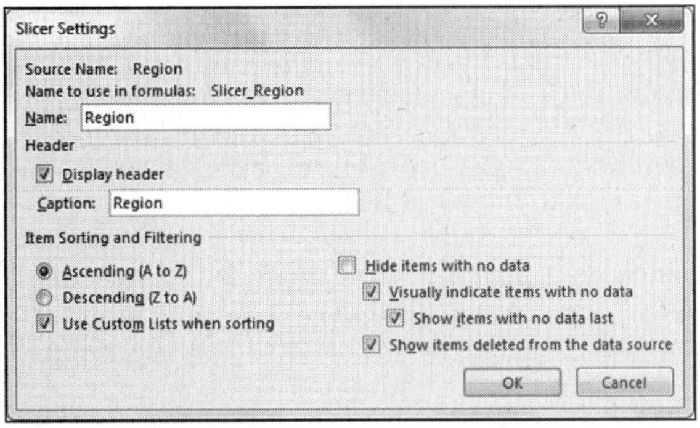

Figure 3-46:
The Slicer
Settings
dialog box.

Controlling Multiple Pivot Tables with One Slicer

Another advantage you gain with slicers is that each slicer can be tied to
more than one pivot table; that is to say, any filter you apply to your slicer
can be applied to multiple pivot tables.

To connect the slicer to more than one pivot table, simply right-click the
slicer and select Report Connections. This opens the Report Connections

dialog box, shown in Figure 3-47. Place a check mark next to any pivot table that you want to filter using the current slicer.

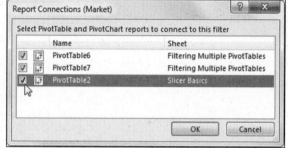

Figure 3-47: Choose the pivot tables to be filtered by this slicer.

At this point, any filter you apply to the slicer is applied to all connected pivot tables. Controlling the filter state of multiple pivot tables is a powerful feature, especially in reports that run on multiple pivot tables.

Creating a Timeline Slicer

The Timeline slicer works in the same way a standard slicer does, in that it lets you filter a pivot table using a visual selection mechanism rather than the old Filter fields. The difference is that the Timeline slicer is designed to work exclusively with date fields, providing an excellent visual method to filter and group the dates in the pivot table.

To create a Timeline slicer, the pivot table must contain a field where *all* data is formatted as a date. It's not enough to have a column of data that contains a few dates. All values in the date field must be a valid date and formatted as such.

To create a Timeline slicer, follow these steps:

1. **Place the cursor anywhere inside the pivot table, and then click the Analyze tab on the Ribbon. There, click the Insert Timeline command, shown in Figure 3-48.**

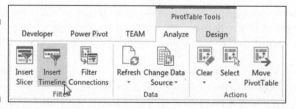

Figure 3-48: Inserting a Timeline slicer.

The Insert Timelines dialog box, shown in Figure 3-49, appears, showing you all available date fields in the chosen pivot table.

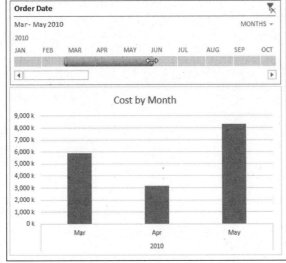

Figure 3-49: Select the date fields for which you want slicers created.

2. **In the Insert Timelines dialog box, select the date fields for which you want to create the timeline.**

After the Timeline slicer is created, you can filter the data in the pivot table and pivot chart, using this dynamic data-selection mechanism. Figure 3-50 demonstrates how selecting Mar, Apr, and May in the Timeline slicer automatically filters the pivot chart.

Figure 3-50: Click a date selection to filter the pivot table or pivot chart.

Figure 3-51 illustrates how you can expand the slicer range with the mouse to include a wider range of dates in your filtered numbers.

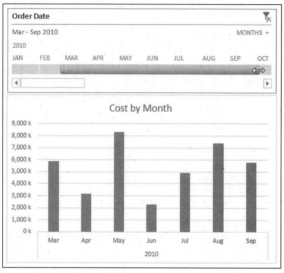

Figure 3-51: You can expand the range on the Timeline slicer to include more data in the filtered numbers.

Want to quickly filter the pivot table by quarters? Well, that's easy with a Timeline slicer. Simply click the time period drop-down menu and select Quarters. As you can see in Figure 3-52, you can also switch to Years or Days, if needed.

Timeline slicers are not *backward compatible;* they are usable only in Excel 2013 and Excel 2016. If you open a workbook with Timeline slicers in Excel 2010 or previous versions, the Timeline slicers are disabled.

Figure 3-52: Quickly switch among Quarters, Years, Months, and Days.

Chapter 4

Using External Data with Power Pivot

*I*n Chapter 2, I start an exploration of Power Pivot by showing you how to load the data already contained within the workbook you're working on. But as you discover in this chapter, you're not limited to using only the data that already exists in your Excel workbook.

Power Pivot has the ability to reach outside the workbook and import data found in external data sources. Indeed, what makes Power Pivot powerful is its ability to consolidate data from disparate data sources and build relationships between them. You can theoretically create a Power Pivot data model that contains some data from a SQL Server table, some data from a Microsoft Access database, and even data from a one-off text file.

In this chapter, I help you continue your journey by taking a closer look at the mechanics of importing external data into your Power Pivot data models.

This chapter has no associated sample file. But don't worry: You can easily translate the information found here to your own data sources.

Loading Data from Relational Databases

One of the more common data sources used by Excel analysts is the relational database. It's not difficult to find an analyst who frequently uses data from Microsoft Access, SQL Server, or Oracle databases. In this section, I walk you through the steps for loading data from external database systems.

Loading data from SQL Server

SQL Server databases are some of the most commonly used for the storing of enterprise-level data. Most SQL Server databases are managed and maintained by the IT department. To connect to a SQL Server database, you have to work with your IT department to obtain Read access to the database you're trying to pull from.

After you have access to the database, open the Power Pivot window and click the From Other Sources command button on the Home tab. This opens the Table Import Wizard dialog box, shown in Figure 4-1. There, select the Microsoft SQL Server option and then click the Next button.

Figure 4-1:
Open the
Table Import
Wizard and
select
Microsoft
SQL Server.

The Table Import Wizard now asks for all the information it needs to connect to your database (see Figure 4-2). On this screen, you need to provide the information for the options described in this list:

- **Friendly Connection Name:** The Friendly Name field allows you to specify your own name for the external source. You typically enter a name that is descriptive and easy to read.

- **Server Name:** This is the name of the server that contains the database you're trying to connect to. You get this from your IT department when you gain access. (Your server name will be different from the one shown in Figure 4-2.)

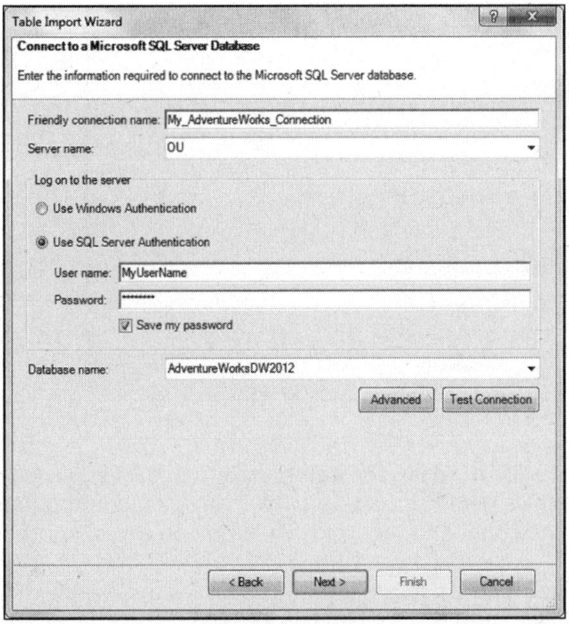

Figure 4-2:
Provide the basic information needed to connect to the target database.

✔ **Log On to the Server:** These are your login credentials. Depending on how your IT department gives you access, you select either Windows Authentication or SQL Server Authentication. Windows Authentication essentially means that the server recognizes you by your windows login. SQL Server Authentication means that the IT department created a distinct username and password for you. If you're using SQL Server Authentication, you need to provide a username and password.

✔ **Save My Password:** You can select the check box next to Save My Password if you want your username and password to be stored in the workbook. Your connections can then remain refreshable when being used by other people. This option obviously has security considerations, because anyone can view the connection properties and see your username and password. You should use this option only if your IT department has set you up with an application account (an account created specifically to be used by multiple people).

✔ **Database Name:** Every SQL Server can contain multiple databases. Enter the name of the database you're connecting to. You can get it from your IT department whenever someone gives you access.

After you enter all the pertinent information, click the Next button to see the next screen, shown in Figure 4-3. You have the choice of selecting from a list of tables and views or writing your own custom query using SQL syntax. In most cases, you choose the option to select from a list of tables.

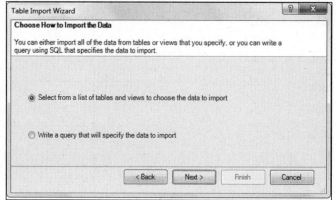

Figure 4-3:
Choose to
select from
a list of
tables and
views.

The Table Import Wizard reads the database and shows you a list of all available tables and views (see Figure 4-4). Tables have an icon that looks like a grid, and views have an icon that looks like a box on top of another box.

The idea is to place a check mark next to the tables and views you want to import. In Figure 4-4, note the check mark next to the FactInternetSales table. The Friendly Name column allows you to enter a new name that will be used to reference the table in Power Pivot.

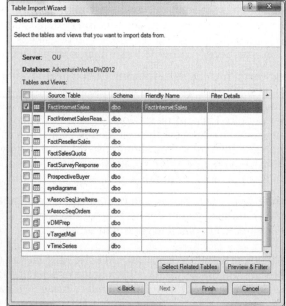

Figure 4-4:
The Table
Import
Wizard
offers up a
list of tables
and views.

Importing tables versus importing views

You may recall from reading Chapter 1 that views are query objects that are built to extract subsets of data from database tables based on certain predefined conditions. (That's a mouthful!) Views are typically created by someone familiar with the database as a kind of canned reporting mechanism that outputs a ready-to-use data set.

There are pros and cons to importing tables versus views.

Tables come with the benefit of defined relationships. When you import tables, Power Pivot can recognize the relationships between the tables and automatically duplicate the relationships in the data model. Tables are also more transparent, allowing you to see all the raw unfiltered data. However, when you import tables, you have to have some level of understanding of the database schema and how the values within the tables are utilized in context of the organization's business rules. In addition, importing a table imports all the columns and records; whether you need them or not. To keep the size of your Power Pivot data model manageable, this often forces you to take the extra step of explicitly filtering out the columns you don't need.

Views are often cleaner data sets because they are already optimized to include only the columns and data that are necessary. In addition, you don't need to have an intimate knowledge of the database schema. Someone with that knowledge has already done the work for you — joined the correct tables, applied the appropriate business rules, and optimized output, for example. What you lose with views, however, is the ability for Power Pivot to automatically recognize and build relationships within the data model. Also, if you don't have the rights to open the views in Design mode, you lose transparency because you cannot see exactly what the view is doing to come up with its final output.

In terms of which is better to use — tables or views — it's generally considered a best practice to use views whenever possible. They not only provide you with cleaner, more user-friendly data but can also help streamline your Power Pivot data model by limiting the amount of data you import. Regardless, using tables is by no means frowned upon and is often the only option because of the lack of database rights or availability of predefined views. You will even find yourself importing both tables and views from the same database.

In Figure 4-4, you see the Select Related Tables button. After you select one or more tables, you can click this button to tell Power Pivot to scan for, and automatically select, any other tables that have a relationship with the table(s) you've already selected. This feature is handy to have when sourcing large databases with dozens of tables.

Importing a table imports all columns and records for that table. This can have an impact on the size and performance of your Power Pivot data model. You will often find that you need only a handful of the columns from the tables you import. In these cases, you can use the Preview & Filter button.

Click the table name to highlight it in blue (refer to Figure 4-4), and then click the Preview & Filter button. The Table Import Wizard opens the Preview Selected Table screen, shown in Figure 4-5. You can see all columns available in the table, with a sampling of rows.

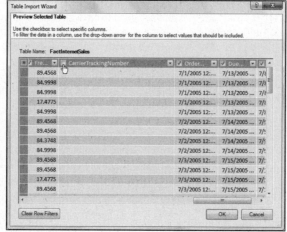

Figure 4-5:
The Preview
& Filter
screen
allows you
to filter out
columns you
don't need.

Each column header has a check box next to it, indicating that the column will be imported with the table. Removing the check mark tells Power Pivot to not include that column in the data model.

You also have the option to filter out certain records. Figure 4-6 demonstrates that clicking on the drop-down arrow for any of the columns opens a Filter menu that allows you to specify criterion to filter out unwanted records. This works just like the standard filtering in Excel. You can select and deselect the data items in the filtered list, or, if there are too many choices, you can apply a broader criteria by clicking Date Filters above the list. (If you're filtering a textual column, it's Text Filters.)

After you finish selecting your data and applying any needed filters, you can click the Finish button on the Table Import Wizard to start the import process. The import log, shown in Figure 4-7, shows the progress of the import and summarizes the import actions taken after completion.

The final step in loading data from SQL Server is to review and create any needed relationships. Open the Power Pivot window and click the Diagram View command button on the Home tab. Power Pivot opens the diagram screen (see Figure 4-8), where you can view and edit relationships as needed.

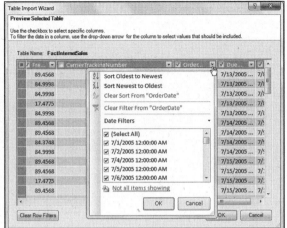

Figure 4-6:
Use the
drop-down
arrows in
each
column to
filter out
unneeded
records.

Figure 4-7:
The last
screen of
the Table
Import
Wizard
shows you
the progress
of your
import
actions.

Don't panic if you feel like you've botched the column-and-record filtering on your imported Power Pivot table. Simply select the worrisome table in the Power Pivot window and open the Edit Table Properties dialog box (choose Design➪Table Properties). Note that this dialog box is basically the same Preview & Filter screen you encounter in the Import Table Wizard (refer to Figure 4-5). From here, you can select columns you originally filtered out, edit record filters, clear filters, or even use a different table/view.

Chapter 2 tells you more about relationships.

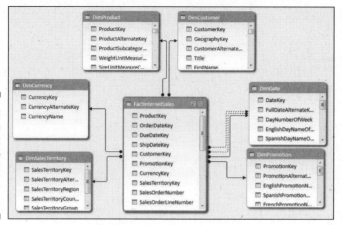

Figure 4-8:
Be sure to
review and
create any
needed
relation-
ships.

Loading data from Microsoft Access databases

Because Microsoft Access has traditionally been made available with the
Microsoft Office suite of applications, Access databases have long been used
by organizations to store and manage mission-critical departmental data.
Walk into any organization, and you will likely find several Access databases
that contain useful data.

Unlike SQL Server databases, Microsoft Access databases are typically found
on local desktops and directories. This means you can typically import data
from Access without the help of your IT department.

Open the Power Pivot window and click the From Other Sources command
button on the Home tab. This opens the Table Import Wizard dialog box,
shown in Figure 4-9. Select the Microsoft Access option, and then click the
Next button.

The Table Import Wizard asks for all the information it needs to connect to
your database (see Figure 4-10).

On this screen, you need to provide the information for these options:

✔ **Friendly Connection Name:** The Friendly Name field allows you to specify your own name for the external source. You typically enter a name
that is descriptive and easy to read.

✔ **Database Name:** Enter the full path of your target Access database. You
can use the Browse button to search for and select the database you
want to pull from.

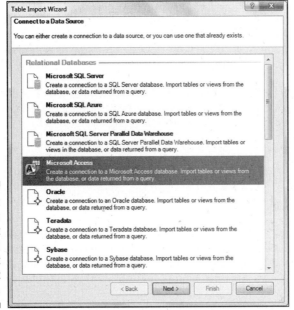

Figure 4-9:
Open the
Table Import
Wizard and
select
Microsoft
Access.

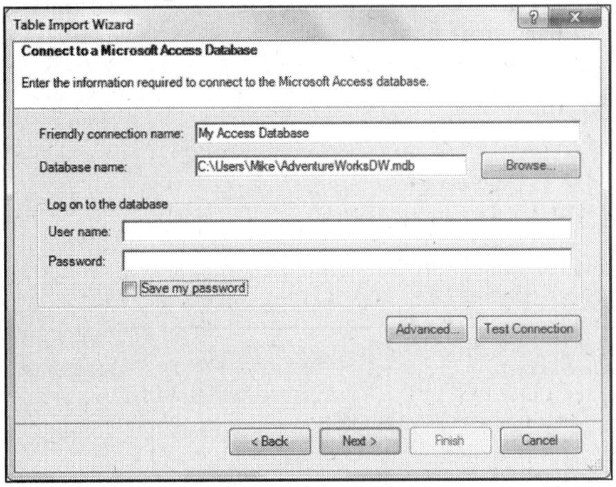

Figure 4-10:
Provide the
basic
information
needed to
connect to
the target
database.

✔ **Log On to the Database:** Most Access databases aren't password protected. But if you're connecting one that does require a username and password, enter your login credentials.

✔ **Save My Password:** You can select the check box next to Save My Password if you want your username and password to be stored in the workbook. Then your connections can remain "refreshable" when being used by other people. Keep in mind that anyone can view the connection properties and see your username and password.

Because Access databases are essentially desktop files (.mdb or .accdb), they're susceptible to being moved, renamed, or deleted. Be aware that the connections in your workbook are hard coded, so if you do move, rename, or delete your Access database, you can no longer connect it.

At this point, you can click the Next button to continue with the Table Import Wizard. From here on out, the process is virtually identical to importing SQL Server data, covered in the last section (starting at Figure 4-3).

Loading data from other relational database systems

Whether your data lives in Oracle, Dbase, or MySQL, you can load data from virtually any relational database system. As long as you have the appropriate database drivers installed, you have a way to connect Power Pivot to your data.

Open the Power Pivot window and click the From Other Sources command button on the Home tab. This opens the Table Import Wizard dialog box, shown in Figure 4-11. The idea is to select the appropriate relational database system. If you need to import data from Oracle, select Oracle. If you need to import data from Sybase, select Sybase.

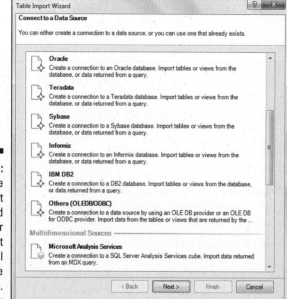

Figure 4-11:
Open the Table Import Wizard and select your target relational database system.

Connecting to any of these relational systems takes you through roughly the same steps as importing SQL Server data, earlier in this chapter. You may see some alternative dialog boxes based on the needs of the database system you select.

Understandably, Microsoft cannot possibly create a named connection option for every database system out there. So you may not find your database system listed. In this case, simply select the Others option (OLEDB/ODBC). Selecting this option opens the Table Import Wizard, starting with a screen asking you to enter or paste the connection string for your database system (see Figure 4-12).

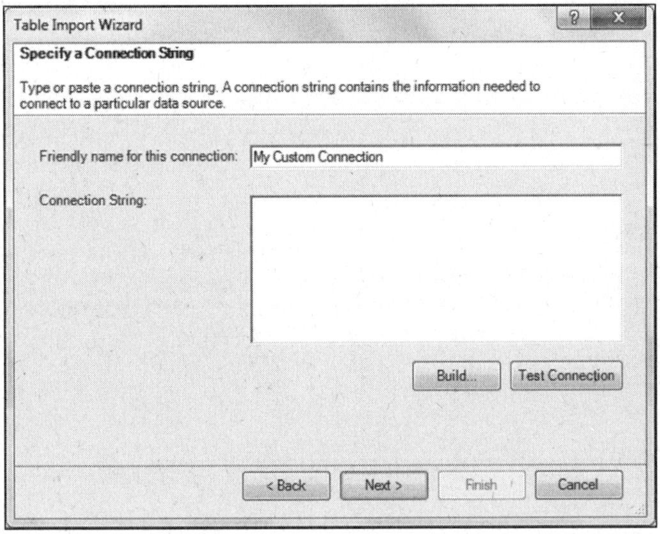

Figure 4-12: Enter the connection string for your database system.

You may be able to get this connection string from your IT department. If you're having trouble finding the correct syntax for your connection string, you can use the Build button to create the string via a set of dialog boxes. Pressing the Build button opens the Data Link Properties dialog box, shown in Figure 4-13.

Start with the Provider tab, selecting the appropriate driver for your database system. The list you see on your computer will be different from the list shown in Figure 4-13. Your list will reflect the drivers you have installed on your own machine.

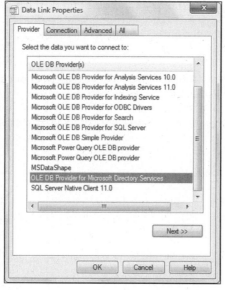

Figure 4-13:
Use the
Data Link
Properties
dialog box
to configure
a custom
connection
string
to your
relational
database
system.

After selecting a driver, move through each tab on the Data Link Properties dialog box and enter the necessary information. When it's complete, click OK to return to the Table Import Wizard, where you see the connection string input box populated with the connection string needed to connect to your database system (see Figure 4-14).

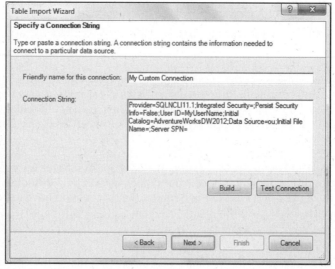

Figure 4-14:
The Table
Import
Wizard
displays the
final syntax
for your
connection
string.

Again, from here on out, the process is virtually identical to importing SQL Server data, as covered earlier in this chapter (starting at Figure 4-3).

To connect to any database system, you must have that system's drivers installed on your PC. Because SQL Server and Access are Microsoft products, their drivers are virtually guaranteed to be installed on any PC with Windows installed. The drivers for other database systems, however, need to be explicitly installed — typically, by the IT department either at the time the machine is loaded with corporate software or upon demand. If you don't see the needed drivers for your database system, contact your IT department.

Loading Data from Flat Files

The term *flat file* refers to a file that contains some form of tabular data without any sort of structural hierarchy or relationship between records. The most common types of flat files are Excel files and text files. Whether anyone likes to admit it or not, a ton of important data is maintained in flat files. In this section, I tell you how to import these flat file data sources into the Power Pivot data model.

Loading data from external Excel files

In Chapter 2, I show you how to create linked tables by loading Power Pivot with the data contained within the same workbook. Linked tables have a distinct advantage over other types of imported data in that they immediately respond to changes in the source data within the workbook. If you change the data in one of the tables in the workbook, the linked table within the Power Pivot data model automatically changes. The real-time interactivity you get with linked tables is especially helpful if you're making frequent changes to your data.

The drawback to linked tables is that the source data must be stored in the same workbook as the Power Pivot data model. This isn't always possible. You'll encounter plenty of scenarios where you need to incorporate Excel data into your analysis, but that data lives in another workbook. In these cases, you can use Power Pivot's Table Import Wizard to connect to external Excel files.

Open the Power Pivot window and click the From Other Sources command button on the Home tab. This opens the Table Import Wizard dialog box, shown in Figure 4-15. Select the Excel File option and then click the Next button.

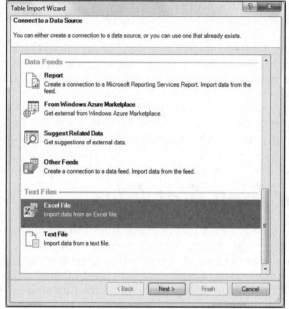

Figure 4-15:
Open the
Table Import
Wizard and
select
Excel File.

The Table Import Wizard asks for all the information it needs to connect to your target workbook (see Figure 4-16).

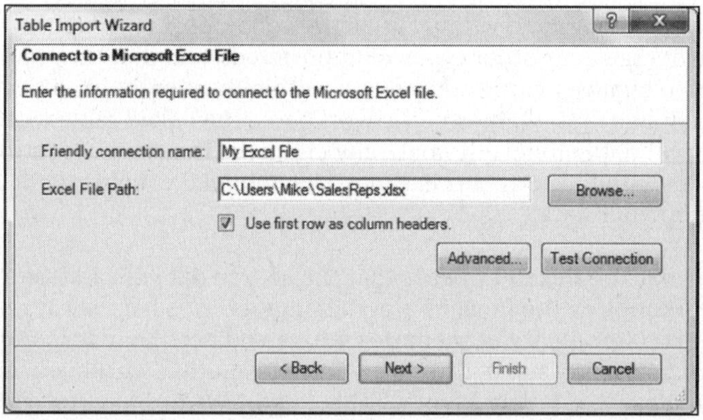

Figure 4-16:
Provide the
basic
information
needed to
connect to
the target
workbook.

On this screen, you need to provide the following information:

✔ **Friendly Connection Name:** In the Friendly Connection Name field, you specify your own name for the external source. You typically enter a name that is descriptive and easy to read.

✔ **Excel File Path:** Enter the full path of your target Excel workbook. You can use the Browse button to search for and select the workbook you want to pull from.

✔ **Use First Row as Column Headers:** In most cases, your Excel data will have column headers. Select the check box next to Use First Row As Column Headers to ensure that your column headers are recognized as headers when imported.

After you enter all the pertinent information, click the Next button to see the next screen, shown in Figure 4-17. You see a list of all worksheets in the chosen Excel workbook. In this case, you have only one worksheet. Place a check mark next to the worksheets you want to import. The Friendly Name column allows you to enter a new name that will be used to reference the table in Power Pivot.

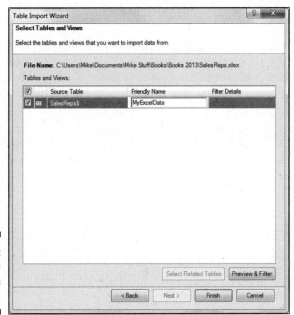

Figure 4-17:
Select the
worksheets
to import.

When reading from external Excel files, Power Pivot cannot identify individual table objects. As a result, you can select only entire worksheets in the Table Import Wizard (shown in Figure 4-17). Keeping this in mind, make sure to import worksheets that contain a single range of data.

As discussed earlier in this chapter, in the section "Loading Data from Relational Databases," you can use the Preview & Filter button to filter out unwanted columns and records, if needed. Otherwise, continue with the Table Import Wizard to complete the import process.

As always, be sure to review and create relationships to any other tables you've loaded into the Power Pivot data model.

Loading external Excel data doesn't give you the same interactivity you get with linked tables. As with importing database tables, the data you bring from an external Excel file is simply a snapshot. You need to refresh the data connection to see any new data that may have been added to the external Excel file (see "Refreshing and Managing External Data Connections," later in this chapter).

Loading data from text files

The text file is another type of flat file used to distribute data. This type of file is commonly output from legacy systems and websites. Excel has always been able to consume text files. With Power Pivot, you can go further and integrate them with other data sources.

Open the Power Pivot window and click the From Other Sources command button on the Home tab. This opens the Table Import Wizard dialog box shown in Figure 4-18. Select the Text File option and then click the Next button.

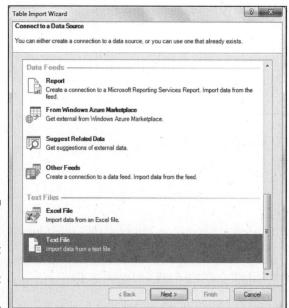

Figure 4-18: Open the Table Import Wizard and select Excel File.

The Table Import Wizard asks for all the information it needs to connect to the target text file (see Figure 4-19).

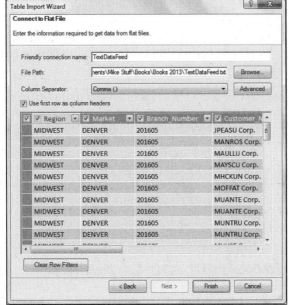

On this screen, you provide the following information:

- **Friendly Connection Name:** The Friendly Connection Name field allows you to specify your own name for the external source. You typically enter a name that is descriptive and easy to read.

- **File Path:** Enter the full path of your target text file. You can use the Browse button to search for and select the file you want to pull from.

- **Column Separator:** Select the character used to separate the columns in the text file. Before you can do this, you need to know how the columns in your text file are delimited. For instance, a comma-delimited file will have commas separating its columns. A tab-delimited file will have tabs separating the columns. The drop-down list in the Table Import Wizard includes choices for the more common delimiters: Tab, Comma, Semicolon, Space, Colon, and Vertical bar.

- **Use First Row as Column Headers:** If your text file contains header rows, be sure to select the check box next to Use First Row as a Column Headers. This ensures that the column headers are recognized as headers when imported.

Notice that you see an immediate preview of the data in the text file. Here, you can filter out any unwanted columns by simply removing the check mark next to the column names. You can also use the drop-down arrows next to each column to apply any record filters.

Clicking the Finish button immediately starts the import process. Upon completion, the data from your text file will be part of the Power Pivot data model. As always, be sure to review and create relationships to any other tables you've loaded into Power Pivot.

Anyone who's worked with text files in Excel knows that they're notorious for importing numbers that look like numbers, but are really coded as text. In standard Excel, you use Text to Columns to fix these kinds of issues. Well, this can be a problem in Power Pivot, too.

When importing text files, take the extra step of verifying that all columns have been imported with the correct data formatting. You can use the formatting tools found on the Power Pivot window's Home tab to format any column in the data model.

Loading data from the Clipboard

Power Pivot includes an interesting option for loading data straight from the Clipboard — that is to say, pasting data you've copied from some other place. This option is meant to be used as a one-off technique to quickly get useful information into the Power Pivot data model.

As you consider this option, keep in mind that there is no real data source. It's just you manually copying and pasting. You have no way to refresh the data, and you have no way to trace back to where you copied the data from.

Imagine that you've received the Word document shown in Figure 4-20. You like the nifty table of holidays within the document, and you believe it would be useful in your Power Pivot data model.

Figure 4-20:
You can copy data straight out of Microsoft Word.

Day	Date	Holiday
Wednesday	1/1/2013	New Year's Day
Monday	1/20/2013	Martin Luther King's Birthday
Monday	2/17/2013	Presidents Day
Sunday	4/20/2013	Easter
Monday	5/26/2013	Memorial Day
Friday	7/4/2013	Independence Day
Monday	9/1/2013	Labor Day
Monday	10/13/2013	Columbus Day
Tuesday	11/11/2013	Veterans Day
Thursday	11/27/2013	Thanksgiving Day
Friday	11/28/2013	Friday after Thanksgiving
Wednesday	12/25/2013	Christmas Day

You can copy the table and then go to the Power Pivot window and click the Paste command on the Home tab. This opens the Past Preview dialog box, shown in Figure 4-21, where you can review what exactly will be pasted. You won't see many options here. You can specify the name that will be used to reference the table in Power Pivot, and you can specify whether the first row is a header.

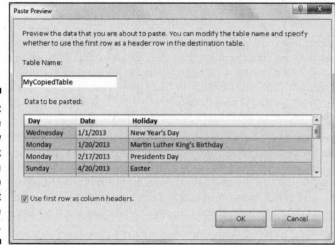

Figure 4-21:
The Paste Preview dialog box gives you a chance to see what you're pasting.

Clicking the OK button imports the pasted data into Power Pivot without a lot of fanfare. At this point, you can adjust the data formatting and create the needed relationships.

Loading Data from Other Data Sources

At this point, I've covered the data sources that are most important to a majority of Excel analysts. Still, there are a few more data sources that Power Pivot is able to connect to and load data from. I touch on some of these data sources later in this book, though others remain out of scope.

Although these data sources are not likely to be used by your average analyst, it's worth dedicating a few lines to each one, if only to know that they exist and are available if ever you should need them:

✔ **Microsoft SQL Azure:** SQL Azure is a cloud-based relational database service that some companies use as an inexpensive way to gain the benefits of SQL Server without taking on the full cost of hardware, software, and IT staff. Power Pivot can load data from SQL Azure in much the same way as the other relational databases I talk about in this chapter.

✔ **Microsoft SQL Parallel Data Warehouse:** SQL Parallel Data Warehouse (SQL PDW) is an appliance that partitions very large data tables into separate servers and manages query processing between them. SQL PDW is used to provide scalability and performance for big data analytics. From a Power Pivot perspective, it's no different than connecting to any other relational database.

✔ **Microsoft Analysis Services:** Analysis Services is Microsoft's OLAP (Online Analytical Processing) product. The data in Analysis Services is traditionally stored in a multidimensional cube.

✔ **Report:** The curiously named Report data source refers to SQL Server Reporting Services reports. In a very basic sense, Reporting Services is a business intelligence tool used to create stylized PDF-style reports from SQL Server data. In the context of Power Pivot, a Reporting Services Report can be used as a data-feed service, providing a refreshable connection to the underlying SQL Server data.

✔ **From Windows Azure Marketplace:** Windows Azure Marketplace is an OData (Open Data Protocol) service that provides both free and paid data sources. Register for a free Azure Marketplace account and you get instant access to governmental data, industrial market data, consumer data, and much more. You can enhance your Power Pivot analyses by loading the data from the Azure marketplace using this connection type.

✔ **Suggested Related Data:** This data source reviews the content of the Power Pivot data model and, based on its findings, suggests Azure Marketplace data that you may be interested in.

✔ **Other Feeds:** The Other Feeds data source allows you to import data from OData web services into Power Pivot. OData connections are facilitated by XML Atom files. Point the OData connection to the URL of the .atomsvcs file and you essentially have a connection to the published web service.

Refreshing and Managing External Data Connections

When you load data from an external data source into Power Pivot, you essentially create a static snapshot of that data source at the time of creation. Power Pivot uses that static snapshot in its Internal Data Model.

As time goes by, the external data source may change and grow with newly added records. However, Power Pivot is still using its snapshot, so it can't incorporate any of the changes in your data source until you take another snapshot.

The action of updating the Power Pivot data model by taking another snapshot of your data source is called *refreshing* the data. You can refresh manually, or you can set up an automatic refresh.

Manually refreshing Power Pivot data

On the home tab of the Power Pivot window, you see the Refresh command. Click the drop-down arrow below it to see two options shown in Figure 4-22: Refresh and Refresh All.

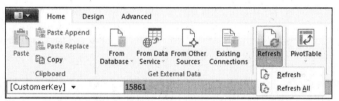

Figure 4-22: Power Pivot allows you to refresh one table or all tables.

Use the Refresh option to refresh the Power Pivot table that's active. That is to say, if you're on the Dim_Products tab in Power Pivot, clicking Refresh reaches out to the external SQL Server and requests an update for only the Dim_Products table. This works nicely when you need to strategically refresh only certain data sources.

Use the Refresh All option to refresh all tables in the Power Pivot data model.

Setting up automatic refreshing

You can configure your data sources to automatically pull the latest data and refresh Power Pivot.

Go to the Data tab on the Excel Ribbon, and select the Connections command. The Workbook Connections dialog box, shown in Figure 4-23, opens. Select the data connection you want to work with and then click the Properties button.

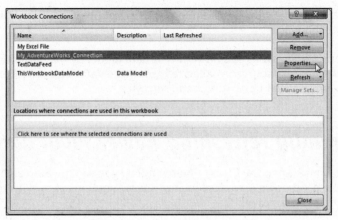

With the Properties dialog box open, select the Usage tab. Here, you'll find an option to refresh the chosen data connection every X minutes and an option to refresh the data connection when the Excel work is opened (see Figure 4-24):

- ✔ **Refresh Every X Minutes:** Placing a check next to this option tells Excel to automatically refresh the chosen data connection a specified number of minutes. This refreshes all tables associated with that connection.

- ✔ **Refresh Data When Opening the File:** Placing a check mark next to this option tells Excel to automatically refresh the chosen data connection after opening of the workbook. This refreshes all tables associated with that connection as soon as the workbook is opened.

Preventing Refresh All

Earlier in this section, you see that you can refresh all connections that feed Power Pivot, by using the Refresh All command (refer to Figure 4-22). Well, there are actually two more places where you can click Refresh All in Excel: on the Data tab in the Excel Ribbon and on the Analyze tab you see when working in a pivot table.

In Excel 2010, these two buttons refreshed only standard pivot tables and workbook data connections, and the Power Pivot refresh buttons affected only Power Pivot. They now all trigger the same operation. So clicking any Refresh All button anywhere in Excel essentially completely reloads Power Pivot, refreshes all pivot tables, and updates all workbook data connections. If your Power Pivot data model imports millions of lines of data from an external data source, you may well want to avoid using the Refresh All feature.

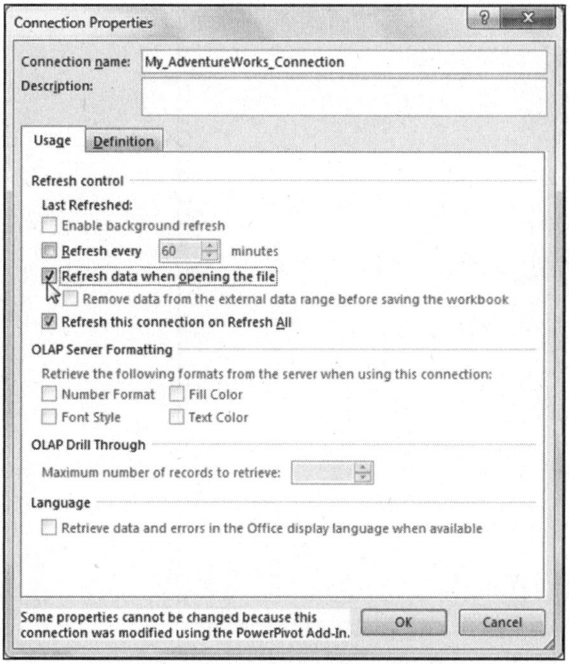

Figure 4-24:
The Proper-
ties dialog
box lets you
configure
the chosen
data
connection
to refresh
automati-
cally.

Luckily, you have a way to prevent certain data connections from refreshing when Refresh All is selected. Go to the Data tab on the Excel Ribbon and
select the Connections command. This opens the Workbook Connections
dialog box, where you select the data connection you want to configure, and
then click the Properties button.

When the Properties dialog box has opened, select the Usage tab and then
remove the check mark next to the Refresh This Connection on Refresh All
(as shown in Figure 4-25).

Editing the data connection

In certain instances, you may need to edit the source data connection after
you've already created it. Unlike refreshing, where you simply take another
snapshot of the same data source, editing the source data connection allows

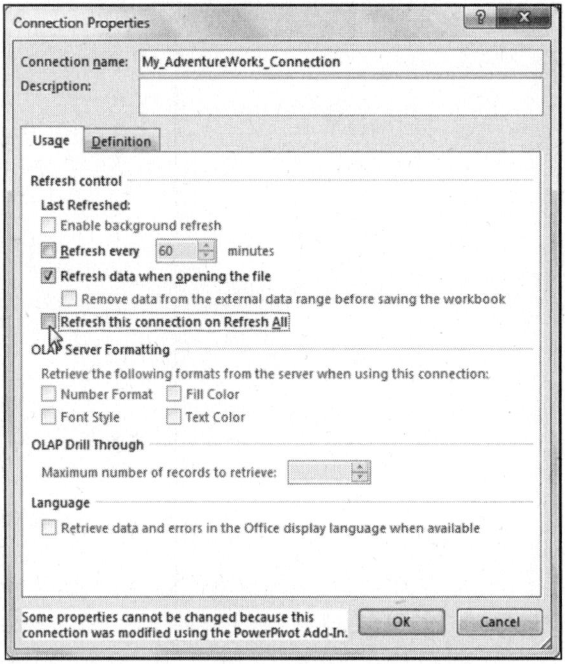

Figure 4-25:
The Properties dialog box lets you configure the chosen data connection to ignore the Refresh All command.

you to go back and reconfigure the connection itself. Here are a few reasons you may need to edit the data connection:

- The location or server or data source file has changed.
- The name of the server or data source file has changed.
- You need to edit your login credentials or authentication mode.
- You need to add tables you left out during initial import.

In the Power Pivot window, go to the Home tab and click the Existing Connections command button. The Existing Connections dialog box, shown in Figure 4-26, opens. Your Power Pivot connections are under the Power Pivot Data Connections subheading. Choose the data connection that needs editing.

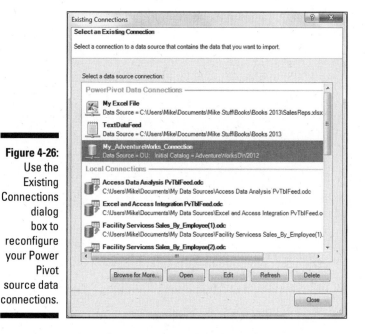

Figure 4-26:
Use the
Existing
Connections
dialog
box to
reconfigure
your Power
Pivot
source data
connections.

After your target data connection is selected, look to the Edit and Open buttons. The button you click depends on what you need to change:

✔ **Edit button:** Lets you reconfigure the server address, file path, and authentication settings.

✔ **Open button:** Lets you import a new table from the existing connection, which is handy when you've inadvertently missed a table during the initial loading of data.

Chapter 5

Working Directly with the Internal Data Model

*I*n the preceding chapters, you use the Power Pivot add-in to work with the Internal Data Model. But as you'll see in this chapter, you can use a combination of pivot tables and Excel data connections to directly interact with the Internal Data Model, without the Power Pivot add-in.

This is useful if you're using versions of Excel that don't come supplied with the Power Pivot add-in, such as when you're using Microsoft Office, either Home or Small Business edition. Every Excel 2013 and 2016 workbook comes with an Internal Data Model.

You can find the sample files for this chapter on this book's companion website at `www.dummies.com/go/excelpowerpivotpowerqueryfd`. These include the `Chapter 5 Sample File.xlsx` Excel workbook and the `Facility Services.accdb` Access database.

Directly Feeding the Internal Data Model

Imagine that you have the Transactions table you see in Figure 5-1, and on another worksheet you have an Employees table (see Figure 5-2) that contains information about the employees.

	A	B	C	D
1	Sales_Rep	Invoice_Date	Sales_Amount	Contracted Hours
2	4416	1/5/2007	111.79	2
3	4416	1/5/2007	111.79	2
4	160006	1/5/2007	112.13	2
5	6444	1/5/2007	112.13	2
6	160006	1/5/2007	145.02	3
7	52661	1/5/2007	196.58	4
8	6444	1/5/2007	204.20	4
9	51552	1/5/2007	225.24	3
10	55662	1/6/2007	86.31	2
11	1336	1/6/2007	86.31	2
12	60224	1/6/2007	86.31	2
13	54564	1/6/2007	86.31	2
14	56146	1/6/2007	89.26	2
15	5412	1/6/2007	90.24	1

Figure 5-1: This table shows transactions by employee number.

	A	B	C	D
1	Employee_Number	Last_Name	First_Name	Job_Title
2	21	SIOCAT	ROBERT	SERVICE REPRESENTATIVE 3
3	42	BREWN	DONNA	SERVICE REPRESENTATIVE 3
4	45	VAN HUILE	KENNETH	SERVICE REPRESENTATIVE 2
5	104	WIBB	MAURICE	SERVICE REPRESENTATIVE 2
6	106	CESTENGIAY	LUC	SERVICE REPRESENTATIVE 2
7	113	TRIDIL	ROCH	SERVICE REPRESENTATIVE 2
8	142	CETE	GUY	SERVICE REPRESENTATIVE 3
9	145	ERSINEILT	MIKE	SERVICE REPRESENTATIVE 2
10	162	GEBLE	MICHAEL	SERVICE REPRESENTATIVE 2
11	165	CERDANAL	ALAIN	SERVICE REPRESENTATIVE 3
12	201	GEIDRIOU	DOMINIC	TEAMLEAD 1

Figure 5-2: This table provides information on employees: first name, last name, and job title.

You need to create an analysis that shows sales by job title. This would normally be difficult given the fact that sales and job title are in two separate tables. But with the Internal Data Model, you can follow these simple steps:

1. **Click inside the Transactions data table and start a new pivot table by choosing Insert ⇨ Pivot Table from the Ribbon.**

2. **In the Create PivotTable dialog box, select the Add This Data to the Data Model option (see Figure 5-3).**

3. **Click inside the Employees data table and start a new pivot table.**

   Again, be sure to select the Add This Data to the Data Model option, as shown in Figure 5-4.

   Notice that in Figures 5-3 and 5-4, the Create PivotTable dialog boxes are referencing named ranges. That is to say, each table was given a specific name. When you're adding data to the Internal Data Model, it's a best practice to name the data tables. This way, you can easily recognize your tables in the Internal Data Model.

   If you don't name your tables, the Internal Data Model shows them as Range1, Range2, and so on.

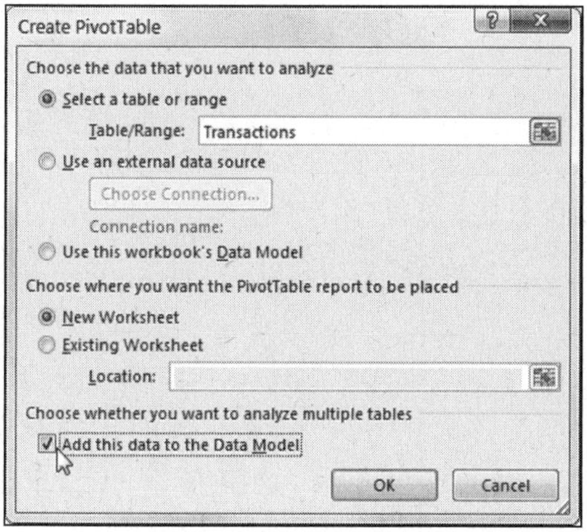

Figure 5-3:
When you
create a
new pivot
table from
the Trans-
actions
table, be
sure to
select Add
This Data to
the Data
Model.

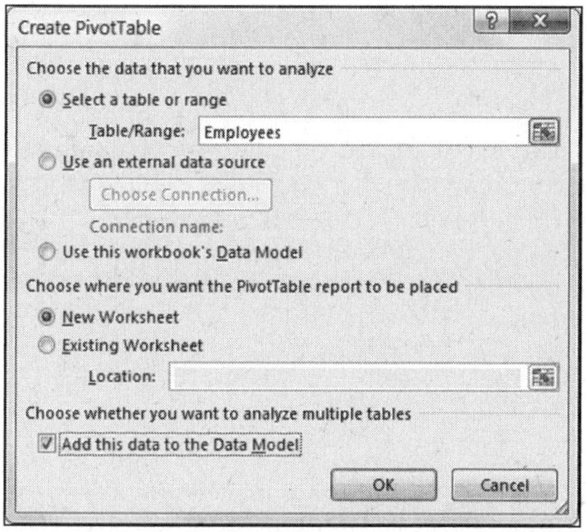

Figure 5-4:
Create a
new pivot
table from
the Employ-
ees table,
and select
Add This
Data to the
Data Model.

4. **To give the data table a name, simply highlight all data in the table, and then select Formulas ⇨ Define Name command from the Ribbon. In the dialog box, enter a name for the table.**

    Repeat for all other tables.

5. **After both tables have been added to the Internal Data Model, open the PivotTable Fields list and choose the ALL selector, as shown in Figure 5-5.**

    This step shows both ranges in the field list.

6. **Build out the pivot table as normal. In this case, Job_Title is placed in the Row area, and Sales_Amount goes to the Values area.**

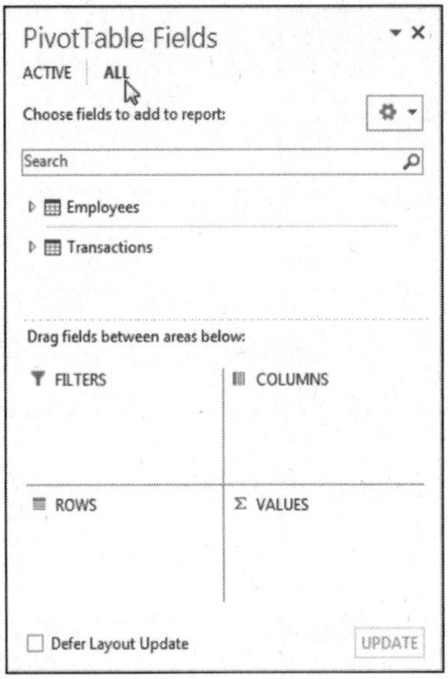

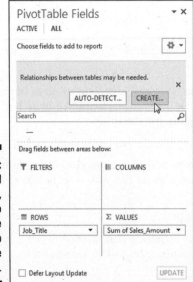

Figure 5-5:
Select ALL
in the
PivotTable
Fields list to
see both
tables in the
Internal
Data Model.

As you can see in Figure 5-6, Excel immediately recognizes that you're using two tables from the Internal Data Model and prompts you to create a relationship between them. You have the option to let Excel autodetect the relationships between your tables or to click the Create button. Always create the relationships yourself, to avoid any possibility of Excel getting it wrong.

Figure 5-6:
When Excel
prompts you,
choose to
create the
relationship
between the
two tables.

7. Click the Create button.

Excel opens the Create Relationship dialog box, shown in Figure 5-7. There, you select the tables and fields that define the relationship. In Figure 5-7, you can see that the Transactions table has a Sales_Rep field. It's related to the Employees table via the Employee_Number field.

After you create the relationship, you have a single pivot table that effectively uses data from both tables to create the analysis you need. Figure 5-8 illustrates that, by using the Excel Internal Data Model, you've achieved the goal of showing sales by job title.

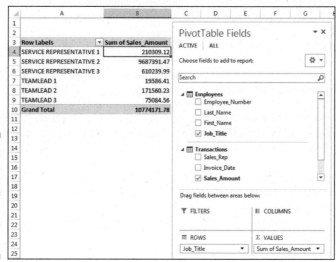

The limitations of Power Pivot-driven pivot tables

Pivot tables built on top of Power Pivot or the Internal Data Model come with limitations that could be showstoppers in terms of your reporting needs. Here's a quick rundown of the limitations you should consider before deciding to base your pivot table reporting on Power Pivot or the Internal Data Model:

- ✔ The Group feature is disabled for Power Pivot–driven pivot tables. You can't roll dates into months, quarters, or years, for example.

- ✔ In a standard pivot table, you can double-click a cell in the pivot to drill into to the rows that make up the figure in that cell. In Power Pivot–driven pivot tables, however, you see only the first 1,000 rows.

- ✔ Power Pivot–driven pivot tables don't allow you to create the traditional Calculated Fields and Calculated Items found in standard Excel pivot tables.

- ✔ Workbooks that use the Power Pivot data model can't be refreshed or configured if opened in a version of Excel earlier than Excel 2013.

- ✔ You can't use custom lists to automatically sort the data in your Power Pivot–driven pivot tables.

- ✔ Neither the Product nor Count Numbers summary calculations are available in Power Pivot–driven pivot tables.

In Figure 5-7, you see that the lower-right drop-down is named Related Column (Primary). The term *primary* means that the Internal Data Model uses this field from the associated table as the primary key.

A *primary key* is a field that contains only unique non-null values (no duplicates or blanks). Primary key fields are necessary in the data model to prevent aggregation errors and duplications. Every relationship you create must have a field designated as the primary key.

The Employees table (in the scenario in Figure 5-7) must have all unique values in the Employee_Number field, with no blanks or null values. This is the only way that Excel can ensure data integrity when joining multiple tables.

After you assign tables to the Internal Data Model, you might need to adjust the relationships between the tables. To make changes to the relationships in an Internal Data Model, click the Data tab on the Ribbon and select the Relationships command. The Manage Relationships dialog box, shown in Figure 5-9, opens.

Figure 5-9:
The Manage Relation-ships dialog box enables you to make changes to the relation-ships in the Internal Data Model.

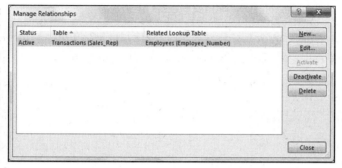

Here, you'll find the following commands:

- **New:** Create a new relationship between two tables in the Internal Data Model.
- **Edit:** Alter the selected relationship.
- **Activate:** Enforce the selected relationship, telling Excel to consider the relationship when aggregating and analyzing the data in the Internal Data Model.
- **Deactivate:** Turn off the selected relationship, telling Excel to ignore the relationship when aggregating and analyzing the data in the Internal Data Model.
- **Delete:** Remove the selected relationship.

Adding a New Table to the Internal Data Model

You can add a new table to the Internal Data Model in one of two ways, as described in this section.

The easiest way is to create a pivot table from the new table and then choose the Add This Data to the Internal Data Model option. Excel adds the table to the Internal Data Model and produces a pivot table. After the table has been added, you can open the Manage Relationships dialog box and create the needed relationship.

The second, and more flexible, method is to define the table manually and add it to the Internal Data Model. Here's how:

1. Place the cursor inside the data table and select Insert Table.

The Create Table dialog box, shown in Figure 5-10, opens.

Figure 5-10:
Converting
the range
into a
defined
table.

2. Specify the range for your data and click the OK button.

Excel turns that range into a defined table that the Internal Data Model can recognize.

3. On the Table Tools Design tab, change the Table Name field (in the Properties group), as shown in Figure 5-11.

Pick a name that's appropriate and easy to remember.

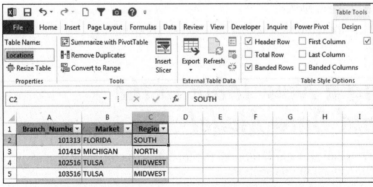

Figure 5-11:
Give the
newly
created
table a
friendly
name.

4. From the Data tab on the Ribbon, select Connections.

The Workbook Connections dialog box opens, as shown in Figure 5-12.

5. Click the drop-down list next to Add and choose the Add to the Data Model option.

The Existing Connections dialog box opens.

Figure 5-12:
Open the
Workbook
Connections
dialog box
and select
Add to the
Data Model.

6. **On the Tables tab, find and select the newly created table, as shown in
   Figure 5-13. Click the Open button to add it to the Internal Data Model.**

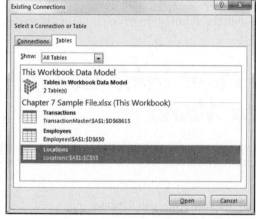

Figure 5-13:
Select the
newly
created
table and
click the
Open
button.

At this point, all pivot tables built on the Internal Data Model are updated
to reflect the new table. Be sure to open the Manage Relationships dialog
box and create the needed relationship.

Removing a Table from the Internal Data Model

You might find that you want to remove a table or data source altogether
from the Internal Data Model. To do so, click the Data tab on the Ribbon and
then click the Connections command. The Workbook Connections dialog
box, shown in Figure 5-14, opens.

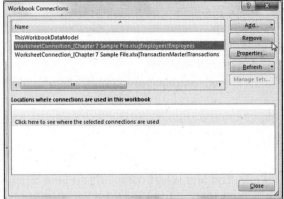

Figure 5-14:
Use the
Workbook
Connections
dialog box
to remove
any table
from
the Internal
Data Model.

Click the table you want to remove from the Internal Data Model (Employees, in this case) and then click the Remove button.

Creating a New Pivot Table Using the Internal Data Model

In certain instances, you may want to create a pivot table from scratch using the existing Internal Data Model as the source data. Here are the steps to do so:

1. **Choose Insert ⇨ PivotTable from the Ribbon.**

   The Create PivotTable dialog box opens.

2. **Select the Use an External Data Source option, as shown in Figure 5-15, and then click the Choose Connection button.**

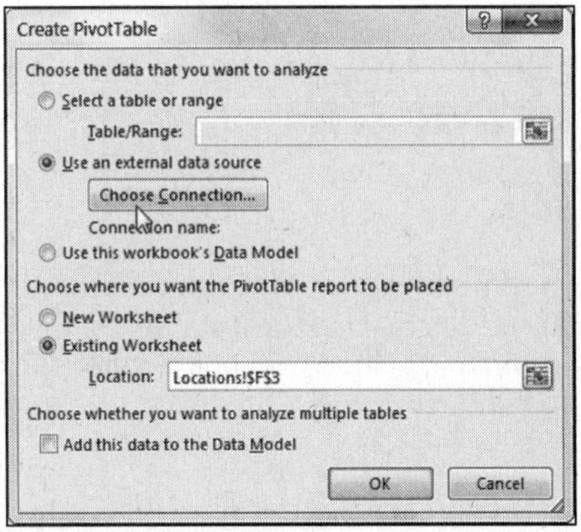

Figure 5-15:
Open the
Create
PivotTable
dialog box
and choose
the external
data-source
option.

You see the Existing Connections dialog box, as shown in Figure 5-16.

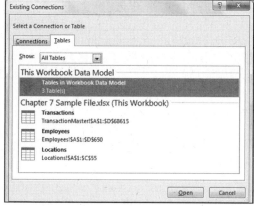

Figure 5-16:
Use the
Existing
Connections
dialog box
to select the
Data Model
as the data
source for
your pivot
table.

3. **On the Tables tab, select Tables in Workbook Data Model, and then click the Open button.**

   You return to the Create PivotTable dialog box.

4. **Click the OK button to create the pivot table.**

   If all goes well, you see the PivotTable Fields dialog box with all tables that are included in the Internal Data Model, as shown in Figure 5-17.

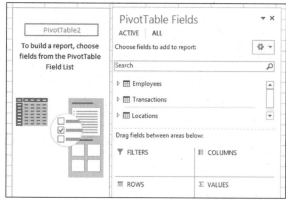

Figure 5-17:
The newly
created
pivot table
shows all
tables in the
Internal
Data Model.

Filling the Internal Data Model with Multiple External Data Tables

Suppose you have an Access database that contains a normalized set of tables. You want to analyze the data in that database in Excel, so you decide to use the new Excel Internal Data Model to expose the data you need through a pivot table.

To accomplish this task, follow these steps:

1. **Click the Data tab on the Ribbon and click the From Access command, as shown in Figure 5-18.**

File
Home
Insert
Page Layout
Formulas
Data
From Access
From Web
From Text
From Other Sources
Existing Connections
Get External Data
Show Queries
From Table
New Query
Recent Sources
Get & Transform

Figure 5-18: Click the From Access button to get data from your Access database.

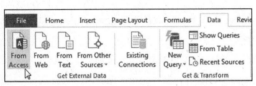

2. **Browse to your target Access database and open it.**

   The Select Table dialog box opens.

3. **Place a check mark next to the Enable Selection of Multiple Tables option (see Figure 5-19).**

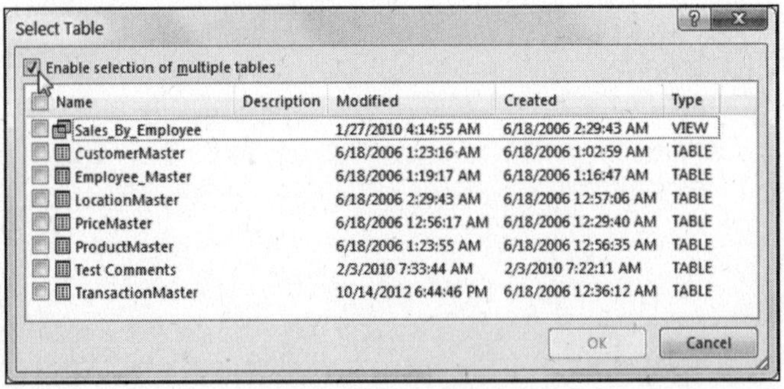

Select Table
Enable selection of multiple tables
Name
Description
Modified
Created
Type
Sales_By_Employee 1/27/2010 4:14:55 AM 6/18/2006 2:29:43 AM VIEW
CustomerMaster 6/18/2006 1:23:16 AM 6/18/2006 1:02:59 AM TABLE
Employee_Master 6/18/2006 1:19:17 AM 6/18/2006 1:16:47 AM TABLE
LocationMaster 6/18/2006 2:29:43 AM 6/18/2006 12:57:06 AM TABLE
PriceMaster 6/18/2006 12:56:17 AM 6/18/2006 12:29:40 AM TABLE
ProductMaster 6/18/2006 1:23:55 AM 6/18/2006 12:56:35 AM TABLE
Test Comments 2/3/2010 7:33:44 AM 2/3/2010 7:22:11 AM TABLE
TransactionMaster 10/14/2012 6:44:46 PM 6/18/2006 12:36:12 AM TABLE
OK
Cancel

Figure 5-19: Enable the selection of multiple tables.

4. **Place a check mark next to each table that you want to import into the Internal Data Model, as shown in Figure 5-20. Then click OK.**

   The Import Data dialog box opens.

Figure 5-20:
Select the
tables you
want import
into the
Internal
Data Model,
and then
click OK.

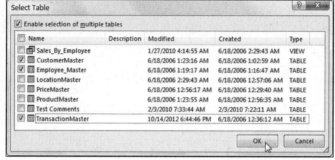

5. **Click the drop-down arrow next to Properties, and remove the check mark next to the Import Relationships Between Tables option, as shown in Figure 5-21.**

Figure 5-21:
Click to
deselect the
Import Rela-
tionships
Between
Tables
option.

This step ensures that Excel doesn't introduce a potential error by misinterpreting how the tables are related. In other words, you'll want to create relationships yourself.

6. **Still in the Import Data dialog box, choose the PivotTable Report option and click OK to create the base pivot.**

7. **Click the Data tab on the Ribbon and choose the Relationships command.**

   This step opens the Manage Relationships dialog box.

8. **Create the needed relationships, as shown in Figure 5-22, and then click Close.**

You now have a pivot table based on external data imported into the Internal Data Model (see Figure 5-23). At this point, you can use the Pivot Table Field list to build the pivot table.

In just a few a few clicks, you have created a powerful platform to build and maintain pivot table analysis based on data in an Access database!

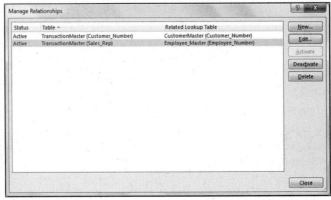

Figure 5-22: Create the needed relationships for the tables you just imported.

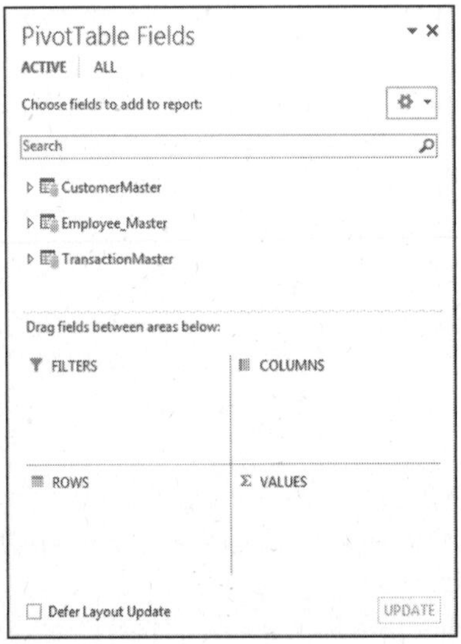

Figure 5-23: You're ready to build the pivot table analysis based on multiple external data tables.

Chapter 6

Adding Formulas to Power Pivot

In This Chapter

▶ Creating, formatting, and hiding your own calculated columns

▶ Creating calculated columns by using DAX

▶ Creating calculated measures

▶ Breaking out of pivot tables with cube functions

*W*hen analyzing data with Power Pivot, you often find the need to expand your analysis to include data based on calculations that are not in the original dataset. Power Pivot has a robust set of functions (called *DAX* functions) that allow you to perform mathematical operations, recursive calculations, data lookups, and much more.

This chapter introduces you to DAX functions and provides the ground rules for building your own calculations in Power Pivot data models.

Enhancing Power Pivot Data with Calculated Columns

Calculated columns are columns you create to enhance a Power Pivot table with your own formulas. When you enter calculated columns directly in the Power Pivot window, they become part of the source data you use to feed your pivot table. Calculated columns work at the row level. That is to say, the formulas you create in a calculated column perform their operations based on the data in each individual row. For example, if you have a Revenue column and a Cost column in your Power Pivot table, you could create a new column that calculates [Revenue] minus [Cost]. This simple calculation is valid for each row in the data set.

Calculated measures are used to perform more complex calculations that work on an aggregation of data. These calculations are applied directly to a pivot table, creating a sort of virtual column that can't be seen in the Power Pivot window. Calculated measures are needed whenever you need to calculate based on an aggregated grouping of rows — for example, the sum of [Year2] minus the sum of [Year1].

Creating your first calculated column

Creating a calculated column works much like building formulas in an Excel table. Follow these steps to create a calculated column:

1. **Activate the Power Pivot window (click the Manage command button on the Power Pivot Ribbon tab), and then select the Invoice Details tab.**

   In the table, you see an empty column on the far right, labeled Add Column.

2. **Click on the first blank cell in that column.**

3. **On the Formula bar, enter the following formula (as shown in Figure 6-1):**

   ```
   =[UnitPrice]*[Quantity]
   ```

Figure 6-1: Start the calculated column by entering an operation on the Formula bar.

	InvoiceNumber	Quantity	UnitCost	UnitPrice	Total Revenue	
	[Total Revenue] ▾	fx =[UnitPrice]*[Quantity]				
1	ORDST1022	1	59.29	119.95	119.95	
2	ORDST1015	1	3290.55	6589.95	6589.95	
3	ORDST1016	10	35	34.95	349.5	
4	ORDST1017	50	91.59	189.95	9497.5	
5	ORDST1018	1	59.29	119.95	119.95	
6	INV1010	1	674.5	1349.95	1349.95	
7	INV1011	1	91.25	189.95	189.95	
8	INV1012	1	303.85	609.95	609.95	
9	ORDST1020	1	59.29	119.95	119.95	
10	ORDST1021	1	59.29	119.95	119.95	

4. **Press Enter.**

   The formula populates the entire column, and Power Pivot automatically renames the column to Calculated Column 1.

5. **Double-click on the column label and rename the column Total Revenue.**

   You can rename any column in the Power Pivot window by double-clicking the column name and entering a new name. Alternatively, you can right-click any column and choose the Rename option.

You can build calculated columns by clicking instead of typing. For example, rather than manually enter =[UnitPrice]*[Quantity], you can enter the equal sign (=), click the UnitPrice column, type the asterisk (*), and then click the Quantity column. You can also enter your own static data. For example, you can enter a formula to calculate a 10-percent tax rate by entering =[UnitPrice]*1.10.

Each calculated column you create is automatically available in any pivot table connected to the Power Pivot Data Model. You don't have to take any action to get your calculated columns into the pivot table. Figure 6-2 shows the Total Revenue calculated column in the PivotTable Fields List. These calculated columns can be used just as you would use any other field in the pivot table.

Row Labels	▼ Sum of Total Revenue
Aaron Fitz Electrical	45668.4
Adam Park Resort	6238.5
Advanced Paper Co.	131930.45
Advanced Tech Satellite System	2278.7
American Science Museum	6357.8
Associated Insurance Company	1299.8
Astor Suites	174604.55
Atmore Retirement Center	39.95
Baker's Emporium Inc.	18418
Blue Yonder Airlines	26138.3
Boyle's Country Inn's	1829.85
Breakthrough Telemarketing	91437
Castle Inn Resort	239.9
Central Communications LTD	36816.2
Central Distributing	9637.8
Central Illinois Hospital	10229.9
Communication Connections	928.85
Computerized Phone Systems	239.9

PivotTable Fields ▾ ✕

ACTIVE | ALL

Choose fields to add to report: ⚙ ▾

Search 🔍

▲ 🎬 InvoiceDetails
☐ InvoiceNumber
☐ Quantity
☐ UnitCost
☐ UnitPrice
☑ Total Revenue
▷ 🎬 InvoiceHeader

Drag fields between areas below:

▼ FILTERS   ▥ COLUMNS

Figure 6-2: Calculated columns automatically show up in the PivotTable Fields List.

If you need to edit the formula in a calculated column, find the calculated column in the Power Pivot window, click the column, and then make changes directly on the Formula bar.

See Chapter 2 for a refresher on how to create a pivot table from Power Pivot.

Formatting calculated columns

You often need to change the formatting of Power Pivot columns to appropriately match the data within them. For example, you may want to show numbers as currency, remove decimal places, or display dates in a certain way.

You're by no means limited to formatting only calculated columns. The following steps can be used to format any column you see in the Power Pivot window:

1. **In the Power Pivot window, click on the column you want to format.**

2. **Go to the Home tab of the Power Pivot window and find the Formatting group (see Figure 6-3).**

3. **Use the option to alter the formatting of the column as you see fit.**

Figure 6-3:
You can use the formatting tools found on the Power Pivot window's Home tab to format any column in the Data Model.

	InvoiceNumber	Quantity	UnitCost	UnitPrice	Total Revenue	Add Column
1	ORDST1022	1	59.29	119.95	$119.95	
2	ORDST1015	1	3290.55	6589.95	$6,589.95	
3	ORDST1016	10	35	34.95	$349.50	
4	ORDST1017	50	91.59	189.95	$9,497.50	
5	ORDST1018	1	59.29	119.95	$119.95	
6	INV1010	1	674.5	1349.95	$1,349.95	
7	INV1011	1	91.25	189.95	$189.95	
8	INV1012	1	303.85	609.95	$609.95	
9	ORDST1020	1	59.29	119.95	$119.95	
10	ORDST1021	1	59.29	119.95	$119.95	

[Total Revenue] ▾ f_x =[UnitPrice]*[Quantity]

Data Type : Auto (Decimal Number)
Format : Currency

Veteran Excel pivot table users know that changing pivot table number formats one data field at a time is a pain. One fantastic feature of Power Pivot formatting is that any format you apply to the columns in the Power Pivot window is automatically applied to all pivot tables connected to the Data Model.

Referencing calculated columns in other calculations

As with all calculations in Excel, Power Pivot allows you to reference a calculated column as a variable in another calculated column. Figure 6-4 illustrates this concept with a new calculated column named Gross Margin. Notice that on the Formula bar, the calculation is using the [Total Revenue] calculated column that you create earlier in this chapter.

Figure 6-4:
The new Gross Margin calculation is using the previously created [Total Revenue] and calculated column.

f_x =[Total Revenue]-([UnitCost]*[Quantity])

Quantity	UnitCost	UnitPrice	Total Revenue	Gross Margin
1	59.29	119.95	$119.95	60.66
1	3290.55	6589.95	$6,589.95	3299.4
10	35	34.95	$349.50	-0.5
50	91.59	189.95	$9,497.50	4918
1	59.29	119.95	$119.95	60.66
1	674.5	1349.95	$1,349.95	675.45
1	91.25	189.95	$189.95	98.7
1	303.85	609.95	$609.95	306.1
1	59.29	119.95	$119.95	60.66
1	59.29	119.95	$119.95	60.66

Hiding calculated columns from end users

Because calculated columns can reference each other, you can imagine creating columns simply as helper columns for other calculations. You may not want your end users to see these columns in your client tools. (In this context, *client tools* refers to pivot tables, Power View dashboards, and Power Map.)

Similar to hiding columns on an Excel worksheet, Power Pivot allows you to hide any column. (It doesn't have to be a calculated column.) To hide columns, select the columns you want hidden, right-click the selection, and then choose the Hide from Client Tools option (as shown in Figure 6-5).

	UnitCost	UnitPrice	Total Revenue	Gross Margin	
1	59.29	119.95	$	Create Relationship...	
1	3290.55	6589.95	$6,	Navigate to Related Table	
10	35	34.95	$	Copy	
50	91.59	189.95	$9,	Insert Column	
1	59.29	119.95	$	Delete Columns	
1	674.5	1349.95	$1,	Rename Column	
1	91.25	189.95	$	Freeze Columns	
1	303.85	609.95	$	Unfreeze All Columns	
1	59.29	119.95	$	Hide from Client Tools	
1	59.29	119.95	$	Column Width...	
1	179.85	359.95	$	Filter	
1	3.29	9.95		Description...	

Figure 6-5:
Right-click and select Hide from Client Tools.

When a column is hidden, it doesn't show as an available selection in the PivotTable Fields List. However, if the column you're hiding is already part of the pivot report (meaning you've already dragged it onto the pivot table), hiding the column doesn't automatically remove it from the report. Hiding merely affects the ability to see the column in the PivotTable Fields List.

Note in Figure 6-6 that Power Pivot recolors columns based on their attributes. Hidden columns are subdued and grayed-out, whereas calculated columns that are not hidden have a darker (black) header.

To unhide columns, select the hidden columns in the Power Pivot window, right-click on the selection, and then choose the Unhide from Client Tools option.

Figure 6-6:
Hidden
columns are
grayed-out,
and
calculated
columns
have darker
headings.

UnitCost	UnitPrice	Total Revenue	Gross Margin
59.29	119.95	$119.95	60.66
3290.55	6589.95	$6,589.95	3299.4
35	34.95	$349.50	-0.5
91.59	189.95	$9,497.50	4918
59.29	119.95	$119.95	60.66
674.5	1349.95	$1,349.95	675.45
91.25	189.95	$189.95	98.7
303.85	609.95	$609.95	306.1
59.29	119.95	$119.95	60.66
59.29	119.95	$119.95	60.66

Utilizing DAX to Create Calculated Columns

Data Analysis Expressions, or DAX, is essentially the formula language that
Power Pivot uses to perform calculations within its own construct of tables
and columns. The DAX formula language comes supplied with its own set
of functions. Some of these functions can be used in calculated columns for
row-level calculations, and others are designed to be used in calculated
measures to aggregate operations.

In this section, I touch on some of the DAX functions that you can leverage in
calculated columns.

DAX has more than 150 different functions. The examples of DAX that I demonstrate in this chapter are meant to give you a sense of how calculated
columns and calculated measures work. A full overview of DAX is beyond the
scope of this book. If, after reading this chapter, you want to read more about
DAX, however, pick up *The Definitive Guide to DAX,* by Alberto Ferrari and
Marco Russo. Ferrari and Russo provide an excellent overview of DAX that is
comprehensive but easy to understand.

Identifying DAX functions that are safe for calculated columns

Earlier in this chapter, you use the Formula bar within the Power Pivot
window to enter calculations. Next to the Formula bar, you may have noticed
the Insert Function button: the button labeled *fx*. It's similar to the Insert
Function button in Excel. Clicking this button opens the Insert Function
dialog box, shown in Figure 6-7. Using this dialog box, you can browse, search
for, and insert the available DAX functions.

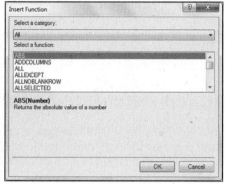

Figure 6-7:
The Insert Function dialog box shows you all available DAX functions.

As you look through the list of DAX functions, notice that many of them look like the common Excel functions that most people are familiar with. But make no mistake: They aren't Excel functions. Whereas Excel functions work with cells and ranges, these DAX functions are designed to work at the table and column levels.

To understand what I mean, start a new calculated column on the Invoice Details tab. Click on the Formula bar and type a good old SUM function: SUM([Gross Margin]). The result is shown in Figure 6-8.

	f_x =sum([Gross Margin])				
Cost	UnitPrice	Total Revenue	Gross Margin	Calculated Column 1	
59.29	119.95	$119.95	60.66	928378.069999998	
3290.55	6589.95	$6,589.95	3299.4	928378.069999998	
35	34.95	$349.50	-0.5	928378.069999998	
91.59	189.95	$9,497.50	4918	928378.069999998	
59.29	119.95	$119.95	60.66	928378.069999998	
674.5	1349.95	$1,349.95	675.45	928378.069999998	
91.25	189.95	$189.95	98.7	928378.069999998	
303.85	609.95	$609.95	306.1	928378.069999998	
59.29	119.95	$119.95	60.66	928378.069999998	
59.29	119.95	$119.95	60.66	928378.069999998	

Figure 6-8:
The DAX SUM function can only sum the column as a whole.

As you can see, the SUM function sums the entire column. This is because Power Pivot and DAX are designed to work with tables and columns. Power Pivot has no construct for cells and ranges. It doesn't even have column letters and row numbers on its grid. Though you would normally reference a range (as in an Excel SUM function), DAX basically takes the entire column.

The bottom line is that not all DAX functions can be used with calculated columns. Because a calculated column evaluates at the row level, only DAX functions that evaluate single data points can be used in a calculated column.

Here's a good rule of thumb: If the function requires an array or a range of cells as an argument, it isn't viable in a calculated column.

So, functions such as SUM, MIN, MAX, AVERAGE, and COUNT don't work in calculated columns. Functions that require only single data-point arguments work quite well in calculated columns: functions such as YEAR, MONTH, MID, LEFT, RIGHT, IF, and IFERROR.

Building DAX-driven calculated columns

To demonstrate the usefulness of employing a DAX function to enhance calculated columns, let's return to the walk-through example. Go to the Power Pivot window and select the InvoiceHeader tab on the Ribbon. If you've accidentally closed the Power Pivot window, you can open it by clicking the Manage command button on the Power Pivot Ribbon tab.

The InvoiceHeader tab, shown in Figure 6-9, contains an InvoiceDate column. Although this column is valuable in the raw table, the individual dates aren't convenient when analyzing the data with a pivot table. It would be beneficial to have a column for Month and a column for Year. This way, you could aggregate and analyze the data by month and year.

Figure 6-9: DAX functions can help enhance the invoice header data with Year and Month time dimensions.

	InvoiceDate	InvoiceNumber	CustomerID	Add Column
1	5/8/2005 12:00:00 AM	ORDST1025	BAKERSEM0001	
2	4/12/2007 12:00:00 AM	STDINV2251	BAKERSEM0001	
3	5/8/2005 12:00:00 AM	ORDST1026	AARONFIT0001	
4	4/12/2007 12:00:00 AM	STDINV2252	AARONFIT0001	
5	5/7/2004 12:00:00 AM	ORD1002	METROPOL0001	
6	2/10/2004 12:00:00 AM	INV1024	AARONFIT0001	
7	2/15/2004 12:00:00 AM	INV1025	AARONFIT0001	
8	5/10/2004 12:00:00 AM	ORDPH1005	LECLERC0001	
9	5/8/2004 12:00:00 AM	ORD1000	MAGNIFIC0001	

For this endeavor, you use the DAX functions YEAR( ), MONTH( ), and FORMAT( ) to add some time dimensions to the Data Model. Follow these steps:

1. **In the InvoiceHeader table, click on the first blank cell in the empty column labeled Add Column, on the far right.**

2. **On the Formula bar, type** =YEAR([InvoiceDate]) **and then press Enter.**

   Power Pivot automatically renames the column to Calculated Column 1.

3. **Double-click on the column label and rename the column** Year.

4. **Starting in the next column, click on the first blank cell in the empty column labeled Add Column, on the far right.**

5. **On the Formula bar, type** =MONTH([InvoiceDate]), **and then press Enter.**

   Power Pivot automatically renames the column to Calculated Column 1.

6. **Double-click on the column label and rename the column** Month.

7. **Starting in the next column, click on the first blank cell in the empty column labeled Add Column, on the far right.**

8. **On the Formula bar, type** =FORMAT([InvoiceDate],"mmm") **and then press Enter.**

   Power Pivot automatically renames the column to Calculated Column 1.

9. **Double-click on the column label and rename the column** Month Name.

After completing these steps, you should have three new calculated columns similar to the ones shown in Figure 6-10.

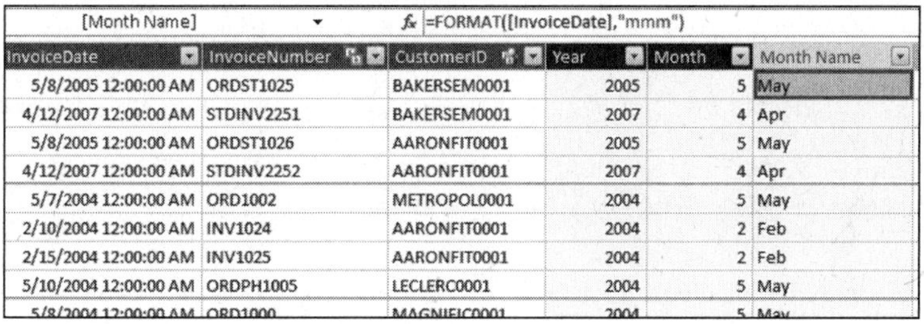

Figure 6-10:
Using DAX
functions to
supplement
a table with
Year,
Month, and
Month
Name
columns.

[Month Name]	▼	*f_x* =FORMAT([InvoiceDate],"mmm")				
InvoiceDate	InvoiceNumber	CustomerID	Year	Month	Month Name
5/8/2005 12:00:00 AM	ORDST1025	BAKERSEM0001	2005	5	May
4/12/2007 12:00:00 AM	STDINV2251	BAKERSEM0001	2007	4	Apr
5/8/2005 12:00:00 AM	ORDST1026	AARONFIT0001	2005	5	May
4/12/2007 12:00:00 AM	STDINV2252	AARONFIT0001	2007	4	Apr
5/7/2004 12:00:00 AM	ORD1002	METROPOL0001	2004	5	May
2/10/2004 12:00:00 AM	INV1024	AARONFIT0001	2004	2	Feb
2/15/2004 12:00:00 AM	INV1025	AARONFIT0001	2004	2	Feb
5/10/2004 12:00:00 AM	ORDPH1005	LECLERC0001	2004	5	May
5/8/2004 12:00:00 AM	ORD1000	MAGNIFIC0001	2004	5	May

As I mention earlier in this chapter, creating calculated columns automatically makes them available through the PivotTable Fields List (see Figure 6-11).

One of the more annoying aspects of Power Pivot is that it doesn't inherently know how to sort months. Unlike standard Excel, Power Pivot doesn't use the built-in custom lists that define the order of month names. Whenever you create a calculated column such as [Month Name] and place it into your pivot table, Power Pivot puts those months in alphabetical order, as shown in Figure 6-12.

The fix for this problem is fairly easy. Open the Power Pivot window and select the Home tab. There, click the Sort by Column command button. The Sort by Column dialog box the opens, as shown in Figure 6-13.

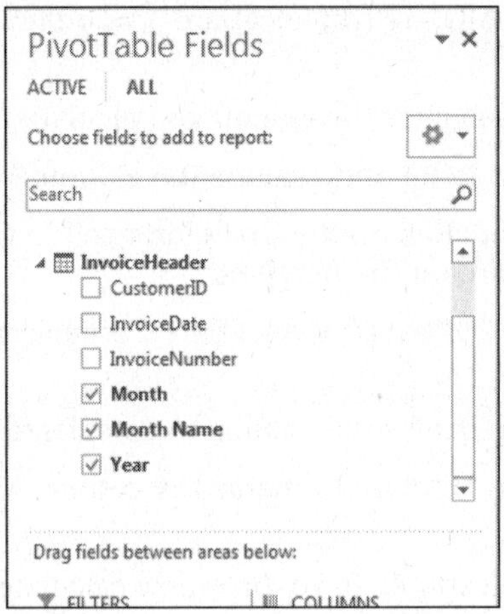

Figure 6-11:
DAX calcu-
lations are
immediately
available
in any
connected
pivot table.

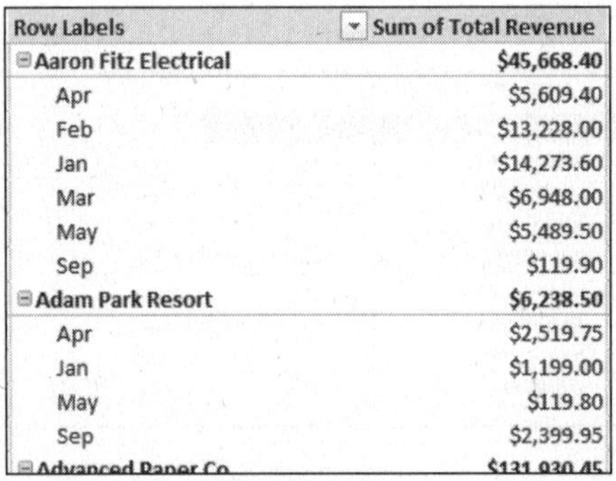

Figure 6-12:
Month
names in
Power
Pivot-driven
pivot tables
don't auto-
matically
sort in
month
order.

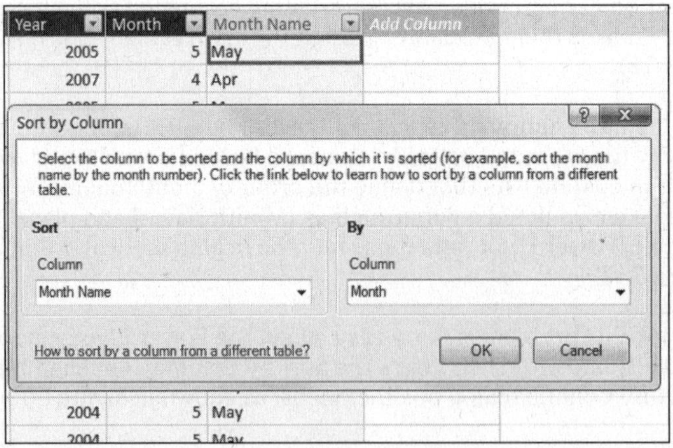

Row Labels	Sum of Total Revenue
⊟Aaron Fitz Electrical	$45,668.40
Apr	$5,609.40
Feb	$13,228.00
Jan	$14,273.60
Mar	$6,948.00
May	$5,489.50
Sep	$119.90
⊟Adam Park Resort	$6,238.50
Apr	$2,519.75
Jan	$1,199.00
May	$119.80
Sep	$2,399.95
⊟Advanced Paper Co	$131,930.45

Figure 6-13:
The Sort by
Column
dialog box
lets you
define how
columns are
sorted.

The idea is to select the column you want sorted and then select the column you want to sort by. In this scenario, you want to sort Month Name by month.

After you confirm the change, it initially appears as though nothing has happened. The reason is that the sort order you defined isn't for the Power Pivot window. The sort order is applied to the pivot table. You can switch over to Excel to see the result in the pivot table (see Figure 6-14).

Row Labels	Sum of Total Revenue
Aaron Fitz Electrical	**$45,668.40**
Jan	$14,273.60
Feb	$13,228.00
Mar	$6,948.00
Apr	$5,609.40
May	$5,489.50
Sep	$119.90
Adam Park Resort	**$6,238.50**
Jan	$1,199.00
Apr	$2,519.75
May	$119.80
Sep	$2,399.95
Advanced Paper Co	$131,930.45

Figure 6-14: The month names now show in the correct month order.

Referencing fields from other tables

Sometimes, the operation you're trying to perform with a calculated column requires you to utilize fields from other tables within the Power Pivot Data Model. For example, you may need to account for a customer-specific discount amount from the Customers table (see Figure 6-15) when creating a calculated column in the InvoiceDetails table.

Custom...	CustomerName	Discount Amount	Address
1	DOLLISCO0001	Dollis Cove Resort	11 %	765 Kingway
2	GETAWAYI0001	Getaway Inn	10 %	234 E Cannon Ave.
3	HOMEFURN0001	Home Furnishings Limited	25 %	234 Heritage Ave.
4	JOHNSONK0001	Johnson, Kimberly	12 %	5678 S. 42nd Ave.
5	KELLYCON0001	Kelly Consulting	5 %	123 Yeo
6	KENSINGT0001	Kensington Gardens Resort	13 %	12345 Redmond Rd
7	HAMPTONV0001	Hampton Village Eatery	20 %	234 Hampton Villa
8	HEALTHYC0001	Healthy Concepts	11 %	1234 Westown Roa
9	LECLERC0001	LeClerc & Associates	8 %	4321 West Broadw
10	LEISURET0001	Leisure & Travel Consultants	6 %	City 123

Figure 6-15: The discount amount in the Customers table can be used in a calculated column in another table.

To accomplish this, you can use a DAX function named RELATED. Similar to VLOOKUP in standard Excel, the RELATED function allows you to look up values from one table in order to use them in another.

Follow these steps to create a new calculated column that displays a discounted amount for each transaction in the InvoiceDetails table:

1. **In the InvoiceDetails table, click on the first blank cell in the empty column labeled Add Column, on the far right.**

2. **On the Formula bar, type** =RELATED(.

   As soon as you enter the open parenthesis, a menu of available fields (shown in Figure 6-16) is displayed. Note that the items in the list represent the table name followed by the field name in brackets. In this case, you're interested in the Customers[Discount Amount] field.

   The RELATED function leverages the relationships you defined when creating the Data Model in order to perform the lookup. So this list of choices contains only the fields that are available based on the relationships you defined.

Figure 6-16:
Use the
RELATED
function to
look up a
field from
another
table.

	X	✓	ƒx	=RELATED(				
				RELATED(ColumnName)				
UnitCost		UnitPrice				Gross Margin		Add Column
59.29		119.	Customers[Address]			60.66		
3290.55		6589.	Customers[City]			3299.4		
35		34.	Customers[Country]			-0.5		
91.59		189.	Customers[CustomerID]			4918		
59.29		119.	Customers[CustomerName]			60.66		
674.5		1349.	Customers[Discount Amount]			675.45		
91.25		189.	Customers[State]			98.7		
303.85		609.	Customers[Zip]			306.1		
59.29		119.	'Invoice Header'[Calculated Column 1]			60.66		
59.29		119.	'Invoice Header'[CustomerID]			60.66		

3. **Double-click the Customers[Discount Amount] field and then press Enter.**

   Power Pivot automatically renames the column to Calculated Column 1.

4. **Double-click on the column label and rename the column** Discount%.

5. **Starting in the next column, click on the first blank cell in the empty column labeled Add Column, on the far right.**

6. **On the Formula bar, type** =[UnitPrice]*[Quantity]*(1-[Discount%]) **and then press Enter.**

   Power Pivot automatically renames the column to Calculated Column 1.

7. **Double-click on the column label and rename the column** Discounted Revenue.

The reward for your efforts is a new column that uses the discount percent from the Customers table to calculate discounted revenue for each transaction. Figure 6-17 illustrates the new calculated column.

	Total Revenue	Discount%	Discounted Revenue
9.95	$119.95	0.13	$104.36
9.95	$6,589.95	0.11	$5,865.06
4.95	$349.50	0.09	$318.05
9.95	$9,497.50	0.06	$8,927.65
9.95	$119.95	0.09	$109.15
9.95	$1,349.95	0.15	$1,147.46
9.95	$189.95	0.17	$157.66
9.95	$609.95	0.05	$579.45
9.95	$119.95	0.11	$106.76
9.95	$119.95	0.16	$100.76
9.95	$359.95	0.15	$305.96
9.95	$9.95	0.11	$8.86
9.95	$5,999.95	0.07	$5,579.95

Figure 6-17: The final discount amount calculated column using the Discount% column from the Customers table.

In the example from the preceding section, you first create a Discount% column using the RELATED function, and then you use that column in another calculated column to calculate the discount amount.

You don't necessarily have to create multiple calculated columns to accomplish a task like this one. You could instead nest the RELATED function into the discount amount calculation. The following line shows the syntax for the nested calculation:

```
=[UnitPrice]*[Quantity]*
```

```
(1-RELATED(Customers[Discount Amount]))
```

As you can see, *nesting* simply means to embed functions within a calculation. In this case, rather than use the RELATED function in a separate Discount% field, you can embed it directly into the discounted revenue calculation.

Nesting functions can definitely save time and even improve performance in larger data models. On the other hand, complicated nested functions can be harder to read and understand.

Understanding Calculated Measures

You can enhance the functionality of your Power Pivot reports by using a kind of calculation called a calculated measure. *Calculated measures* are not applied to the Power Pivot window like calculated columns. Instead, they're applied directly to the pivot table, creating a sort of virtual column that isn't visible in the Power Pivot window. You use calculated measures when you need to calculate based on an aggregated grouping of rows.

Creating a calculated measure

Imagine that you want to show the difference in unit costs between the years 2007 and 2006 for each of your customers. Think about what technically has to be done to achieve this calculation: You have to figure out the sum of unit costs for 2007, determine the sum of unit costs for 2006, and then subtract the sum of 2007 from the sum of 2006. This calculation simply can't be completed using calculated columns. Using calculated measures is the only way to calculate the cost variance between 2007 and 2006.

Follow these steps to create a calculated measure:

1. **Start with a pivot table created from a Power Pivot Data Model.**

    The Chapter 6 Sample File.xlsx workbook contains the Calculated Measures tab with a pivot table already created.

2. **Click the Power Pivot tab on the Excel Ribbon, and choose Measures⇨New Measure.**

    This step opens the Measure dialog box, shown in Figure 6-18.

Figure 6-18: Creating a new calculated measure.

Measure	
Table name:	InvoiceDetails
Measure name:	2007 Cost
Description:	
Formula: f_x	Check formula

```
=CALCULATE(
        SUM(InvoiceDetails[UnitCost]),
        YEAR(InvoiceHeader[InvoiceDate])=2007
        )
```

Formatting Options

Category:
General
Number
Currency
Date
TRUE/FALSE

Symbol: $
Decimal places: 2
☑ Use 1000 separator (,)

OK   Cancel

3. **In the Measure dialog box, set the following inputs:**

   - *Table name:* Choose the table you want to contain the calculated measure when looking at the PivotTable Fields List. Don't sweat this decision too much. The table you select has no bearing on how the calculation works. It's simply a preference on where you want to see the new calculation within the PivotTable Fields List.

   - *Measure name:* Give the calculated measure a descriptive name.

   - *Description:* Enter a friendly description to document what the calculation does.

   - *Formula:* Enter the DAX formula that will calculate the results of the new field.

     In this example, you use the following DAX formula:

     ```
     =CALCULATE(
              SUM(InvoiceDetails[UnitCost]),
              YEAR(InvoiceHeader[InvoiceDate])=2007
              )
     ```

     This formula uses the CALCULATE function to sum the Total Revenue column from the InvoiceDetails table, where the Year column in the InvoiceHeader is equal to 2007.

   - *Formatting Options:* Specify the formatting for the calculated measure results.

4. **Click the Check Formula button to ensure that there are no syntax errors.**

   If your formula is well formed, you see the message `No errors in formula`. If the formula has errors, you see a full description.

5. **Click the OK button to confirm the changes and close the dialog box.**

   You see your newly created calculated measure in the pivot table.

6. **Repeat Steps 2–5 for any other calculated measure you need to create.**

In this example, you need a measure to show the 2006 cost:

```
=CALCULATE(
         SUM(InvoiceDetails[UnitCost]),
         YEAR(InvoiceHeader[InvoiceDate])=2006
         )
```

You also need a measure to calculate the variance:

```
=[2007 Revenue]-[2006 Revenue]
```

Figure 6-19 illustrates the newly created calculated measures. The calculated measures are applied to each customer, displaying the variance between their 2007 and 2006 costs. As you can see, each calculated measure is available for selection in the PivotTable Fields List.

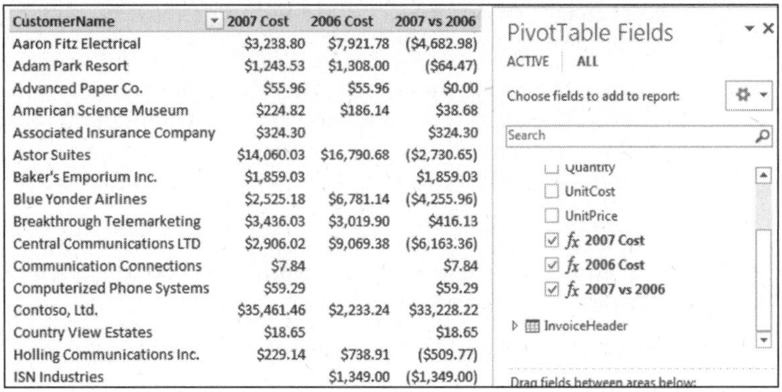

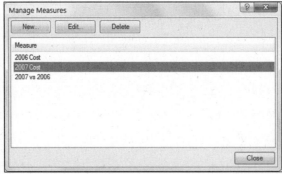

CustomerName 2007 Cost 2006 Cost 2007 vs 2006
Aaron Fitz Electrical $3,238.80 $7,921.78 ($4,682.98)
Adam Park Resort $1,243.53 $1,308.00 ($64.47)
Advanced Paper Co. $55.96 $55.96 $0.00
American Science Museum $224.82 $186.14 $38.68
Associated Insurance Company $324.30 $324.30
Astor Suites $14,060.03 $16,790.68 ($2,730.65)
Baker's Emporium Inc. $1,859.03 $1,859.03
Blue Yonder Airlines $2,525.18 $6,781.14 ($4,255.96)
Breakthrough Telemarketing $3,436.03 $3,019.90 $416.13
Central Communications LTD $2,906.02 $9,069.38 ($6,163.36)
Communication Connections $7.84 $7.84
Computerized Phone Systems $59.29 $59.29
Contoso, Ltd. $35,461.46 $2,233.24 $33,228.22
Country View Estates $18.65 $18.65
Holling Communications Inc. $229.14 $738.91 ($509.77)
ISN Industries $1,349.00 ($1,349.00)
PivotTable Fields
ACTIVE
ALL
Choose fields to add to report:
Search
UnitCost
UnitPrice
2007 Cost
2006 Cost
2007 vs 2006
InvoiceHeader

Figure 6-19: Calculated measures can be seen in the PivotTable Fields List.

Always attempt to achieve readability by using carriage returns and spaces. In Figure 6-18, the DAX calculation is entered with carriage returns and spaces. This is purely for readability purposes. DAX ignores white spaces and isn't case sensitive, so it's quite forgiving on how you structure the calculation.

Editing and deleting calculated measures

You may find that you need to either edit or delete a calculated measure. You can do so by following these steps:

1. **Click anywhere inside the pivot table, click the Power Pivot tab on the Excel Ribbon, and choose Measures➪Manage Measures.**

   This step opens the Manage Measures dialog box, shown in Figure 6-20.

Manage Measures
New...
Edit...
Delete
Measure
2006 Cost
2007 Cost
2007 vs 2006
Close

Figure 6-20: The Manage Measures dialog box lets you edit or delete your calculated measures.

2. **Select the target calculated measure, and click one of these two buttons:**

- *Edit:* Opens the Measure dialog box, where you can make changes to the calculation setting.

- *Delete:* Opens a message box asking you to confirm that you want to remove the measure. After you confirm, the calculated measure is removed.

Free Your Data With Cube Functions

Cube functions are Excel functions that can be used to access the data in a Power Pivot Data Model outside the constraints of a pivot table. Although cube functions aren't technically used to create calculations themselves, they can be used to free PowerPivot data so that it can be used with formulas you may have in other parts of your Excel spreadsheet.

One of the easiest ways to start exploring cube functions is to allow Excel to convert your Power Pivot pivot table into cube functions. The idea is to tell Excel to replace all cells in the pivot table with a formula that connects back to the Power Pivot Data Model.

Follow these steps to create your first set of cube functions:

1. **Start with a pivot table created from a Power Pivot model.**

   The `Chapter 6 Sample File.xlsx` workbook contains a Cube Functions tab with a pivot table already created.

2. **Place the cursor anywhere inside the pivot table, and then select Analyze ⇨ Convert to Formulas, as shown in Figure 6-21.**

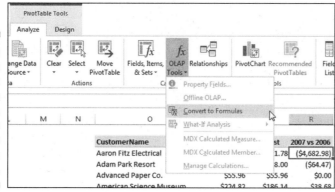

Figure 6-21: Select the Convert to Formulas option to convert the pivot table to cube formulas.

3. **In the Measure dialog box, set the following inputs: Table Name, Measure Name, Formula, and Formatting Options.**

After a second or two, the cells that formerly housed a pivot table are now homes for cube formulas. The Formula bar, shown in Figure 6-22, illustrates the cube functions.

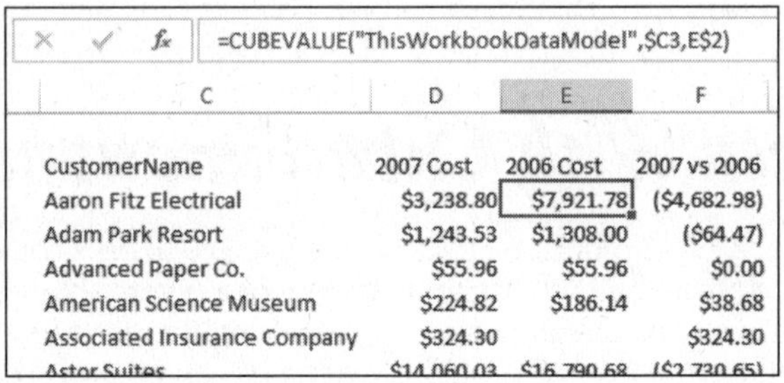

Figure 6-22:
These cells
are now a
series of
cube
functions!

		f_x	=CUBEVALUE("ThisWorkbookDataModel",$C3,E$2)	
	C	D	E	F
CustomerName		2007 Cost	2006 Cost	2007 vs 2006
Aaron Fitz Electrical		$3,238.80	$7,921.78	($4,682.98)
Adam Park Resort		$1,243.53	$1,308.00	($64.47)
Advanced Paper Co.		$55.96	$55.96	$0.00
American Science Museum		$224.82	$186.14	$38.68
Associated Insurance Company		$324.30		$324.30
Astor Suites		$14.060.03	$16.790.68	($2.730.65)

If the pivot table contains a report filter field, the dialog box shown in Figure 6-23 opens. This dialog box gives you the option to convert the filter drop-down selectors to cube formulas. If you select this option, the drop-down selectors are removed, leaving a static formula.

If you need to have the filter drop-down selectors intact so you can interactively change the selections in the filter field, leave the Convert Report Filters option deselected.

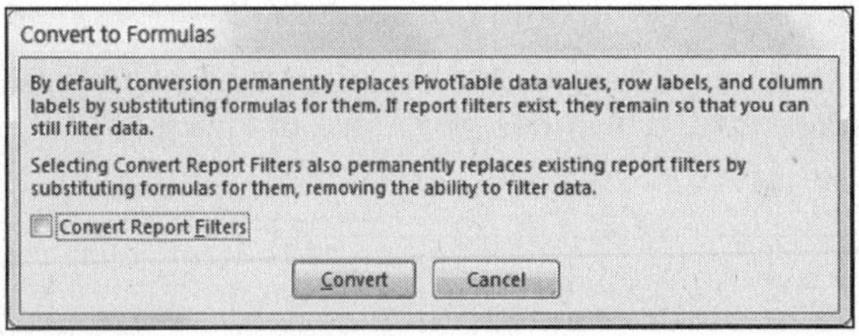

Figure 6-23:
Excel gives
you the
option to
convert your
report filter
fields.

Convert to Formulas

By default, conversion permanently replaces PivotTable data values, row labels, and column labels by substituting formulas for them. If report filters exist, they remain so that you can still filter data.

Selecting Convert Report Filters also permanently replaces existing report filters by substituting formulas for them, removing the ability to filter data.

☐ Convert Report Filters

Convert   Cancel

Why is this capability useful? Well, now that the values you see are no longer part of a pivot table object, you can insert rows and columns, add your own calculations, or combine the data with other formulas in your spreadsheet.

The bottom line is that cube functions give you the flexibility to free your Power Pivot data from the confines of a pivot table and then use it in all sorts of ways by simply moving formulas around.

Chapter 7

Publishing Power Pivot to SharePoint

By publishing your Excel reports and dashboards to SharePoint, you can make them available to others in your organization via a browser and prevent multiple users from having separate versions of your workbooks on their computers. You can also make your Power Pivot reports easier to find, share, and use.

In this chapter, you first discover how SharePoint helps organizations share and collaborate on data. You will then explore the options for publishing your Power Pivot reports to SharePoint.

Understanding SharePoint

SharePoint is Microsoft's premier collaborative server environment, providing tools for sharing documents and data across various organizations within a company's network.

Typically deployed on a company's network as a series of intranet sites, SharePoint lets various departments control their own security, workgroups, documents, and data. As with any other website, a SharePoint site — or an individual page within the site — is accessible by way of a URL that the user can access using a standard web browser.

SharePoint is most often used for the storing of version-controlled documents, such as Word documents and Excel worksheets. In many environments, email is used for passing documents back and forth between users. The potential for mixing up different versions of the same document is considerable. Also, storing multiple copies of the same document takes up a lot of disk space. Because SharePoint provides a single source for storing, viewing, and updating documents, many of these issues are eliminated.

And because SharePoint easily handles virtually any type of document, it is frequently used to consolidate and store various types of documentation (project drawings, videos, schematics, photographs, and workbooks, for example) that are required for large projects where multiple teams must collaborate.

Microsoft chose SharePoint as the platform for Excel publishing because of the significant features built into SharePoint, including these:

- ✔ **Security:** SharePoint supports users and groups of users. Users and groups may be granted or denied access to various parts of a SharePoint website, and designated users may be granted permission to add, delete, or modify the site.

- ✔ **Versioning:** SharePoint automatically maintains a version history of objects and data. Changes can be rolled back to an earlier state at virtually any time. The ability to roll back changes can be granted to individual users, and DBA support is not required.

- ✔ **Recycle bin:** Deleted data and objects are held in a "recycle bin" so that they can be recovered, if necessary. SharePoint supports an Undo feature for its data.

- ✔ **Alerts:** Users and groups can be alerted by email message whenever a specific document in SharePoint is added, deleted, or changed. When granted the proper permissions, users can manage their own alerts.

- ✔ **End-user maintenance:** SharePoint sites are meant to be maintained by their users, without the intervention of IT departments. Although SharePoint pages are not as flexible as typical web pages, a SharePoint developer can add or remove features from pages; change fonts, headings, colors, and other attributes of pages; create subsites and lists; and perform many other maintenance and enhancement tasks.

- ✔ **Other features:** Every SharePoint site includes a number of features, such as a calendar, a task list, and announcements that users may turn off or remove.

Most IT organizations have already implemented a SharePoint environment, so your organization likely already has SharePoint running on its network. No lone user can simply start up a SharePoint site. If you're interested in using SharePoint, contact your IT department to inquire about getting access to a SharePoint site.

Understanding Excel Services for SharePoint

The mechanism that allows for the publishing of Excel documents to SharePoint as interactive web pages is Excel Services.

Excel Services is a broader term to describe these three components:

✔ **Excel Calculation Services:** Serves as the primary engine of Excel services. This component loads Excel documents, runs calculations on the Excel sheet, and runs the refresh process for any embedded data connection.

✔ **Excel Web Access:** Allows users to interact with Excel through a web browser.

✔ **Excel Web Services:** Hosted in SharePoint Services, it provides developers with an application programming interface (API) to build custom applications based on the Excel workbook.

SharePoint requirements and Office 365

The Excel Services SharePoint implementation is available only with SharePoint 2010 or 2013, so you should ensure that your SharePoint site has one of those two versions.

Most Excel analysts work in companies that already have a SharePoint 2010 or 2013 environment. However, if you don't have access to an already existing SharePoint environment, you can check out hundreds of service providers that offer subscription-based SharePoint services. Many of these providers provide volume-based pricing on a subscription model.

In fact, the Microsoft offering, Office 365, is a cloud-based environment that offers subscribers a line of collaborative, Microsoft Office–like tools that can be accessed on the web. Similar to Google Docs or Google Spreadsheets, Microsoft offers Word, Excel, and PowerPoint in Office 365, so you can use Office 365 to publish and host your Excel reports.

Subscribing to a commercial SharePoint service provider may be the fastest and most affordable way to host Microsoft Excel solutions on SharePoint. Again, the only caveat is that the commercial service provider you choose must have SharePoint 2010 or 2013 with Excel Services implemented.

When you publish a workbook to Excel Services, your audience can interact with your Excel file in several ways:

- ✔ View workbooks that contain a data model and Power View reports.
- ✔ Navigate between worksheets.
- ✔ Sort and filter data.
- ✔ Work with pivot tables.
- ✔ Use slicers and pivot table report filters.
- ✔ Refresh data for embedded data connections.

Publishing an Excel Workbook to SharePoint

To take advantage of the functionality afforded by Excel Services, you must have the proper permissions to publish to a SharePoint site that is running Excel Services. To obtain access, speak with your IT department.

After you have access to publish to SharePoint, follow these steps:

1. **Click the File tab on the Excel Ribbon, choose Save As➪Other Web Locations, and then click the Browse button.**

   This step opens the Save As dialog box.

2. **Enter the URL of your SharePoint site in the File Name input box (see Figure 7-1).**

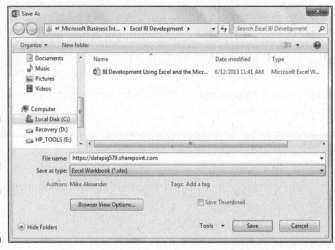

Figure 7-1:
Enter your
SharePoint
URL in the
input box of
the Save As
dialog box.

3. Click the Browser View Options button.

The Browser View Options dialog box opens.

4. Select which parts of the workbook will be available on the web, as shown in Figure 7-2, and then click the OK button.

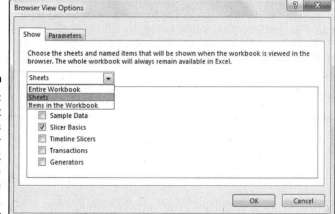

Figure 7-2: Select which parts of your workbook will be available on the web.

You can choose to show the entire workbook, only certain sheets, or only specific objects (charts, and pivot tables, for example). You can also define parameters to allow certain named ranges to be editable in the web browser.

5. Click the Save button to connect to the SharePoint site and see your document library, as shown in Figure 7-3.

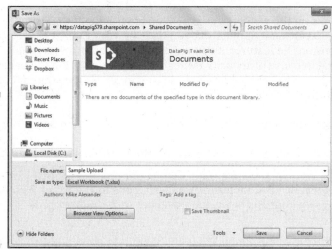

Figure 7-3: Double-click the library where you want to save the file, and click the Save button.

You can think of a document library as a directory on the SharePoint site.

6. Enter a filename in the File Name input box, double-click the library where you want the file saved, and then click the Save button.

After you've published the workbook, you can view it on the web by finding the document in the appropriate library on your SharePoint site. When you open the workbook, it shows up in the browser, with several menu options (see Figure 7-4), as described in the following list:

- ✔ **Edit Workbook:** Either download the workbook or edit the workbook in the browser.

- ✔ **Share:** Email a link to your newly published workbook.

- ✔ **Data:** Refresh any external data connections that are in your workbook.

Figure 7-4:
A workbook, as shown in Excel Services.

Workbooks on the web are running in an environment that is quite different from the Excel client application you have on your PC. Excel Services has limitations on the features it can render in the web browser. Some limitations exist because of security issues, and others exist simply because Excel Services hasn't yet evolved to include the broad set of features that come supplied with standard Excel.

In any case, the following list describes some limitations on Excel Services:

- ✔ **Data validation does not work on the web.** This feature is simply ignored when you publish your workbook to the web.

- ✔ **No form of VBA, including a macro, runs in the Excel Web App.** Your VBA procedures simply don't transfer with the workbook.

✔ **Worksheet protection doesn't work on the web.** Instead, you need to plan for, and use, the Browser View Options dialog box (refer to Figure 7-2).

✔ **Links to external workbooks no longer work after publishing to the web.** Any links or references to other workbooks will no longer work after you publish your file to SharePoint.

✔ **You can use any pivot tables with full fidelity on the web, but you cannot create any new pivot tables while your workbook is on the web.** Create any pivot tables in the Excel client on your PC before publishing on the web.

✔ **OfficeArt doesn't render on the web.** This includes Shape objects, WordArt, SmartArt, diagrams, signature lines, and ink annotations.

Publishing to a Power Pivot Gallery

A *Power Pivot Gallery* is a type of document library that showcases Power Pivot reports and allows for scheduled refresh cycles.

Exploring the Power Pivot Gallery

For your end users, the Power Pivot Gallery provides an attractive portal that serves as a one-stop shop for all the reports and dashboards you publish. For you, the Power Pivot Gallery enables better management of your Power Pivot reports by allowing you to schedule nightly refreshes of the data within them.

Speak with your SharePoint administrator about your organization's SharePoint instance, and ask that person to consider adding a Power Pivot Gallery to the site. After you have access to a Power Pivot Gallery, you can upload your Power Pivot workbooks by following the same steps for publishing a standard workbook to SharePoint (see "Publishing an Excel Workbook to SharePoint" in this chapter).

Figure 7-5 illustrates a typical Power Pivot Gallery. Note that each workbook is shown as a thumbnail, providing users with a snapshot of each report. Clicking a thumbnail opens the report as a web page.

If you have an Office 365 SharePoint subscription, you have no option, unfortunately, for a Power Pivot Gallery, because Office 365 doesn't support it. This situation may change as Microsoft continues to add improvements to Office 365.

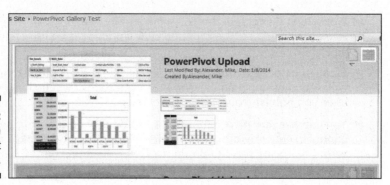

Figure 7-5:
A sample
Power Pivot
Gallery.

Refreshing data connections in published Power Pivot workbooks

You can manually refresh the data connections within your published Power Pivot report by opening the workbook and selecting the Data drop-down menu. As you can see in Figure 7-6, you have the option of refreshing a single connection or all connections in the workbook.

Figure 7-6:
You can use
the Data
drop-down
menu to
manually
refresh data
connections.

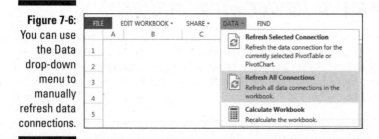

Alternatively, you can use the Power Pivot Gallery to schedule an automatic refresh based on a schedule you define. Simply click the Manage Data icon in the upper-right corner of the target report's shadow box (see Figure 7-7).

SharePoint opens the Manage Data Refresh screen, shown in Figure 7-8. The idea is to configure each setting to set up the schedule you want.

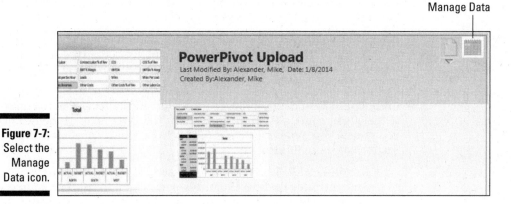

Manage Data

Figure 7-7:
Select the
Manage
Data icon.

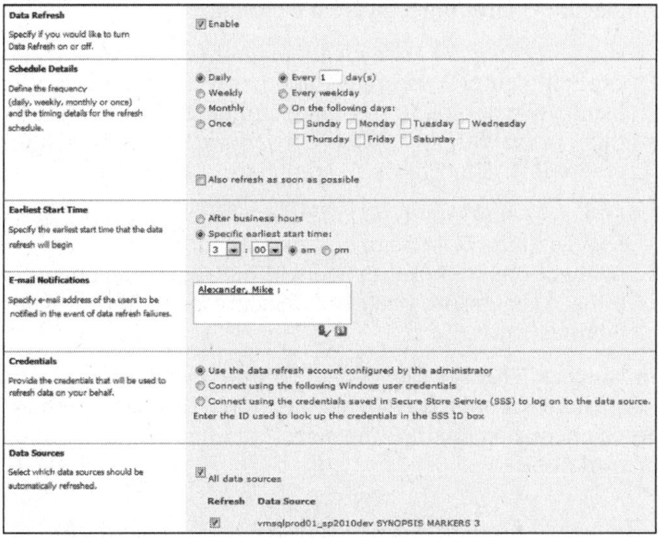

Figure 7-8:
Set up your
schedule.

This list describes each settings section:

- **Data Refresh:** The Data Refresh section holds the On-Off switch for your schedule. Place a check in the Enable Schedule check box to make the schedule active. Remove the check to stop automatic refreshes.

- **Schedule Details:** In the Schedule Details section, you can specify the frequency and intervals of the schedule. In addition to selecting the time intervals, you can refresh as soon as possible. Placing a check mark next to the Also Refresh as Soon as Possible option starts a refresh within a minute. This option is helpful when you want to test the refresh process.

- ✔ **Earliest Start Time:** The Earliest Start Time section lets you specify the time of day to run the refresh process.

- ✔ **E-mail Notifications:** The E-mail Notifications section lets you specify who should receive an email from SharePoint every time the scheduled refresh is run. Individuals who are specified receive an email regardless of whether the process ran successfully.

- ✔ **Credentials:** Most data sources require authentication in order to connect to them (username, password, and so on). The Credentials section lets you specify how authentication is passed to external data sources. This section has these three options:

  - *Use the Data Refresh Account Configured by the Administrator:* Authenticates the SharePoint system account to the data source. You typically have to work with your SharePoint administrator to set up this authentication method and ensure that the data source can use SharePoint's system account.

  - *Connect Using the Following Windows User Credentials:* Lets you explicitly enter a username and password for authentication. Avoid using your personal username and password here. Instead, use this option with an *application account,* which is a "dummy" user created by your database administrators.

  - *Connect Using the Credentials Saved in Secure Store Service (SSS) to Log On to the Data Source:* This authentication option allows data connections to be refreshed without requiring a password. In order to use this option, you need a Secure Store ID from your SharePoint administrator.

- ✔ **Data Sources:** This setting lets you define whether all data connections are refreshed, or only specific connections. Deselecting the All Data Sources check box enables the selection of individual connections in your workbook.

Part II
Wrangling Data with Power Query

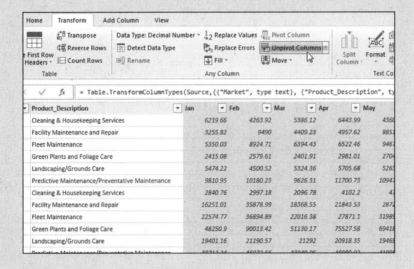

In this part . . .

- ✔ Discover the fundamentals of using Power Query to import and process data from various data sources.

- ✔ Explore Power Query tools and formulas that can automate and simply your data-transformation processes.

- ✔ Uncover methods of merging and appending multiple queries to go beyond simple data imports.

- ✔ Get the skinny on creating your own custom functions to extend the functionality of Power Query.

Chapter 8

Introducing Power Query

• •

• •

*I*n information management, the term ETL (Extract, Transform, Load)
refers to the three separate functions typically required to integrate disparate data sources: extract, transform, and load. The extraction function refers
to the reading of data from a specified source and extracting a desired subset
of data. The transformation function refers to the cleaning, shaping, and
aggregating of data to convert it to the desired structure. The loading function refers to the actual importing or writing of the resulting data to a target
location.

Excel analysts have been manually performing ETL processes for years —
although they rarely call it ETL. Every day, millions of Excel users manually
pull data from a source location, manipulate that data, and integrate it into
their reporting. This process requires lots of manual effort.

Power Query enhances the ETL experience by offering an intuitive mechanism to extract data from a wide variety of sources, perform complex
transformations on that data, and then load the data into a workbook or the
Internal Data Model.

In this chapter, you explore the basics of the Power Query Add-in. You
also get a glimpse of how it can help you save time and automate the steps
needed to ensure that clean data is imported into your reporting models.

Installing and Activating a Power Query Add-In

In Excel 2016, Power Query isn't an add-in — it's a native feature of Excel, just like charts and pivot tables are native features. If you're working with Excel 2016, you don't have to install any additional components. You'll find Power Query in Excel 2016 hidden on the Data tab, in the Get & Transform group (see Figure 8-1).

Figure 8-1:
In Excel
2016, the
Power
Query
commands
are found in
the Get &
Transform
group on the
Data tab.

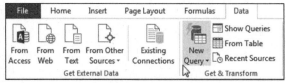

If you're working with Excel 2010 or Excel 2013, you need to explicitly download and install the Power Query add-in. As of this writing, the Power Query add-in is available to you only if you have one of these editions of Office or Excel:

- ✔ **Office 2010 Professional Plus:** Available for purchase through any retailer

- ✔ **Office 2013 Professional Plus:** Available through volume licensing only

- ✔ **Office 365 Pro Plus:** Available with an ongoing subscription to Office365.com

- ✔ **Excel 2013 Stand-alone Edition:** Available for purchase through any retailer

If you have any of these editions, you can install and activate the Power Query add-in. Simply enter the search term *Excel Power Query add-in* into your favorite search engine to find the free installation package.

Note that Microsoft offers Power Query for both Excel 2010 and Excel 2013 in both 32- and 64-bit platforms. Be sure to download the version that matches your version of Excel as well as the platform on which your PC is running.

After the add-in is installed, activate it by following these steps:

1. **Open Excel and look for the Power Query command on the Insert tab (see Figure 8-2).**

   If you see it, the Power Query add-in is already activated. You can skip the remaining steps.

Figure 8-2: In Excel 2010 and 2013, the Power Query add-in is exposed via its own tab on the Ribbon.

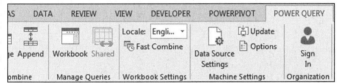

2. **From the Excel Ribbon, choose File ⇨ Options.**

3. **Choose the Add-Ins option on the left, and then look for the Manage drop-down list at the bottom of the dialog box. Select COM Add-Ins and then click Go.**

4. **Look for Power Query for Excel in the list of available COM add-ins. Select the check box next to each one of these options and click OK.**

5. **Close and restart Excel.**

A successful install results in a new Power Query tab on the Excel Ribbon.

Power Query Basics

In this section, I walk you through a simple example of using Power Query. Imagine that you need to import Microsoft Corporation stock prices from the past 30 days by using Yahoo! Finance. For this scenario, you need to perform a web query to pull the data you need from Yahoo! Finance.

Starting the query

To start the query, follow these steps:

1. **If you have Excel 2016, select the New Query command on the Data tab, and then select From Other Sources⇨From Web (see Figure 8-3).**

   If you're working with Excel 2010 or Excel 2013, click the Power Query tab and select the From Web command.

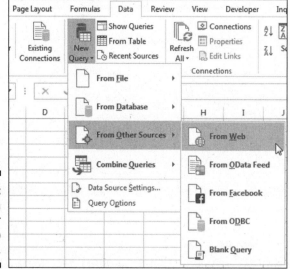

Figure 8-3:
Starting a
Power
Query web
query.

2. **In the dialog box that appears, enter the URL for the data you need, as shown in Figure 8-4.**

   In this example, you type `http://finance.yahoo.com/q/hp?s=MSFT`.

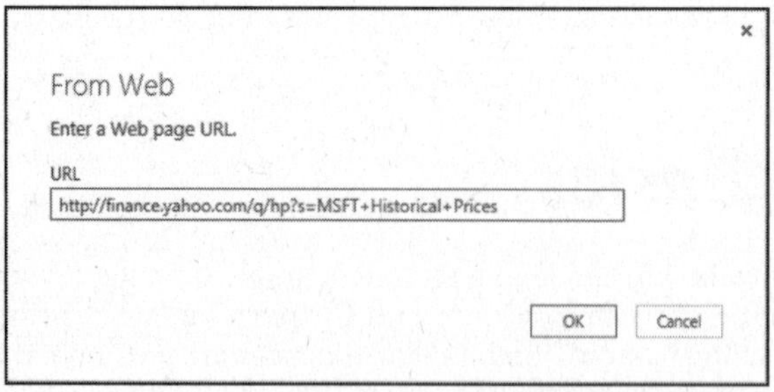

Figure 8-4:
Enter the
target URL
containing
the data you
need.

After a bit of gyrating, the Navigator pane shown in Figure 8-5 appears. You can select the data source that you want to extract. Click on each table to see a preview of the data.

Figure 8-5: Select the correct data source and then click the Edit button.

3. **In this case, Table 4 holds the historical stock data you need, so click Table 4 in the list box on the left and then click the Edit button.**

   You may have noticed that the Navigator pane, shown in Figure 8-5, offers a Load button (next to the Edit button). You can use this button to skip any editing and import your targeted data as is. If you're sure that you won't need to transform or shape your data in any way, click the Load button to import the data directly into the data model or a spreadsheet in your workbook.

   Excel has another From Web command button, on the Data tab in the Get External Data group. This unfortunate duplicate command is the legacy web-scraping capability found in all Excel versions since Excel 2000.

   The Power Query version of the From Web command (choose New Query ⇨ From Other Sources ⇨ From Web) goes beyond simple web scraping. Power Query can pull data from advanced web pages and then manipulate it. Make sure you're using the correct feature when pulling data from the web.

   When you click the Edit button, Power Query activates a new Query Editor window, which contains its own Ribbon and a preview pane that shows a preview of the data (see Figure 8-6). You can apply certain actions to shape, clean, and transform the data before importing.

   The idea is to work with each column shown in the Query Editor, applying the necessary actions that will give you the data and structure you need. You can dive deeper into column actions later in this chapter. For now, continue toward the goal of getting the last 30 days of stock prices for Microsoft Corporation.

Formula bar   Query Settings

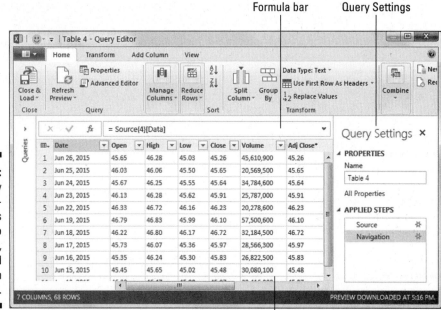

Figure 8-6:
The Query
Editor win-
dow allows
you to
shape,
clean, and
transform
data.

Preview pane

4. **Right-click the Date column to see the available column actions, as
   shown in Figure 8-7. Select Change Type and then Date to ensure that
   the Date field is formatted as a proper date.**

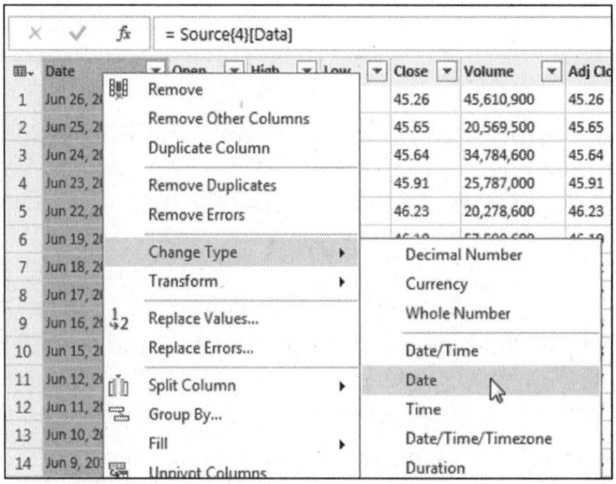

Figure 8-7:
Right-click
the Date
column and
choose to
change the
data type to
a date
format.

5. **Remove all unnecessary columns by right-clicking each one and selecting Remove.**

   (Besides the Date field, the only other columns you need are the High, Low, and Close fields.)

   Alternatively, you can hold down the Ctrl key on the keyboard, select the columns you want to keep, right-click any selected column, and then choose Remove Other Columns (see Figure 8-8).

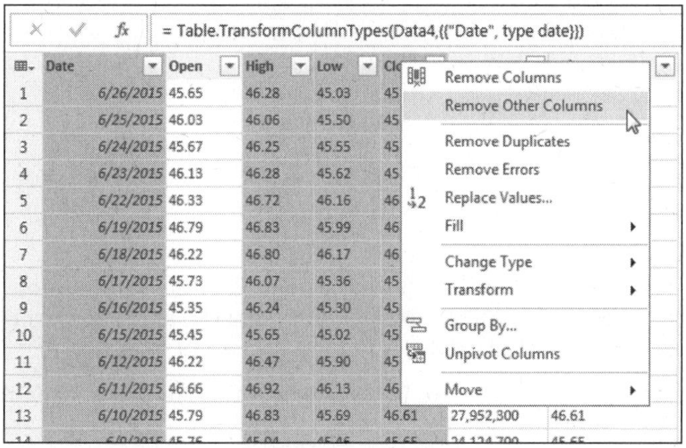

Figure 8-8:
Select
unneeded
columns,
and then
select
Remove
Other
Columns to
get rid of
them.

6. **To ensure that the High, Low, and Close fields are formatted as proper numbers, hold down the Ctrl key on the keyboard, select the three columns, and right-click and choose Change Type ⇨ Decimal Number.**

   After you do this, you may notice that some of the rows show the word *Error.* These are rows that contain text values that could not be converted.

7. **Remove the error rows by selecting Remove Errors from the Table Actions list (next to the Date field), as shown in Figure 8-9.**

8. **After all errors are removed, add a Week Of field that displays which week each date in the table belongs to.**

   Here's how to do this:

   1. *Right-click the Date field and select the Duplicate Column option.*

      A new column is added to the preview.

   2. *Right-click the newly added column, select the Rename option, and then rename the column Week Of.*

Figure 8-9:
You can
click the
Table
Actions icon
to select
actions
(such as
Remove
Errors) that
you want
applied to
the entire
data table.

	Date		High	Low	Close
	Use First Row As Headers		47.81	47.18	47.58
		5/19/2015	Error	Error	Error
	Add Custom Column...				
	Add Index Column	▸	48.22	47.61	48.01
		5/15/2015	48.91	48.05	48.3
	Choose Columns...		48.82	48.03	48.72
	Remove Duplicates		48.32	47.57	47.63
		5/12/2015	47.68	46.42	47.35
	Keep Top Rows...		47.91	47.37	47.37
	Keep Bottom Rows...				
	Keep Range of Rows...	5/8/2015	47.98	47.52	47.75
		5/7/2015	47.09	46.16	46.7
	Remove Top Rows...	5/6/2015	47.77	46.02	46.28
	Remove Bottom Rows...	5/5/2015	48.16	47.31	47.6
	Remove Alternate Rows...	5/4/2015	48.87	48.18	48.24
	Remove Errors	5/1/2015	48.88	48.4	48.66
		4/30/2015	49.54	48.6	48.64
	Merge Queries...	4/29/2015	49.31	48.5	49.06
	Append Queries				

9. **Select the Transform tab on the Power Query Ribbon, look to the right to find the Date & Time Column group, and then choose Date ⇨ Week ⇨ Start of the Week, as shown in Figure 8-10.**

Excel transforms the date to display the start of the week for a given date.

Figure 8-10:
The Power
Query
Ribbon can
be used to
apply trans-
formation
actions
such as
displaying
the start of
the week
for a given
date.

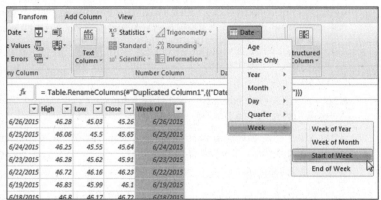

10. **When you've finished configuring your Power Query feed, save and output the results.**

To do this, click the Close & Load drop-down menu on the Home tab of the Power Query Ribbon to reveal the two options shown in Figure 8-11:

- *Close & Load:* Saves your query and outputs the results as an Excel table to a new worksheet in your workbook.

- *Close & Load To:* Opens the Load To dialog box, where you can choose to output the results to a specific worksheet or to the Data Model. Alternatively, you can choose to save the query only as a query connection, and then you can use the query in various in-memory processes without needing to output the results.

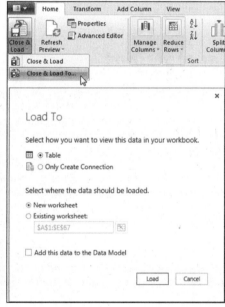

Figure 8-11:
The Load To dialog box gives you more control over how the results of queries are used.

At this point, you have a table similar to the one shown in Figure 8-12, which can be used to produce the pivot table you need.

Take a moment to appreciate what Power Query allowed you to do just now. With a few clicks, you searched the Internet, found some base data, shaped the data to keep only the columns you needed, and even manipulated that data to add an extra Week Of dimension to the base data. This is what Power Query is about: enabling you to easily extract, filter, and reshape data without the need for any programmatic coding skills.

Figure 8-12:
Your final
query pulled
from the
Internet:
trans-
formed, put
into an
Excel table,
and ready to
use in a
pivot table.

	A	B	C	D	E
1	Date	High	Low	Close	Week Of
2	6/26/2015	46.28	45.03	45.26	6/21/2015
3	6/25/2015	46.06	45.5	45.65	6/21/2015
4	6/24/2015	46.25	45.55	45.64	6/21/2015
5	6/23/2015	46.28	45.62	45.91	6/21/2015
6	6/22/2015	46.72	46.16	46.23	6/21/2015
7	6/19/2015	46.83	45.99	46.1	6/14/2015
8	6/18/2015	46.8	46.17	46.72	6/14/2015
9	6/17/2015	46.07	45.36	45.97	6/14/2015
10	6/16/2015	46.24	45.3	45.83	6/14/2015
11	6/15/2015	45.65	45.02	45.48	6/14/2015
12	6/12/2015	46.47	45.9	45.97	6/7/2015
13	6/11/2015	46.92	46.13	46.44	6/7/2015
14	6/10/2015	46.83	45.69	46.61	6/7/2015
15	6/9/2015	45.94	45.46	45.65	6/7/2015

Understanding query steps

Power Query uses its own formula language (known as the "M" language) to codify your queries. As with macro recording, each action you take when working with Power Query results in a line of code being written into a query step. Query steps are embedded M code that allow your actions to be repeated each time you refresh your Power Query data.

You can see the query steps for your queries by activating the Query Settings pane. While in the Query Editor window, you choose View⇨Query Settings. You can also place a check mark in the Formula Bar option to enhance your analysis of each step with a formula bar that displays the syntax for the given step.

The Query Settings pane appears to the right of the preview pane, as shown in Figure 8-13. The formula bar is located directly above the preview pane.

Each query step represents an action you took to get to a data table. You can click on any step to see the underlying M code in the Power Query formula bar. For example, clicking the step called Removed Errors reveals the code for that step in the formula bar.

When you click on a query step, the data shown in the preview pane shows you what the data looked like up to and including the step you clicked. For example, in Figure 8-13, clicking the step before the Removed Other Columns step lets you see what the data looked like before you removed the non-essential columns.

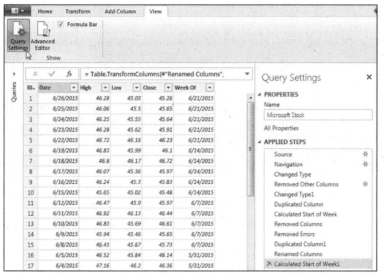

Figure 8-13:
You can view and manage query steps in the Applied Steps section of the Query Settings pane.

You can right-click on any step to see a menu of options for managing your query steps. Figure 8-14 illustrates the following options:

- **Edit Settings:** Edit the arguments or parameters that defines the selected step.

- **Rename:** Give the selected step a meaningful name.

- **Delete:** Remove the selected step. Be aware that removing a step can cause errors if subsequent steps depend on the deleted step.

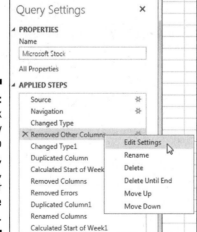

Figure 8-14:
Right-click on any query step to edit, rename, delete, or move the step.

Viewing the Advanced Query Editor

Power Query gives you the option to view and edit a query's embedded M code directly. While in the Query Editor window, click the View tab on the Ribbon and select Advanced Editor. The Advanced Editor dialog box is little more than a space for you to type your own M code. Advanced users can use the M language to extend the capabilities of Power Query by directly coding their own steps in the Advanced Editor. We touch on the M language in Chapter 12 of this book.

- ✔ **Delete Until End:** Remove the selected step and all following steps.

- ✔ **Move Up:** Move the selected step up in the order of steps.

- ✔ **Move Down:** Move the selected step down in the order of steps.

- ✔ **Extract Previous:** Create a new query using the steps prior to the selected step. This feature is covered in Chapter 11.

Refreshing Power Query data

Power Query data is in no way connected to the source data used to extract it. A Power Query data table is merely a snapshot. In other words, as the source data changes, Power Query doesn't automatically keep up with the changes; you need to intentionally refresh your query.

If you chose to load your Power Query results to an Excel table in the existing workbook, you can manually refresh by right-clicking on the table and selecting the Refresh option.

If you chose to load your Power Query data to the Internal Data Model, you need to open the Power Pivot window, select your Power Query data, and then click the Refresh command on the Home tab of the Power Query window.

To get a bit more automated with the refreshing of queries, you can configure your data sources to automatically refresh the Power Query data. To do so, follow these steps:

1. **From the Data tab on the Excel Ribbon, select the Connections command.**

   The Workbook Connections dialog box appears.

2. **Select the Power Query data connection you want to refresh and then click the Properties button.**

   The Properties dialog box opens.

3. **Select the Usage tab.**

4. **Set the options to refresh the chosen data connection:**

   • *Refresh Every X Minutes:* Tells Excel to automatically refresh the chosen data every specified number of minutes. Excel refreshes all tables associated with that connection.

   • *Refresh Data When Opening the File:* Tells Excel to automatically refresh the chosen data connection after opening the workbook. Excel refreshes all tables associated with that connection as soon as the workbook is opened.

These refresh options are useful when you want to ensure that your customers are working with the latest data. Of course, setting these options does not preclude the ability the manually refresh the data using the Refresh command on the Home tab.

Managing existing queries

As you add various queries to a workbook, you need a way to manage them. Excel accommodates this need by offering the Workbook Queries pane, which enables you to edit, duplicate, refresh, and generally manage all existing queries in the workbook. Open the Workbook Queries pane by selecting the Show Queries command on the Data tab of the Excel ribbon.

You need to find the query you want to work with and then right-click it to take any one of the actions described in the following list (see Figure 8-15):

✔ **Edit:** Open the Query Editor, where you can modify the query steps.

✔ **Delete:** Delete the selected query.

✔ **Refresh:** Refresh the data in the selected query.

✔ **Load To:** Activate the Load To dialog box, where you can redefine where the selected query's results are used.

✔ **Duplicate:** Create a copy of the query.

✔ **Reference:** Create a new query that references the output of the original query.

✔ **Merge:** Merge the selected query with another query in the workbook by matching specified columns.

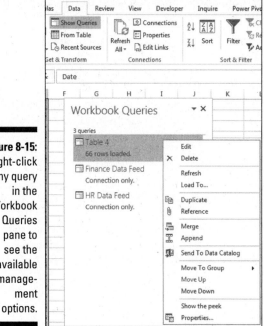

Figure 8-15:
Right-click any query in the Workbook Queries pane to see the available management options.

✔ **Append:** Append the results of another query in the workbook to the selected query.

✔ **Send to Data Catalog:** Publish and share the selected query via a Microsoft Power BI server that your IT department sets up and manages.

✔ **Move to Group:** Move the selected query into a logical group that you create for better organization.

✔ **Move Up:** Move the selected query up in the Workbook Queries pane.

✔ **Move Down:** Move the selected query down in the Workbook Queries pane.

✔ **Show the Peek:** Show a preview of the query results for the selected query.

✔ **Properties:** Rename the query and add a friendly description.

The Workbook Queries pane is especially useful when your workbook contains several queries. Think of it as a kind of table of contents that allows you to easily find and interact with the queries in your workbook.

Understanding Column-Level Actions

Right-clicking a column in the Query Editor opens a context menu that shows a full list of the actions you can take. You can also apply certain actions to multiple columns at one time by selecting two or more columns before right-clicking. Figure 8-16 shows the available column-level actions, and Table 8-1 describes their purpose, as well as a few other actions that are available only on the Query Editor Ribbon.

Figure 8-16:
Right-click any column to see the column-level actions you can use to transform the data.

All column-level actions available in Power Query are also available on the Query Editor Ribbon, so you can either choose the convenience of right-clicking to quickly select an action or use the more visual Ribbon menu. A few useful column-level actions are found only on the Ribbon, as described in Table 8-1.

Table 8-1	Column-Level Actions	
Action	*Purpose*	*Available with Multiple Columns?*
Remove	Remove the selected column from the Power Query data.	Yes
Remove Other Columns	Remove all non-selected columns from the Power Query data.	Yes

(continued)

Table 8-1 *(continued)*

Action	Purpose	Available with Multiple Columns?
Duplicate Column	Create a duplicate of the selected column as a new column placed on the far right end of the table. The name given to the new column is Copy of X, where X is the name of the original column.	No
Remove Duplicates	Remove all rows from the selected column where the values duplicate earlier values. The row with the first occurrence of a value isn't removed.	Yes
Remove Errors	Remove rows containing errors in the selected column.	Yes
Change Type	Change the data type of the selected column to any of these types: Binary, Date, Date/Time, Date/Time/Timezone, Duration, Logical, Number, Text, Time, or Using Locale (which localizes data types to the country you specify).	Yes
Transform	Change the way values in the column are rendered. You can choose from the following options: Lowercase, Uppercase, Capitalize Each Word, Trim, Clean, Length, JSON, and XML. If the values in the column are date/time values, the options are Date, Time, Day, Month, Year, or Day of Week. If the values in the column are number values, the options are Round, Absolute Value, Factorial, Base-10 Logarithm, Natural Logarithm, Power, and Square Root.	Yes
Replace Values	Replace one value in the selected column with another specified value.	Yes
Replace Errors	Replace unsightly error values with your own, friendlier text.	Yes
Group By	Aggregate data by row values. For example, you can group by state and either count the number of cities in each state or sum the population of each state.	Yes
Fill	Fill empty cells in the column with the value of the first non-empty cell. You have the option to fill up or fill down.	Yes
Unpivot Columns	Transpose the selected columns from column-oriented to row-oriented or vice versa.	Yes
Rename	Rename the selected column to a name you specify.	No

Action	Purpose	Available with Multiple Columns?
Move	Move the selected column to a different location in the table. You have these choices for moving the column: Left, Right, To Beginning, and To End.	Yes
Drill Down	Navigate to the contents of the column. This option is used with tables that contain metadata representing embedded information.	No
Add as New Query	Create a new query with the content of the column, by referencing the original query in the new one. The name of the new query is the same as the column header of the selected column.	No
Split Column (Ribbon only)	Split the value of a single column into two or more columns, based on a number of characters or a given delimiter, such as a comma, semicolon, or tab.	No
Merge Column (Ribbon only)	Merge the values of two or more columns into a single column that contains a specified delimiter, such as a comma, semicolon, or tab.	Yes

Understanding Table Actions

While you're in the Query Editor, Power Query lets you apply certain actions to an entire data table. You can see the available table-level actions by clicking the Table Actions icon, shown in Figure 8-17.

Figure 8-17:
Click the Table Actions icon in the upper-left corner of the Query Editor Preview pane to see the table-level actions you can use to transform the data.

Table 8-2 lists the table-level actions and describes the primary purpose of each one.

Table 8-2	Table-Level Actions
Action	*Purpose*
Use First Row as Headers	Replace each table header name with the values in the first row of each column.
Add Custom Column	Insert a new column after the last column of the table. The values in the new column are determined by the value or formula you define.
Add Index Column	Insert a new column containing a sequential list of numbers starting from 1, 0, or another specified value you define.
Choose Columns	Choose the columns you want to keep in the query results.
Remove Duplicates	Remove all rows where the values in the selected columns duplicate earlier values. The row with the first occurrence of a value set isn't removed.
Keep Top Rows	Remove all but the top N number of rows. You specify the number threshold.
Keep Bottom Rows	Remove all but the bottom N number of rows. You specify the number threshold.
Keep Range of Rows	Remove all rows except the ones that fall within a range you specify.
Remove Top Rows	Remove the top N rows from the table.
Remove Bottom Rows	Remove the bottom N rows from the table.
Remove Alternate Rows	Remove alternate rows from the table, starting at the first row to remove and specifying the number of rows to remove and the number of rows to keep.
Remove Errors	Remove rows containing errors in the selected columns.
Merge Queries	Create a new query that merges the current table with another query in the workbook by matching specified columns.
Append Queries	Create a new query that appends the results of another query in the workbook to the current table.

All table-level actions available in Power Query are also available on the Query Editor Ribbon, so you can either choose the convenience of right-clicking to quickly select an action or use the more visual Ribbon menu.

Chapter 9

Power Query Connection Types

Microsoft has invested a great deal of time and resources in ensuring that Power Query has the ability to connect to a wide array of data sources. Whether you need to pull data from an external website, a text file, a database system, Facebook, or a web service, Power Query can accommodate most, if not all, of your source data needs.

You can see all available connection types by clicking on the New Query drop-down arrow on the Data tab. As Figure 9-1 illustrates, Power Query offers the ability to pull from a wide array of data sources, as described in this list:

- ✔ **From File:** Pulls data from specified Excel files, text files, CSV files, XML files, or folders

- ✔ **From Database:** Pulls data from a database such as Microsoft Access, SQL Server, or SQL Server Analysis Services

- ✔ **From Azure:** Pulls data from Microsoft's Azure Cloud service

- ✔ **From Other Sources:** Pulls data from a wide array of Internet, cloud, and other ODBC data sources

In this chapter, I help you explore the various connection types that can be leveraged to import external data.

Figure 9-1:
Power
Query has
the ability to
connect to a
wide array
of text,
database,
and Internet
data
sources.

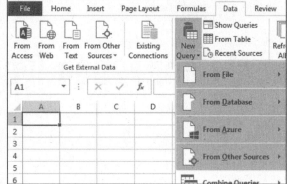

Importing Data from Files

Organizational data is often stored in files such as text files, CSV files, and even other Excel workbooks. It's not uncommon to use these kinds of files as data sources for data analysis. Power Query offers several connection types that enable the importing of data from external files.

The files you import don't necessarily have to be on your own PC. You can import files on network drives as well as in cloud repositories such as Google Drive and Microsoft OneDrive.

Getting data from Excel workbooks

You can import data from other Excel workbooks by selecting Data ⇨ New Query ⇨ From File ⇨ From Workbook from the Excel Ribbon.

Excel opens the Import Data dialog box, shown in Figure 9-2. Use this dialog box to browse for the Excel file you want to work with. Note that you can import any kind of Excel file, including macro-enabled workbooks and template workbooks.

Power Query won't bring in charts, pivot tables, shapes, VBA code, or any other objects that may exist within a workbook. Power Query simply imports the data found in the used cell ranges of the workbook.

After you've selected a file, the Navigator pane activates (see Figure 9-3), showing you all the data sources available in the workbook.

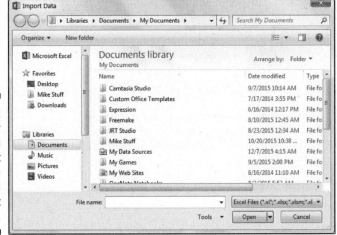

Figure 9-2:
Browse for the Excel file that contains the data you want imported.

The idea here is to select the data source you want and then either load or edit the data using the buttons at the bottom of the Navigator pane. Click the Load button to skip any editing and import your targeted data as is. Click the Edit button if you want to transform or shape before completing the import.

In terms of Excel workbooks, a *data source* is either a worksheet or a defined named range. The icons next to each data source let you distinguish which sources are worksheets and which are named ranges. In Figure 9-3, the source named MyNamedRange is a defined named range, and the source named National Parks is a worksheet.

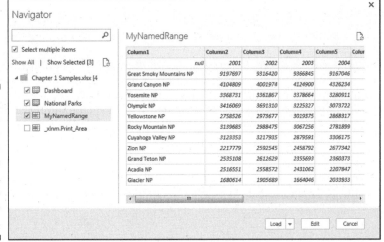

Figure 9-3:
Select the data sources you want to work with, and then click the Load button.

You can import multiple sources at a time by selecting the Select Multiple Items check box and then placing a check mark next to each worksheet and named range that you want imported.

Getting data from CSV and text files

Text files are commonly used to store and distribute data because of their inherent ability to hold many thousands of bytes of data without having an inflated file size. Text files can do this by foregoing all the fancy formatting, leaving only the text.

A *comma-separated value (CSV)* file is a kind of text file that contains commas to delimit (separate) values into columns of data.

Text files

To import a text file, select Data⇨New Query⇨From File⇨From Text on the Excel Ribbon. Excel opens the Import Data dialog box, where you can browse for, and select, a text file.

Excel has another From Text command button on the Data tab, under the Get External Data group. This duplicate command is actually the legacy import capability found in all Excel versions. The Power Query version is much more powerful, allowing you to shape and transform text data before importing. Be sure to use the correct Power Query version of the From Text feature.

Power Query opens the Query Editor to show you the contents of the text file you just imported. As you can see in Figure 9-4, text files are imported as a table with one column containing a row for each line in the text file.

The idea here is to apply any changes you want to make to the data and then click the Close & Load command on the Home tab to complete the import.

Some text files are structured as tab-delimited files. Similar to comma-separated (CSV) files, tab-delimited text files contain tab characters that separate text values into columns of data. Power Query recognizes tab-delimited text files and imports these files into a table that contains a separate column for each tab delimiter.

CSV files

To import a CSV file, go to the Excel Ribbon and select Data⇨New Query⇨From File⇨From CSV. Excel opens the Import Data dialog box, where you can browse for and select your target CSV file.

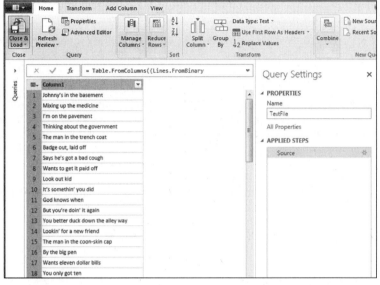

Figure 9-4:
Text files
are brought
into the
Query Editor,
where you
can apply
your edits
and then
click the
Close &
Load
command to
complete
the import.

Power Query opens the Query Editor to show you the contents of the CSV file you just imported. Power Query excels at recognizing the correct delimiters in CSV files and typically does a good job of importing the data correctly.

For example, Row 5 in the sample CSV file illustrated in Figure 9-5 contains the value Johnson, Kimberly. Power Query contains the intelligence to know that the comma in that value is not an actual delimiter. So all the columns are separated correctly.

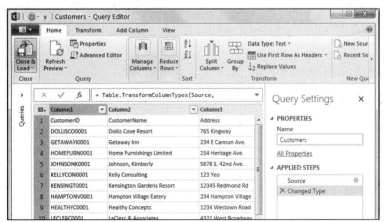

Figure 9-5:
CSV files
are brought
into the
Query Editor,
where you
can apply
your edits
and then
click the
Close &
Load
command to
complete
the import.

You can use the Query Editor to apply any edits you may need and then click the Close & Load command on the Home tab to import the CSV data.

Getting data from XML files

XML files are a family of text files that contain data wrapped in *markup* (tags that denote structure and meaning). These tags essentially make XML files *machine-readable,* which essentially means that any application or web-based solution designed to read XML files can discern the structure and content of the data within.

The markup tags found in XML files are quite robust and make importing XML files a bit tricky. Without getting too geeky, some XML files are *attribute-based:* They contain simple markup defining a table of columns and rows. Other XML files are *element-based:* They contain a wide array of complex markup defining intricate hierarchical tables with many levels of data.

Power Query has the built-in intelligence to handle any kinds of XML file just fine, but you often need to dig for the data you want imported.

Depending on the markup within, Power Query starts you off with either the Navigator pane or the Query Editor. Although this can be a bit jarring at first, you can quickly get the gist of drilling into the data you need.

You can start importing an XML file by going to the Excel Ribbon and selecting Data➪New Query➪From File➪From XML. Excel opens the Import Data dialog box, where you can browse for, and select, the target XML file.

You can import an XML file from the web by simply entering the URL of the file into the Import Data dialog box. For example, you can enter the following line to get to the FinalXMLOutput file found on datapigtechnologies.com:

```
www.datapigtechnologies.com/FinalXMLOutput.xml
```

Attribute-based XML files

If the XML file you've pointed to is attribute-based, Power Query opens the Query Editor and shows the highest-level content it finds. You often see a single row of high-level attributes, similar to Figure 9-6.

You can get to the data within the XML file in one of two ways:

- ✔ Click on the Table hyperlink to drill into the next level of data.
- ✔ Click on the Expand icon to view select the fields found in the next level of data (see Figure 9-7). Simply select the fields you want to see, and then click the OK button.

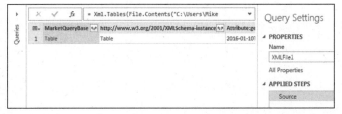

Figure 9-6:
Attribute-
based XML
files often
start with
one line of
high-level
values.

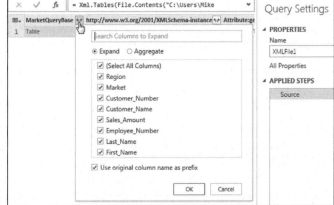

Figure 9-7:
Click the
Expand icon
to view and
drill into the
next layer
of data.

Every XML file is different, so don't anticipate drilling down (expanding to the next level of data, as shown in Figure 9-7) any specific number of times. For some files, you may have to drill down only one level. Other files may require you to drill into several layers before getting to the data you need.

After you drill into the data you need, you can click the Close & Load command on the Home tab to complete the import.

Element-based XML files

If the XML file you've pointed to is element-based, Power Query opens the Navigator pane. As you can see in Figure 9-8, you need to drill into a varying number of elements to get to the element that contains the data you're looking for.

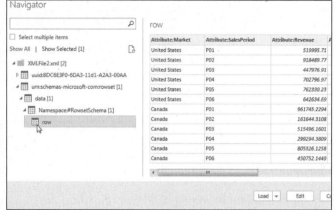

Figure 9-8:
Element-
based XML
files are
initially
displayed
in the
Navigator
pane.

After you find the correct data layer, you can select the data source you want
and then use the buttons at the bottom of the Navigator pane to either load
or edit the data.

Getting data from folders

Power Query has the ability to use the Windows file system as a data source,
enabling you to import a list of folder contents for a specified directory.
This comes in handy when you need to create a list of all the files in a
particular folder.

From the Excel Ribbon, select Data ➪ New Query ➪ From File ➪ From Folder.
The dialog box shown in Figure 9-9 opens, asking you to enter or browse for
the folder (directory) you want to use.

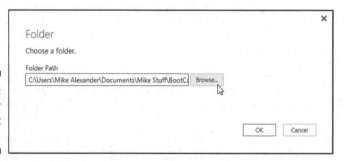

Figure 9-9:
Browse for
the target
folder.

Power Query opens the Query Editor with a new table containing the contents of the specified folder. As Figure 9-10 illustrates, this new table details the key attributes for each file, such as filename, file extension, date created, and date modified. You can even click the Expand icon in the Attributes field and choose to display some of the more advanced attributes for each file.

		fx	= Table.RemoveColumns(Source,{"Date accessed"})	

Name	▼	Extension	▼	Date modified	▼	Date created	▼	Attributes
10 Must Have Excel VBA Skills.xls		.xls		9/14/2012 6:50:20 AM		6/16/2014 7:33:17 AM		
Backup of SlicersDemo.xlk		.xlk		5/19/2011 5:01:06 AM		6/16/2014 7:33:17 AM		
Basic Visualization Techniques.xlsx		.xlsx		9/13/2012 5:53:34 AM		6/16/2014 7:33:18 AM		☑ (Select All Colu
Charting Best Practices.ppt		.ppt		7/25/2014 3:13:56 PM		7/25/2014 3:13:56 PM		☑ Archive
DataPig.odc		.odc		5/19/2011 6:09:54 AM		6/16/2014 7:33:18 AM		☑ Compressed
Excel Keyboard Shortcuts.xls		.xls		2/11/2009 2:43:10 AM		6/16/2014 7:33:18 AM		☑ Content Type
Excel Macros.xlsx		.xlsx		3/28/2012 11:24:36 AM		6/16/2014 7:33:18 AM		☑ Device
ExcelToPowerPoint.xlsm		.xlsm		9/14/2012 6:11:36 AM		6/16/2014 7:33:18 AM		☑ Directory
Forceenablemacros.xls		.xls		9/26/2012 1:14:34 PM		6/16/2014 7:33:18 AM		☑ Encrypted
Interactive Reporting.xls		.xls		5/16/2011 1:19:48 AM		6/16/2014 7:33:18 AM		☑ Hidden
Interactive Reporting.xlsx		.xlsx		5/16/2013 7:24:28 AM		6/16/2014 7:33:18 AM		☑ Kind
Macro Charged PivotTables.xlsm		.xlsm		6/28/2010 7:59:58 AM		6/16/2014 7:33:18 AM		☑ Normal
NorthWind for DAX Tutorials.xlsx		.xlsx		12/7/2015 7:20:21 AM		12/7/2015 6:32:11 AM		☑ NotContentInc

Figure 9-10: Power Query creates a useful list of files.

After you have all the attributes you need, you can click the Close & Load command on the Home tab to complete the import.

The files that are listed include all files contained in subfolders inside the folder you specified. Unfortunately, the resulting output is not hyperlinked back to the actual folder contents. In other words, you can't open the individual files from the query table.

Importing Data from Database Systems

In smart organizations, the task of data management is not performed by Excel; rather, it's performed primarily by database systems such as Microsoft Access and SQL Server. Databases like these not only store millions of rows of data, but also ensure data integrity and allow for the rapid search and retrieval of data by way of queries and views.

A connection for every database type

Power Query offers options to connect to a wide array of database types. Microsoft has been keen to add connection types for as many commonly used databases as it can.

Relational and OLAP databases

Choose Data ➪ New Query ➪ From Database and you see the list of databases shown in Figure 9-11. Power Query has the ability to connect to virtually any database commonly used today: SQL Server, Microsoft Access, Oracle, MySQL, etc.

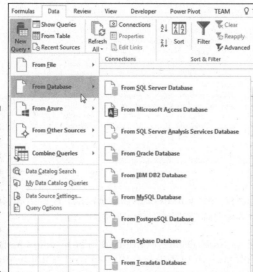

Figure 9-11:
Power Query offers connection types for many of the popular database systems now in use.

Azure databases

If your organization has a Microsoft Azure cloud database or a subscription to Microsoft Azure Marketplace, an entire set of connection types is designed to import data from Azure databases (see Figure 9-12). You can get to these connection types by choosing Data ➪ New Query ➪ From Azure.

ODBC connections to nonstandard databases

If you're using a unique, nonstandard database system that isn't listed under From Database (refer to Figure 9-11) or From Azure (refer to Figure 9-12), not to worry: As long as your database system can be connected to via an ODBC connection string, Power Query can connect to it.

Choose Data ➪ New Query ➪ From Other Data Sources to see a list of other connection types. Click the From ODBC option shown in Figure 9-13 to start a connection to your unique database via an ODBC connection string.

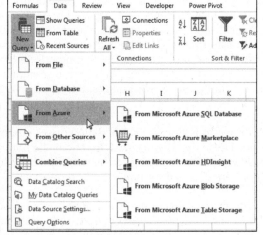

Figure 9-12:
Tools for connection to Microsoft Azure cloud database services.

Getting data from other data systems

In addition to ODBC, Figure 9-13 illustrates other kinds of data systems that can be leveraged by Power Query.

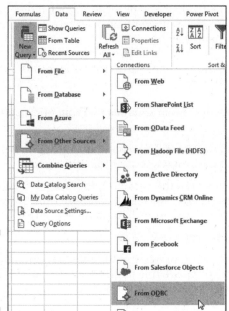

Figure 9-13:
Starting an ODBC connection.

Some of these data systems (SharePoint, Dynamics CRM, Salesforce, and Microsoft Exchange) are popular systems that are used in many organizations to store data, track sales opportunities, and manage emails. Other systems, such as OData Feeds and Hadoop, are less-common services used to work with very large volumes of data. These are often mentioned in conversations about big data. And of course, the From Web option (demonstrated in Chapter 8) is an integral connection type for any analyst who leverages data from the internet.

Clicking any of these connections opens a set of dialog boxes customized for the selected connection. These dialog boxes ask for the basic parameters that Power Query needs in order to connect to the specified data source; parameters such as file path, URL, server name, and credentials.

Each connection type requires its own, unique set of parameters, so each of their dialog boxes is different. Luckily, Power Query rarely needs more than a handful of parameters to connect to any single data source, so the dialog boxes are relatively intuitive and hassle-free.

Walk-through: Getting data from a database

It would be redundant to walk through the process of connection to every type of database available. However, it would be useful to walk through the basic steps of connecting a database.

Here are the steps for connecting to one of the more ubiquitous database systems — Microsoft Access:

1. **Choose Data ⇨ New Query ⇨ From Database ⇨ From Microsoft Access Database.**

2. **Browse for your target database. You can use the Facility Services. accdb database, found in the sample files for this book.**

   After Power Query connects to the database, the Navigator pane, shown in Figure 9-14, activates. There, you see all database objects available to you, including tables and views (or *queries,* in Access lingo).

3. **Click the Sales_By_Employee view.**

   The Navigator pane displays a preview of the Sales_By_Employee data. If you want to transform or shape this data, click the Edit button. In this case, the data looks fine as is.

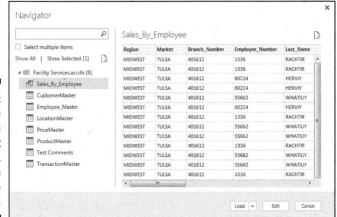

Figure 9-14:
Select the
view you
want
imported,
and then
click the
Load button.

4. Click the Load button to complete the import.

After a bit of processing, Power Query loads the data to a new Excel
worksheet and adds the new query to the Workbook Queries pane,
as shown in Figure 9-15.

You can select multiple tables and views by selecting the Select Multiple
Items check box and then placing a check mark next to each database object
you want imported.

The icon next to each database object distinguishes whether that object is
a table or a view. Views have an icon that looks like two overlapping grids.
See the icon for the Sales_By_Employee view, shown in Figure 9-14, to
get the idea.

Figure 9-15:
The final
imported
database
data.

It's a best practice to use views whenever possible. Views are often cleaner
data sets because they're already optimized to include only the columns and
data that are necessary. (This improves query performance and helps mini-
mize the workbook's file size.) In addition, you don't need to have an intimate

knowledge of the database architecture. Someone with that knowledge has already done the work for you — joined the correct tables, applied the appropriate business rules, and optimized output, for example.

Managing Data Source Settings

Every time you connect to any web-based data source or data source that requires some level of credentials, Power Query *caches* (stores) the settings for that data source.

Suppose that you connect to a SQL Server database, enter all your credentials, and import the data you need. At the moment of successful connection, Power Query caches information about that connection in a file located on your local PC. It includes the connection string, username, password, and privacy settings, for example.

The purpose of all this caching is so that you don't have to reenter credentials every time you need to refresh your queries. That's nifty, but what happens when your credentials are changed? Well, the short answer is those queries will fail until the data source settings are updated.

You can edit data source settings by activating the Data Source Settings dialog box. To do so, choose Data⇨New Query⇨Data Source Settings, as demonstrated in Figure 9-16.

Figure 9-16: Activating the Data Source Settings dialog box.

The Data Source Settings dialog box, shown in Figure 9-17, contains a list of all credentials-based data sources previously used in queries. Select the data source you need to change, and then click the Edit button.

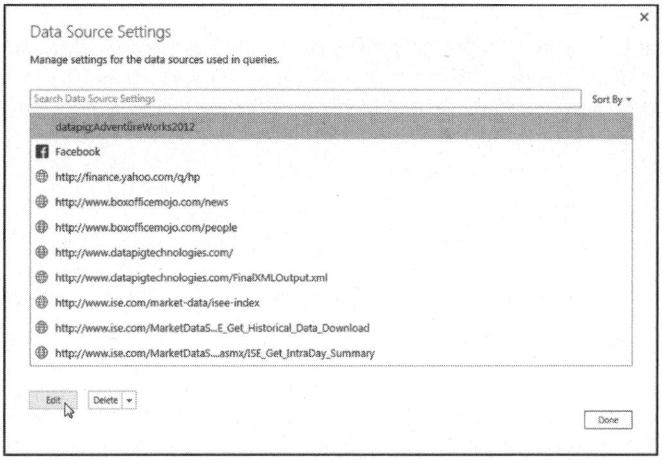

Figure 9-17: Edit a data source by selecting it and clicking the Edit button.

Another dialog box opens — this time, specific to the data source you selected (see Figure 9-18). This dialog box enables you to edit credentials as well as other data privacy settings.

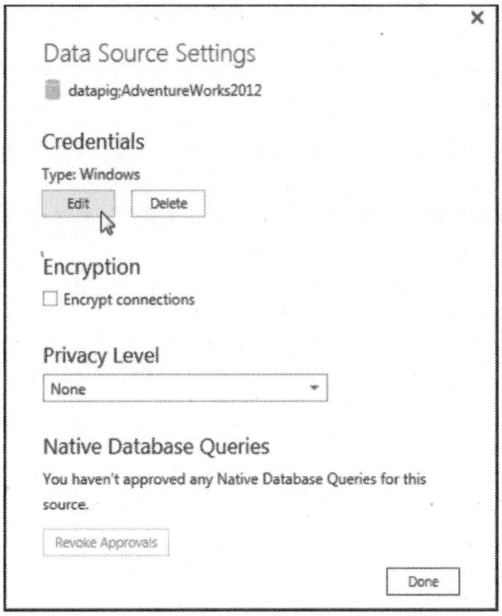

Figure 9-18: The credentials editing screen for your selected data source.

Click the Edit button to make changes to the credentials for the data source. The credentials editing screen will differ based on the data source you're working with, but again, the input dialog boxes are relatively intuitive and easy to update.

Power Query caches data source settings in a file located on your local PC. Even though you may have deleted a particular query, the data source setting is retained for possible future use. This can lead to a cluttered list of old and current data sources. You can clean out old items by selecting the data source in the Data Source Settings dialog box and clicking the Delete button.

Chapter 10

Transforming Your Way to Better Data

Wouldn't it be great if all the data sources you work with were clean and ready to use? Unfortunately, that's not the case — you often receive data that is unpolished, or *raw*. That is to say, the data may have duplicates or blank fields or inconsistent text, for example.

Data transformation generally entails certain actions that are meant to "clean" your data — actions such as establishing a table structure, removing duplicates, cleaning text, removing blanks, and even adding your own calculations.

In this chapter, I introduce you to some of the tools and techniques in Power Query that make it easy for you to clean and massage your data.

You can follow along with the examples in this chapter by downloading the LeadList.txt sample file from www.dummies.com/go/excelpowerpivot powerqueryfd. After you download it, you can import the sample file into Power Query: Select Data ⇨ New Query ⇨ From File ⇨ From Text and then point to LeadList.txt.

Completing Common Transformation Tasks

Many of the unpolished datasets that come to you will require other types of transformation actions. This section covers some of the more common transformation tasks you will have to perform, such as removing duplicates, finding and replacing text, filling empty cells, and splitting or joining text values.

Removing duplicate records

Duplicate records are absolute analysis killers. The effect that duplicate records have on your analysis can be far-reaching, corrupting almost every metric, summary, and analytical assessment you produce. It is for this reason that finding and removing duplicate records should be your first priority when you receive a new dataset.

Before you begin examining the dataset to find and remove duplicate records, consider how you define a duplicate record. Look at the table shown in Figure 10-1, where you see 11 records. Of the 11 records, how many are duplicates?

Figure 10-1: Does this table have duplicate records? It depends on how you define them.

SicCode	PostalCode	CompanyNumber	DollarPotential	City	State	Address
1389	77032	11147805	$9,517.00	houston	tx	6000 n sem heirten pkwy e
1389	77032	11147848	$9,517.00	houston	tx	43410 e herdy rd
1389	77042	11160116	$7,653.00	houston	tx	40642 rachmend ave ste 600
1389	77051	11165400	$9,517.00	houston	tx	5646 helmis rd
1389	77057	11173241	$9,517.00	houston	tx	2514 san filape st ste 6600
1389	77060	11178227	$7,653.00	houston	tx	100 n sem heirten pkwy e ste 100
1389	77073	11190514	$9,517.00	houston	tx	4660 rankan rd # 400
1389	77049	11218412	$7,653.00	houston	tx	4541 mallir read 6
1389	77040	13398882	$18,379.00	houston	tx	3643 wandfirn rd
1389	77040	13399102	$18,379.00	houston	tx	3643 wandfirn rd
1389	77077	13535097	$7,653.00	houston	tx	44160 wisthiamir rd ste 100

If you were to define a duplicate record in Figure 10-1 as a duplication of only the SicCode, you would find 10 duplicate records. That is, of the 11 records shown, 1 record has a unique SicCode, and the other 10 are duplications. Now, if you were to expand your definition of a duplicate record to a duplication of both SicCode and PostalCode, you would find only two duplicates: the duplication of postal codes 77032 and 77040. Finally, if you were to define a duplicate record as a duplication of the unique value of SicCode, PostalCode, and CompanyNumber, you would find no duplicates.

This example shows that having two records with the same value in a column doesn't necessarily mean that you have a duplicate record. It's up to you to determine which field or combination of fields best defines a unique record in the dataset.

After you have a clear idea of which field or fields best make up a unique record in the table, you can remove duplicates easily by using the Remove Duplicates command.

Figure 10-2 illustrates the removal of duplicate rows based on three columns. Note the importance of selecting the columns that define a duplicate. In this case, the combination of Address, CompanyNumber, and CompanyName defines a duplicate record. You select these columns before clicking the Remove Duplicates command on the Home tab of the Power Query ribbon.

Address	CompanyNumber	CompanyName	PostalCode	Type	20 Potential Revenue
66661 624 e realread st	14150640	farist Corp.	53910	DB	4356
30444 6630 midana rd	4633777	mentre Corp.	44333	DB	962
60125 6666 lihagh st	2083985	scett Corp.	18103	DB	21510
22226 po box 130	17762162	canada Corp.	L9R 1V7	DB	441
42466 2200 e santa ana canyen rd ste 524	6103857	rebirt Corp.	92807	DB	4232
66361 46246 n haghway 456	11475365	moxwil Corp.	78750	DB	7196
66361 46246 n haghway 456	11475365	moxwil Corp.	78750	DB	null
66361 46246 n haghway 456	11475365	moxwil Corp.	78750	DB	null
20200 400 ir haghway 4	568358	lancel Corp.	07001	DB	757
20200 400 ir haghway 4	568359	pulca Corp.	07001	DB	757
50100 2 lattilien rd	20087585	qiack Corp.	01432	DB	3420
66600 5400 breinang hwy	2488837	crewn Corp.	21222	DB	22393
45600 po box 4200 stn mean	17703507	dana c Corp.	L4M 5M4	DB	8315
45600 po box 4200 stn mean	17703507	dana c Corp.	L4M 5M4	DB	null

Figure 10-2: Removing duplicate records.

The Remove Duplicates command essentially looks for distinct values in the columns you selected and then removes all records necessary to end up with a unique list of values. If you select only one column before giving the Remove Duplicates command, Power Query uses only one column you selected to determine the unique list of values, which undoubtedly removes too many records — records that aren't truly duplicates. For this reason, be sure to select all columns that define a duplicate.

If you make a mistake and remove duplicates based on the wrong set of columns, don't worry: You can always use the Query Settings pane to delete that step. Right-click on the Removed Duplicates step and select Delete (see Figure 10-3). Alternatively, you can click the X next to the Remove Duplicates step.

Figure 10-3:
Undo the
removal of
records by
deleting the
Removed
Duplicates
step.

If you don't see the Query Settings pane, select View ⇨ Query Settings to activate the Query Settings pane.

Filling in blank fields

There are two kinds of blank values: null and empty string. A *null* is essentially a numerical value of nothing, whereas an empty string is equivalent to entering two quotation marks ("") in a cell.

Blank fields aren't necessarily a bad thing, but having an excessive number of blanks in your data can lead to unexpected problems when analyzing it.

Your job is to decide whether to leave the blanks in the dataset or fill them with actual values. Consider the following best practices:

- ✔ **Use blanks sparingly:** Working with a dataset is a much less daunting task when you don't have to test continually for blank values.

- ✔ **Use alternatives whenever possible:** Represent missing values with some logical missing-value code whenever possible.

- ✔ **Never use null values in number fields:** Use zero instead of null in a currency or a number field that will be used in calculations.

Replacing null values

Power Query shows the word *null* for any null value in your data. Replacing the null values is as simple as selecting the column or columns you want to fix and then selecting the Replace Values command, as shown in Figure 10-4.

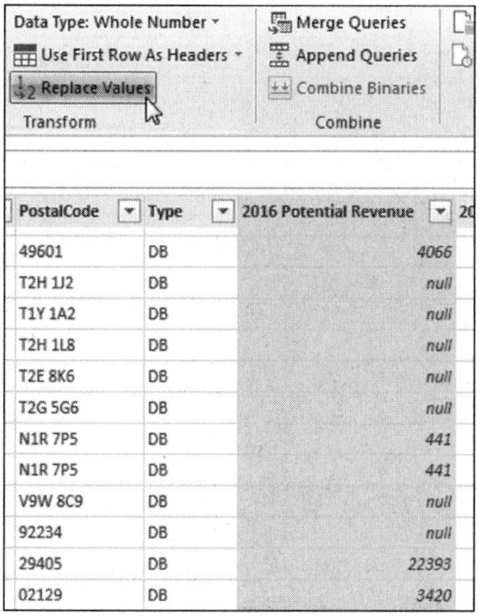

Figure 10-4:
Activating
the Replace
Values
dialog box.

The Replace Values dialog box, shown in Figure 10-5, opens. After you enter the word *null* as the value to find, you can then enter the value you want to use instead. In this case, enter 0 as the Replace With value.

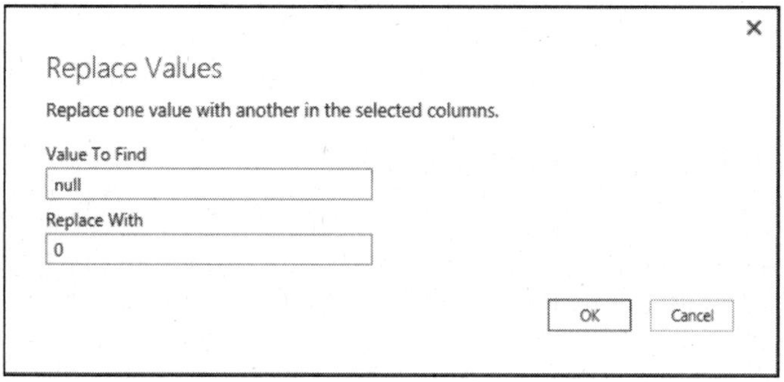

Figure 10-5:
Replacing
null with 0.

Filling in empty strings

To follow best practices, represent missing values in a field with some logical value code whenever possible. For example, in Figure 10-6, I want to tag with the word *Undefined* any record with a missing title in the ContactTitle field.

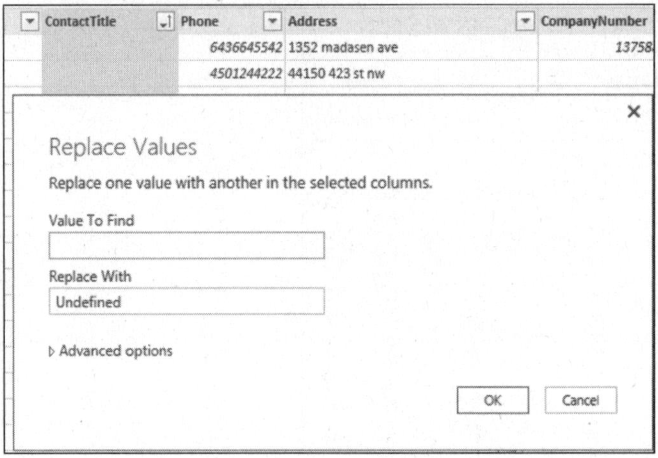

▼ ContactTitle	▼ Phone	▼ Address	▼ CompanyNumber
	6436645542	1352 madasen ave	13758
	4501244222	44150 423 st nw	

Replace Values ✕

Replace one value with another in the selected columns.

Value To Find

[   ]

Replace With

[Undefined   ]

▷ Advanced options

[OK] [Cancel]

Figure 10-6:
Replacing
empty
strings with
the word
Undefined.

You can do so by clicking on ContactTitle, selecting the Replace Values command, and then entering the word *Undefined* in the Replace Values dialog box. As you can see in Figure 10-6, because you're replacing an empty string, there's no need to enter anything in the Value to Find input box.

If you need to adjust or correct the step where you replace values, you can reopen the Replace Values dialog box by clicking the Gear icon next to the name for that step. This is true for any action that requires a dialog box to complete. Clicking on the Gear icon next to any step name opens the appropriate dialog box for that step.

Concatenating columns

You can easily *concatenate* (join) the values in two or more columns. In Power Query, you do this by using the Merge Columns command. The Merge Columns command concatenates the values in two or more fields and outputs the newly merged values into a new column.

First choose the columns you want to concatenate, and then select the Transform tab and then the Merge Columns command, as shown in Figure 10-7.

The Merge Columns dialog box opens, as shown in Figure 10-8. You have the option of choosing from a list of the most commonly used delimiters (comma, space, tab, etc.). You can also select the Custom option to enter your own delimiter. In Figure 10-8, a hyphen (-) is used.

As you can see, you can also name the new column that will be created.

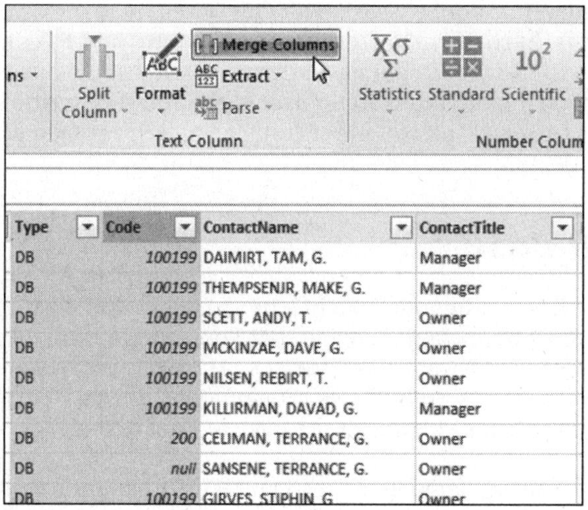

Figure 10-7: Merging the Type and Code fields.

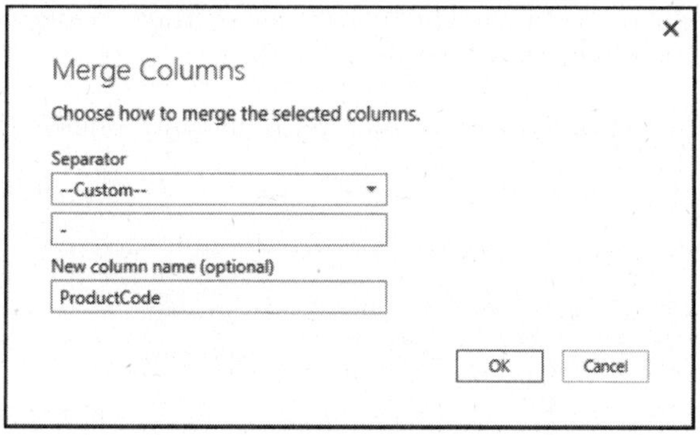

Type		Code		ContactName		ContactTitle	
DB		100199		DAIMIRT, TAM, G.		Manager	
DB		100199		THEMPSENJR, MAKE, G.		Manager	
DB		100199		SCETT, ANDY, T.		Owner	
DB		100199		MCKINZAE, DAVE, G.		Owner	
DB		100199		NILSEN, REBIRT, T.		Owner	
DB		100199		KILLIRMAN, DAVAD, G.		Manager	
DB		200		CELIMAN, TERRANCE, G.		Owner	
DB		null		SANSENE, TERRANCE, G.		Owner	
DB		100199		GIRVES, STIPHIN, G.		Owner	

Figure 10-8: The Merge Columns dialog box.

The reward for your efforts is a new field containing the concatenated values from the original column (see Figure 10-9). The resulting column will be named Merged. You can rename the column by right-clicking it and selecting the Rename option.

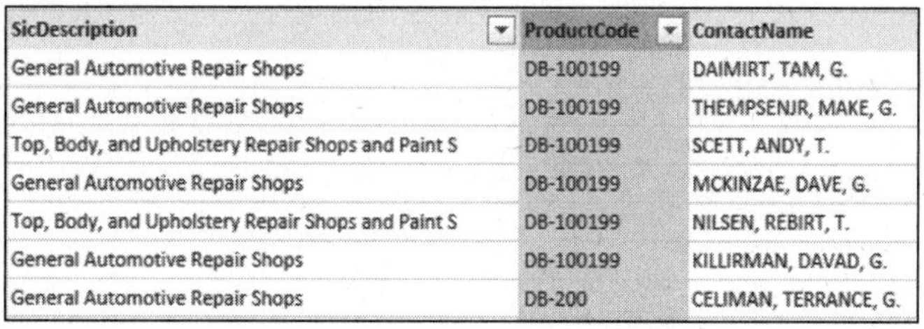

Figure 10-9: The original columns are removed and replaced with a new, merged column.

SicDescription		ProductCode		ContactName
General Automotive Repair Shops		DB-100199		DAIMIRT, TAM, G.
General Automotive Repair Shops		DB-100199		THEMPSENJR, MAKE, G.
Top, Body, and Upholstery Repair Shops and Paint S		DB-100199		SCETT, ANDY, T.
General Automotive Repair Shops		DB-100199		MCKINZAE, DAVE, G.
Top, Body, and Upholstery Repair Shops and Paint S		DB-100199		NILSEN, REBIRT, T.
General Automotive Repair Shops		DB-100199		KILLIRMAN, DAVAD, G.
General Automotive Repair Shops		DB-200		CELIMAN, TERRANCE, G.

This feature is nifty, but notice that Power Query removes the original Type and Code columns. In some instances, you'll definitely want to concatenate values but retain the source columns. In those instances, the answer is to create your own, custom column. Later in this chapter, I describe how to use custom columns to solve this and other transformation problems.

Changing case

Making sure that the text in your data has the correct capitalization may sound trivial, but it's important. Imagine that you receive a customer table that has an address field where all addresses are lowercase. How will that look on labels, form letters, or invoices? Fortunately, Power Query has a few built-in functions that make changing the case of your text a snap.

For example, the ContactName field (see Figure 10-10) contains names that are formatted in all uppercase letters. To change these names to the more appropriate proper case, you can use the Format command found on the Transform tab. The Format command has options for lowercase, uppercase and proper case (capitalize each word).

Selecting the Capitalize Each Word option reformats all values in the selected column to proper case.

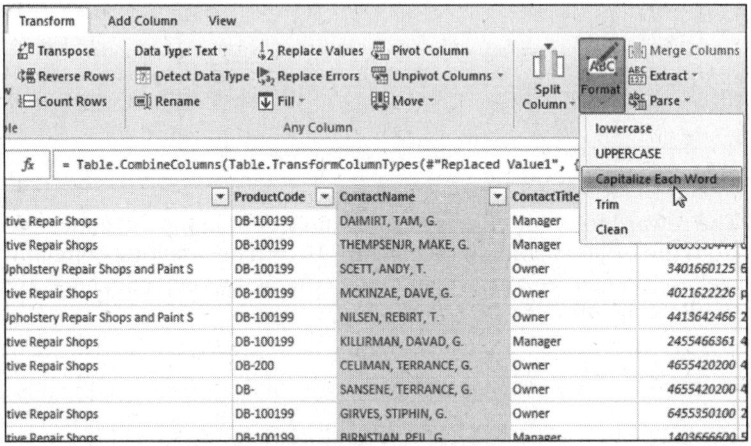

Figure 10-10:
Reformatting
the Contact-
Name field
to proper
case.

Finding and replacing specific text

Imagine that you work in a company named BLVD, Inc. One day, the president of your company informs you that the abbreviation *blvd* on all addresses is now deemed an infringement of your company's trademarked name and must be changed to *Boulevard* as soon as possible. How would you go about meeting this new requirement?

The Replace Values function is ideal in a situation like this. Select the Address field, and then click the Replace Values command on the Home tab.

In the Replace Values dialog box (shown in Figure 10-11), simply fill the Value to Find input box with the value you want to find, and then fill the Replace With input box with the value you want to use as a replacement.

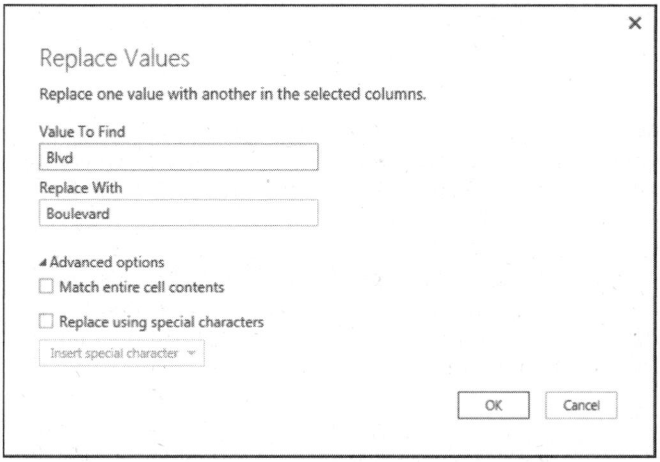

Figure 10-11:
Replacing
text values.

Note that clicking on Advanced Options reveals two optional settings, which are described in this list:

- ✔ **Match entire cell contents:** Selecting this option tells Power Query to replace values that contain only the text entered into the Value to Find field. This option comes in handy when you want to replace zeros (0) with *n/a* but not affect any zeros that are part of a number — only those that are alone in a cell.

- ✔ **Replace Using Special Characters:** Selecting this option allows you to use special invisible characters such as line feed, carriage return, or tab as replacement text. This option is useful when you want to force an indent or reposition the text so that it shows up on two lines.

Trimming and cleaning text

When you receive a dataset from a mainframe system, a data warehouse, or even a text file, it isn't uncommon to have field values that contain leading and trailing spaces. These spaces can cause some abnormal results, especially when you're appending values with leading and trailing spaces to other values that are clean. To demonstrate this concept, look at the dataset in Figure 10-12.

State	SumOfDollarPotential
ca	$26,561,554.00
ny	$7,483,960.00
tx	$13,722,782.00
ca	$12,475,489.00
ny	$827,563.00
tx	$7,669,208.00

Figure 10-12: Leading spaces can cause issues in analysis.

This view is intended to be an aggregate view that displays the sum of the dollar potential for California, New York, and Texas. However, the leading spaces are forcing each state into two sets, preventing you from discerning the accurate totals.

You can easily remove leading and trailing spaces by using the Trim function in Power Query. Figure 10-13 demonstrates how you would update a field to remove the leading and trailing spaces by using the Trim command found on the Transformation tab.

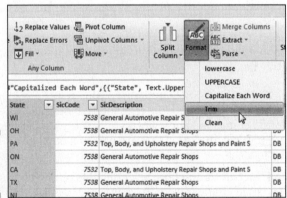

Figure 10-13: The Trim command.

Again, the Trim command is applied to any column or columns you select. So, you can fix multiple columns at a time by simply selecting them before selecting the Trim command.

Figure 10-13 also shows the Clean command (beneath Trim). Whereas Trim removes leading and trailing spaces, the Clean command removes any invisible characters, such as carriage returns and other nonprintable characters that may slip in from external source systems. These characters are typically rendered in Excel as question marks or square boxes. But in Power Query, they show up as spaces.

If the source system that supplies your data has a nasty habit of including strange characters and leading spaces, you can apply the Trim and Clean functions to sanitize the dataset.

 You may already know that the TRIM function in Excel removes the leading spaces, trailing spaces, and excess spaces within the given text. Power Query's Trim function removes leading and trailing spaces, but doesn't touch the excess spaces in the text. If excess spaces are a problem in your data, you can deal with them by using the Replace Values function to replace a given number of spaces with only one space.

Extracting the left, right, and middle values

In Excel, the RIGHT function, the LEFT function, and the MID function allow you to extract portions of a string starting from different positions:

- ✔ **Left:** Returns a specified number of characters, starting from the leftmost character of the string. The required arguments for the Left function are the text you're evaluating and the number of characters you want returned. For example, Left("70056-3504", 5) would return five characters starting from the leftmost character ("70056").

- ✔ **Right:** Returns a specified number of characters starting from the rightmost character of the string. The required arguments for the Right function are the text you're evaluating and the number of characters you want returned. For example, Right("Microsoft", 4) would return four characters starting from the rightmost character ("soft").

- ✔ **Mid:** Returns a specified number of characters starting from a specified character position. The required arguments for the Mid function are the text you're evaluating, the starting position, and the number of characters you want returned. For example, Mid("Lonely", 2, 3) would return either three characters starting from the second character or character number 2 in the string ("one").

Power Query has equivalent functions exposed through the Extract command, found on the Transformation tab (see Figure 10-14). The Extract command allows you to get specified characters from a value.

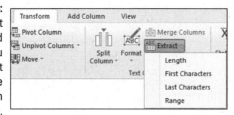

The options under the Extract command are described in this list:

- ✔ **Length:** Transforms a given column into numbers that represent the number of characters in each row (similar to Excel's LEN function).

- ✔ **First Characters:** Transforms a given column to show a specified number of characters from the beginning of text in each row (similar to Excel's LEFT function).

- ✔ **Last Characters:** Transforms a given column to show a specified number of characters from the end of text in each row (similar to Excel's RIGHT function).

- ✔ **Range:** Transforms a given column to show a specified number of characters starting from a specified character position (similar to Excel's MID function).

Applying the Extract command to a column effectively replaces the original text with the results of the operation you choose to apply. That is to say, the original text isn't visible in the table after you apply the Extract command. For this reason, you may want to first copy the column and perform the extraction on the duplicate column.

You can create a copy of a column by right-clicking on the column and selecting Duplicate Column. When the duplicate column is created, it's the last (rightmost) column of the table.

Extracting first and last characters

To extract the first *N* characters of text, highlight the column, select Extract ⇨ First Characters, and then use the dialog box shown in Figure 10-15 to specify the number of characters you want to extract. In this case, the first three characters of the Phone field are extracted.

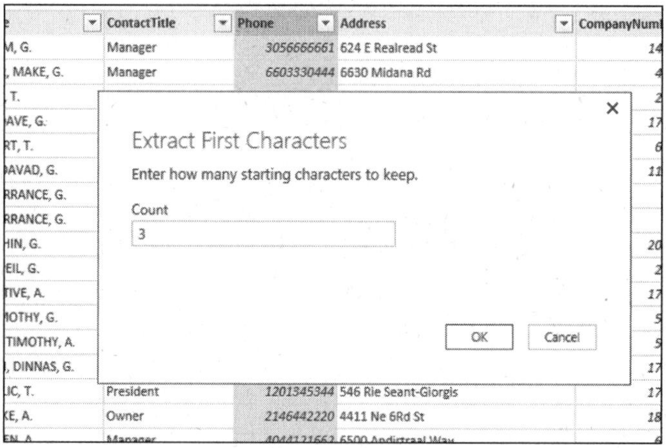

Figure 10-15:
Extracting
the first
three
characters
of the Phone
field.

To extract the last *N* characters of text, highlight the column, select Extract ⇨ Last Characters, and then use the dialog box to specify the number of characters you want extracted.

Extracting middle characters

To extract the middle *N* characters of text, highlight the column and select Extract ⇨ Range. The dialog box shown in Figure 10-16 opens.

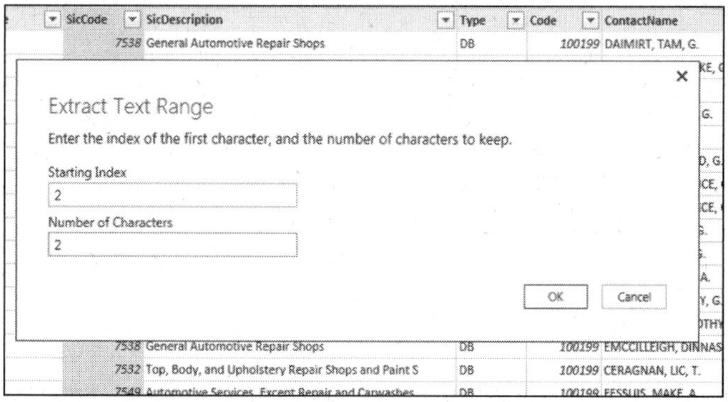

Figure 10-16:
Extracting
the two
middle
characters
of the
SicCode.

The idea here is to tell Power Query to extract a specific number of characters starting from a certain position in the text. For example, the SicCode field is a 4-digit field. If you want to extract the two middle numbers of the SicCode, you would tell Power Query to start at the second character and extract two characters from there.

As you can see in Figure 10-16, the starting index is set to 2 (starting at the second character) and the number of characters is set to 2 (extract two characters from the starting index).

Splitting columns using character markers

Have you ever gotten a dataset where two or more distinct pieces of data were jammed into one field and separated by commas? For example, a field labeled Address may have a single text value that represents address, city, state, and postal code. In a proper dataset, this text would be split into four fields.

In Figure 10-17, you can see that the values in the ContactName field are strings that represent Last name, First name, and Middle initial. Imagine that you need to split this column string into three separate fields.

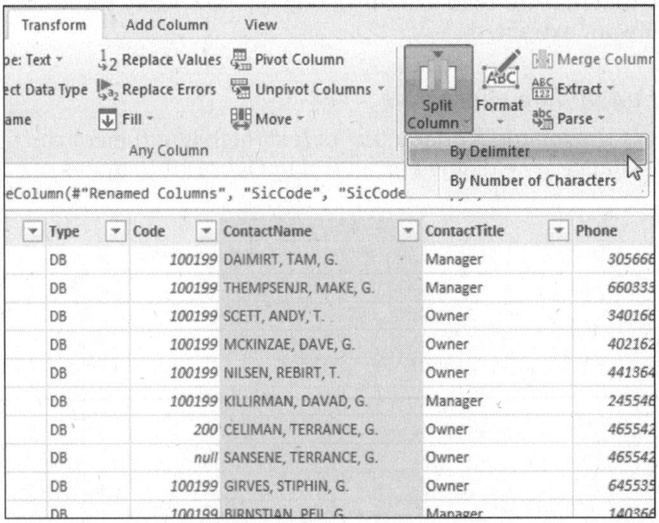

Figure 10-17:
The Split Column command can easily split the Contact-Name Field into three separate columns.

Although this isn't a straightforward undertaking in Excel, it can be done fairly easily with the Split Column command (found on the Transformation tab).

Selecting the Split Column command reveals two options; this list describes what you can do with them:

> ✔ **By Delimiter:** Split a column based on specific characters such as commas, semicolons, or spaces. This option is useful for parsing names or addresses or any field that contains multiple data points separated by delimiting characters.

✔ **By Number of Characters:** Split a column based on a specified number of characters — useful for parsing uniform text at a defined character position.

In the example (refer to Figure 10-17), the contact names are made up of last names, first names, and middle initials, all separated *(delimited)* by commas. So the By Delimiter option is the one I show you how to use.

You can highlight the ContactName field and select Split Column ⇨ By Delimiter to open the Split by Column Delimiter dialog box, shown in Figure 10-18.

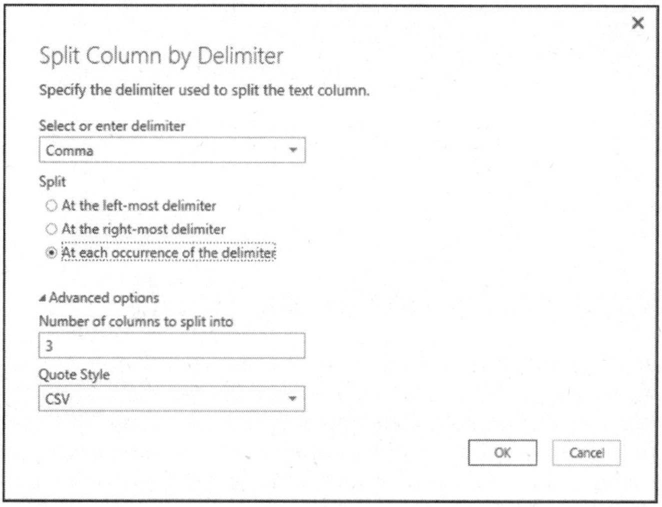

Split Column by Delimiter

Specify the delimiter used to split the text column.

Select or enter delimiter

Comma ▼

Split

○ At the left-most delimiter
○ At the right-most delimiter
⦿ At each occurrence of the delimiter

◢ Advanced options

Number of columns to split into

3

Quote Style

CSV ▼

OK   Cancel

Figure 10-18: Splitting the Contact-Name column at every occurrence of a comma.

This list describes the inputs:

✔ **Select or Enter Delimiter:** Use the drop-down menu to choose the delimiter that will define where the values should be split. If the delimiter isn't listed as a choice on the drop-down list, you can select the Custom option and define your own.

✔ **Split:** Select how you want Power Query to use the specified delimiter. Power Query can split the column only on the first occurrence of the delimiter (the leftmost delimiter) — effectively creating two columns. Alternatively, you can tell Power Query to split the column only on the last occurrence of the delimiter (the rightmost delimiter) — again, creating two columns. The third option is to tell Power Query to split the column at each occurrence of the delimiter.

✔ **Advanced Options:** By default, selecting the option to split the column at each occurrence of the delimiter creates as many columns as there are delimiters. You can use the advanced options to override the default and limit the number of columns to create.

Figure 10-19 shows the new columns created after the ContactName column is split at each comma. As you can see, three new fields are created. You can rename a field by right-clicking the field name and selecting the Rename option.

Code	ContactName.1	ContactName.2	ContactName.3	ContactTitle
100199	DAIMIRT	TAM	G.	Manager
100199	THEMPSENJR	MAKE	G.	Manager
100199	SCETT	ANDY	T.	Owner
100199	MCKINZAE	DAVE	G.	Owner
100199	NILSEN	REBIRT	T.	Owner
100199	KILLIRMAN	DAVAD	G.	Manager
200	CELIMAN	TERRANCE	G.	Owner
null	SANSENE	TERRANCE	G.	Owner
100199	GIRVES	STIPHIN	G.	Owner
100199	BIRNSTIAN	PEIL	G.	Manager
200	MCMANIR	STIVE	A.	Plant Manager
100199	MACHAL	TIMOTHY	G.	Owner
200	YESHANEGA	TIMOTHY	A.	President

Figure 10-19: The Contact-Name field has been split successfully into three columns.

Pivoting and unpivoting fields

You often encounter data sets like the one shown in Figure 10-20, where important headings (like Month) are spread across the top of the table, pulling double duty as column labels and actual data values. This matrix layout is easy to look at in a spreadsheet, but it causes problems when attempting to perform any kind of data analysis that requires aggregation or grouping, for example.

Power Pivot offers an easy way to unpivot and pivot columns, allowing you to quickly convert matrix-style tables to tabular datasets (and vice versa).

	A	B	C	D	E	F	
1	Market	Product_Description	Jan	Feb	Mar	Apr	May
2	BUFFALO	Cleaning & Housekeeping Services	$6,220	$4,264	$5,386	$6,444	$4
3	BUFFALO	Facility Maintenance and Repair	$3,256	$9,490	$4,409	$4,958	$8
4	BUFFALO	Fleet Maintenance	$5,350	$8,925	$6,394	$6,522	$9
5	BUFFALO	Green Plants and Foliage Care	$2,415	$2,580	$2,402	$2,981	$2
6	BUFFALO	Landscaping/Grounds Care	$5,474	$4,501	$5,324	$5,706	$5
7	BUFFALO	Predictive Maintenance/Preventative	$9,811	$10,180	$9,626	$11,701	$10
8	CALIFORNIA	Cleaning & Housekeeping Services	$2,841	$2,997	$2,097	$4,102	
9	CALIFORNIA	Facility Maintenance and Repair	$16,251	$35,879	$18,369	$21,844	$28
10	CALIFORNIA	Fleet Maintenance	$22,575	$36,895	$22,016	$27,871	$31
11	CALIFORNIA	Green Plants and Foliage Care	$48,251	$90,013	$51,130	$75,528	$69
12	CALIFORNIA	Landscaping/Grounds Care	$10,401	$31,101	$21,303	$30,018	$10

Figure 10-20: Matrix layouts are problematic for data analysis.

Unpivot Columns command

The Unpivot Columns command lets you select a set of columns and convert those columns into two columns: one column consisting of the old column labels and another containing the old column data.

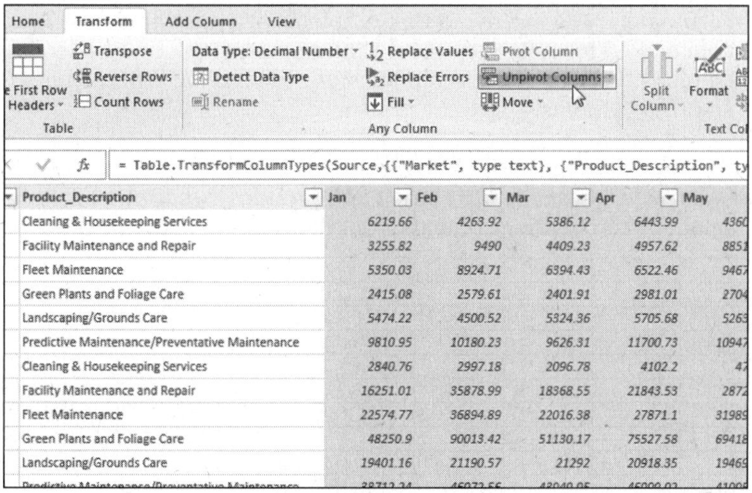

For instance, in Figure 10-21, the month columns can be unpivoted by selecting the months and then clicking the Unpivot Columns command.

Figure 10-21: Unpivoting a matrix-style Month report.

The resulting table is shown in Figure 10-22. Note that the month labels are now entries in a new column named Attribute. The month values are now in a new column named Value. You can, of course rename these columns to Month and Revenue, for example.

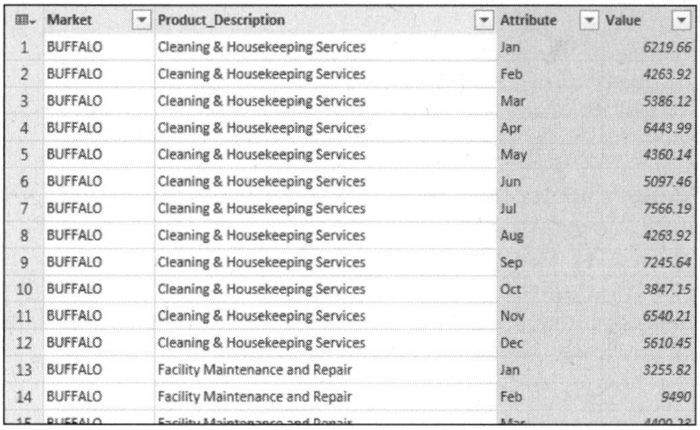

Figure 10-22: All months are now in a tabular format.

Unpivot Other Columns command

As helpful as the Unpivot Columns command is, it has a flaw: You have to explicitly select the months that you want unpivoted. But what if the number of columns is ever growing? What if you unpivot January through June, but next month a new dataset will arrive with July and then August and then September? Because the Unpivot Columns command forces you to essentially hard-code the columns you want unpivoted, you have to redo the unpivot each and every month.

Fortunately, you can avoid this problem with the Unpivot Other Columns command. This nifty command allows you to unpivot by selecting the columns that you want to remain static and telling Power Query to unpivot all other columns.

For instance, Figure 10-23 demonstrates that rather than select the month columns, you can select the Market and Product_Description columns and then select Unpivot Other Columns from the Unpivot Columns drop-down menu.

Figure 10-23: Use Unpivot Other Columns when the number of matrix columns is variable.

Home	Transform	Add Column	View		
	Transpose	Data Type: Text ▾	Replace Values	Pivot Column	
	Reverse Rows	Detect Data Type	Replace Errors	Unpivot Columns	ABC
First Row Headers ▾	Count Rows	Rename	Fill ▾	Unpivot Columns	Format
	Table		Any Column	Unpivot Other Columns	Text

`= Table.TransformColumnTypes(Source,{{"Market", type text}, {"Product_Descrip`

Market	Product_Description	Jan	Feb	Mar
BUFFALO	Cleaning & Housekeeping Services	6219.66	4263.92	5386.1
BUFFALO	Facility Maintenance and Repair	3255.82	9490	4409.2
BUFFALO	Fleet Maintenance	5350.03	8924.71	6394.4
BUFFALO	Green Plants and Foliage Care	2415.08	2579.61	2401.9
BUFFALO	Landscaping/Grounds Care	5474.22	4500.52	5324.3
BUFFALO	Predictive Maintenance/Preventative Maintenance	9810.95	10180.23	9626.3
CALIFORNIA	Cleaning & Housekeeping Services	2840.76	2997.18	2096.7
CALIFORNIA	Facility Maintenance and Repair	16251.01	35878.99	18368.5
CALIFORNIA	Fleet Maintenance	22574.77	36894.89	22016.3
CALIFORNIA	Green Plants and Foliage Care	48250.9	90013.42	51130.1
CALIFORNIA	Landscaping/Grounds Care	19401.16	21190.57	2129
CALIFORNIA	Predictive Maintenance/Preventative Maintenance	38712.24	46072.56	43949.9

Now, it doesn't matter how many new month columns are added or removed each month. Your query always unpivots the correct columns.

TIP

Always use the Unpivot Other Columns option. Even if you don't anticipate new matrix columns, it's always a good bet to use the option that offers more flexibility for those unexpected changes in data.

Pivot Columns command

If you find that you need to transform your data from a tabular layout to a matrix-style layout, you can use the Pivot Columns command.

Simply select the columns that will make up the header labels and values for the new matrix columns, and then select the Pivot Column command, shown in Figure 10-24.

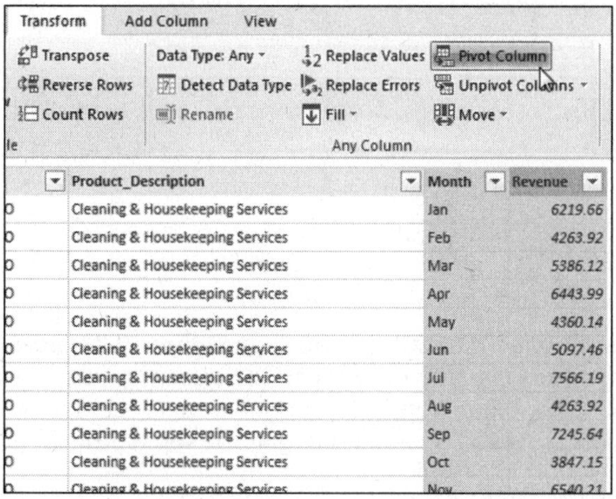

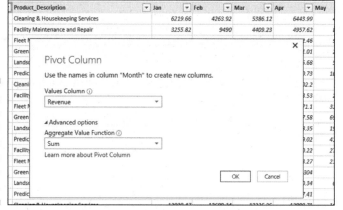

Figure 10-24: Pivoting the Month and Value columns.

Before finalizing the pivot operation, Power Query opens a dialog box (shown in Figure 10-25) to confirm the value column and the aggregation method. By default, Power Query uses the Sum operation to aggregate the data into the matrix format. You can override this default setting by selecting a different operation (count, average, or median, for example). You can even specify that you don't want aggregation performed. Clicking the OK button finalizes the pivot operation.

Figure 10-25: Confirm the aggregation operation to finalize the pivot transformation.

Creating Custom Columns

When transforming your data, you sometimes have to add your own columns to extract key data points, create new dimensions, or even create your own calculations.

You start a new custom column by going to the Add Column tab and clicking the Add Custom Column command (see Figure 10-26). This opens the Add Custom Column dialog box.

Figure 10-26: Adding a custom column.

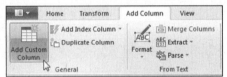

The Add Custom Column dialog box (shown in Figure 10-27) is your workbench for adding your own functionality to the query by using Power Query formulas. That's right: When you add a new custom column, it doesn't do anything until you provide a formula that gives it some utility.

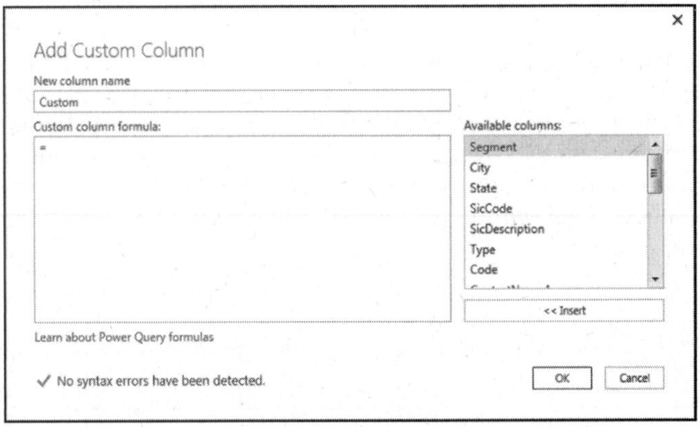

Figure 10-27: The Add Custom Column dialog box.

As for the Add Custom Column dialog box, there's not much to it. The inputs are described in this list:

✔ **New column name:** An input box where you enter a name for the column you're creating.

✔ **Available columns:** A list box that contains the names of all columns in the query. Double-click any column name in this list box to automatically place it in the formula area.

✔ **Custom column formula:** The area where you type the formula.

As in Excel, a formula can be as simple as =1 or as complicated as an if statement that applies some conditional logic. Over the next few sections, I walk you through a few examples of creating custom columns to go beyond the functionality provided via the user interface.

But before diving into building Power Query formulas, you should understand how Power Query formulas differ from those in Excel. Here are some high-level differences to be aware of:

✔ **No cell references.** You can't reach outside the Add Custom Column dialog box to select a range of cells. Power Query formulas work by referencing columns, not cells.

✔ **Excel functions don't work.** The Excel functions you're used to don't work in Power Query. Power Query has many of the same kinds of functions as Excel, but it has its own formula language.

✔ **Everything is case sensitive.** In Excel, you can type in all lowercase or all uppercase letters and your formulas will work. Not so in Power Query. To Power Query, sum, Sum, and SUM are three different items, and only one of them is acceptable.

✔ **Data types matter.** Some fields are text fields, other fields are number fields, and still others are date fields. Excel does a good job of handling formulas that mix fields of differing data types. The Power Query formula language, which is extremely sensitive to data types, doesn't have the built-in intelligence to gracefully handle data type mismatches. Data type issues are resolved with conversion functions, as covered later in this chapter.

✔ **No tool tips or intelligence help.** Excel is quick to throw up a tool tip or a menu of options when you start entering a new formula. Power Query has none of that. As of this writing, Power Query offers only a Learn About Power Query Formulas link to a Microsoft site dedicated to Power Query.

Don't panic. Power Query formulas are not as gloomy as they sound. Let's start with a simple custom column.

Concatenating with a custom column

Earlier in this chapter, I tell you how to concatenate values from two or more columns by using the Merge Columns command. Although this command is easy to use, it results in the original source columns being removed. You will likely want to concatenate values but still retain the source columns.

In these instances, you can create your own custom column. Follow these steps to create a new column that merges the Type and Code columns:

1. **While in the Query Editor, choose Add Column⇨Add Custom Column.**

2. **Place the cursor in the Custom Column Formula area (after the equal sign).**

3. **Find the Type column in the Available Columns list and double-click on it.**

   You see [Type] pop into the formula area.

4. **After [Type], enter the following text:** & "-" &.

   This step ensures that the values in the two columns are separated by a hyphen.

5. **Enter** Number.ToText().

   Number.ToText() is a Power Query function that converts a number to text format on the fly so that it can be used with other text. In this case, because the Code field is formatted as a number, you need convert it on the fly to join it to the Type field. I tell you more about data type conversions later in this chapter.

6. **Place the cursor between the parentheses for the Number.ToText function. Then find the Code column in the Available Columns list and double-click on it.**

   You see [Code] pop into the formula area.

7. **In the New Column Name input, enter** MyFirstColumn.

   At this point, the dialog box should look similar to the one shown in Figure 10-28. Note the message at the bottom of the dialog box: `No syntax errors have been detected`. This message refers to the syntax you entered. Every time you create or adjust a formula, you'll want to ensure that this message states that no errors have been detected.

8. **Click OK to add the custom column.**

If all goes well, you have a new custom column that concatenates two fields. In this basic example, you see the basic foundation of how Power Query formulas work.

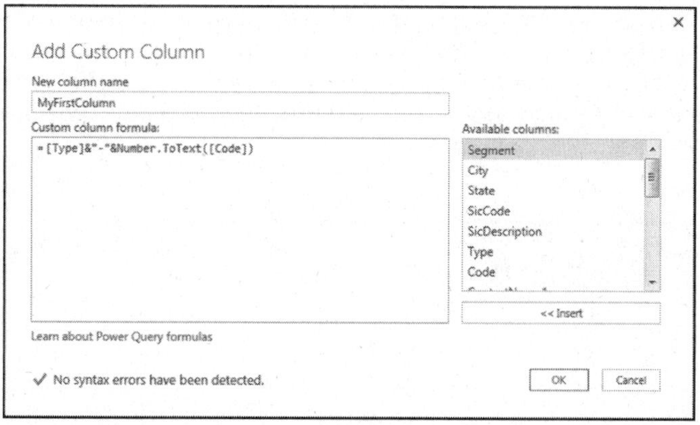

Figure 10-28:
A formula to merge the Type and Code columns.

Understanding data type conversions

When working with formulas in Power Query, you inevitably need to perform some action on fields that have differing data types, as in the exercise in the previous section, where I show you how to merge the Type column (a text field) with the Code column (a numeric field). In that example, you use a conversion function to change the data type of the Code field so that it can be temporarily treated as a text field.

A conversion function does exactly what it sounds like: It converts data from one data type to another.

Table 10-1 lists common conversion functions. As demonstrated in the previous section, you simply wrap these functions around the columns that need converting.

Table 10-1	**Common Conversion Functions**	
Convert From	*To*	*Function*
Date	Text	Date.ToText()
Time	Text	Time.ToText()
Number	Text	Number.ToText()
Text	Number	Number.FromText()
Text Dates	Date	Date.FromText()
Numeric Dates	Date	Date.From()

To find and change the data type for a field, place the cursor in the field and then select the Data Type drop-down menu on the Transform tab (see Figure 10-29). The data type at the top is the type of field the cursor is in. You can edit the data type for the field by selecting a new type from the drop-down list.

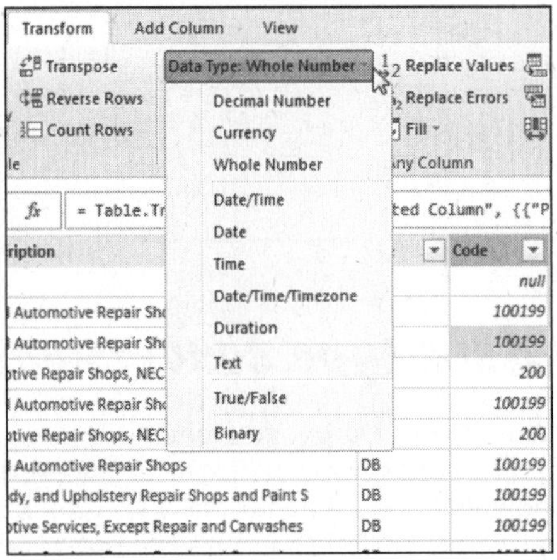

Figure 10-29:
Use the Data Type drop-down menu to discover and select the data type of a given field.

Spicing up custom columns with functions

With a few basic fundamentals and a little knowledge of Power Query functions, you can create transformations that go beyond what you can do by using the Query Editor. In this example, I show you how to use a custom column to pad numbers with zeros.

You may encounter a situation where key fields are required to have a certain number of characters to make the data able to interface with peripheral platforms such as ADP or SAP. Suppose that the CompanyNumber field must be 10 characters long. Those company numbers that aren't ten characters long must be padded with enough leading zeros to create a 10-character string.

The secret to this supplying the proper number of character is to add ten zeros to every company number, regardless of the current length, and then pass them through a function similar to the RIGHT function, which extracts only the rightmost ten characters.

For example, you would first convert company number 29875764 to 000000000029875764; then you would use the RIGHT function to extract only the rightmost ten characters, leaving you with 0029875764.

Although you follow essentially two steps, you can accomplish the same result with only one custom column. Here's how:

1. **While in the Query Editor, choose Add Column ⇨ Add Custom Column.**

2. **Place the cursor in the Custom Column Formula area (after the equal sign).**

3. **Enter ten zeros in quotes (as in "00000000000") followed by an ampersand (&).**

4. **Enter** Number.ToText().

5. **Place the cursor between the parentheses for the Number.ToText function. Then find the CompanyNumber column in the Available Columns list and double-click on it.**

   You see [CompanyNumber] pop into the formula area.

   At this point, the formula area should contain this syntax:

   ```
   "0000000000"&Number.ToText([CompanyNumber])
   ```

   This formula results in nothing more than a concatenation of ten zeros and the CompanyNumber. The goal is to go further and extract only the rightmost ten characters. Unfortunately, the RIGHT function is an Excel function that doesn't work in Power Query. However, Power Query does have an equivalent function named Text.End(). Like the RIGHT function, the Text.End function requires a couple of parameters: the text expression and the number of characters to extract:

   ```
   Text.End([MyText], 10)
   ```

   In this example, the text expression is the formula, and the number of characters to extract is 10.

6. **Enter** Text.End **before your existing formula, and then follow the formula with** ,10.

   Here's the final syntax:

   ```
   Text.End("0000000000"&Number.ToText([Company
        Number]), 10)
   ```

7. **In the New Column Name input, enter** TenDigitCustNumber.

   At this point, the dialog box should look similar to the one shown in Figure 10-30. Again, note the message at the bottom of the dialog box. This message will tell you if you have a syntax error in your formula Make sure that the message at the bottom of the dialog box reads No syntax errors have been detected.

8. **Click OK to apply the custom column.**

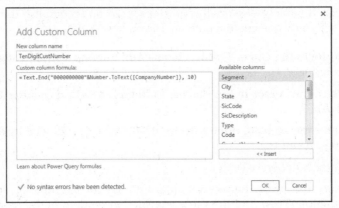

Figure 10-30:
A formula to
create a
consistent
10-digit
padded
Company-
Number.

Table 10-2 lists other Power Query functions that are useful in extending the capabilities of custom columns. Take a moment to examine the list of functions and note how they differ from their Excel equivalents. Remember that Power Query functions are case sensitive.

Table 10-2	Useful Transformation Functions
Excel Function	*Power Query Function*
LEFT([Text], [Number])	Text.Start([Text], [Number])
RIGHT([Text], [Number])	Text.End([Text], [Number])
MID([Text], [StartPosition], [Number])	Text.Range([Text], [StartPosition], [Number])
FIND([Find], [Within])	Text.PositionOf([Within], [Find])+1
IF([Expression], [Result1], [Result2])	if [Expression] then [Result1] else [Result2]
IFERROR([Procedure], [FailResult])	try [Procedure] otherwise [FailResult]

Adding conditional logic to custom columns

As you might notice in Table 10-2, Power Query has a built-in if function. The if function is designed to test for conditions and provide different outcomes based on the results of those tests. In this section, you'll see how you can control the output of your custom columns by utilizing Power Query's if function.

As in Excel, Power Query's `if` function evaluates a specific condition and returns a result based on a true or false determination:

```
if [Expression] then [Result1] else [Result2]
```

In Excel, you think of commas in an `if` function as Then and Else statements. The formula `if`(Babies = 2 , "Twins", "Not Twins") would translate to this: If Babies equals 2, then Twins, else Not Twins In Power Query, you don't use commas. You spell out the entire expression.

You can also use the `if` function to save steps in your analytical processes and, ultimately, save time. For example, you may need to tag customers as either large customers or small customers, based on their dollar potential. You decide to add a custom column that contains either "LARGE" or "SMALL" based on the revenue potential of the customer.

With the help of the `if` function, you can tag all customers with one custom column that uses this formula:

```
if [2016 Potential Revenue]>=10000 then "LARGE" else
       "SMALL"
```

This function tells Power Query to evaluate the [2016 Potential Revenue] field for each record. If the potential record is greater than or equal to 10,000, use the word LARGE; if not, use the word SMALL.

Figure 10-31 demonstrates this `if` statement as it is applied in the Add Custom Column dialog box.

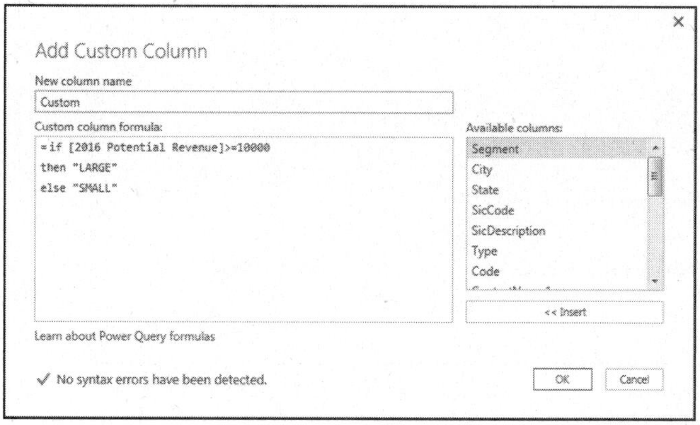

Figure 10-31: Applying an `If` statement in a custom column.

Power Query pays no attention to white space, so you can add as many spaces and carriage returns as you want. As long as the correct case and spelling are used, Power Query doesn't complain.

Figure 10-31 illustrates how separating formulas into separate lines can make them much easier to read.

Grouping and Aggregating Data

In some cases, you may need to transform your data set into compact groups in order to get it into a manageable size of unique values. You may even need to summarize numerical values into an aggregate view. An *aggregate view* is a grouped snapshot of your data that shows sums, averages, counts, and more.

Power Query offers a Group By feature that enables you quickly group data and create aggregate views. Follow these steps to use the Group By feature:

1. **While in the Query Editor, select the Group By command on the Transform tab.**

   The Group By dialog box opens.

2. **From the Group By drop-down menu, select the field you want to group by. Click the plus sign (+) above the Group By drop-down list to add additional fields to grouping.**

   Figure 10-32 shows grouping by State and City.

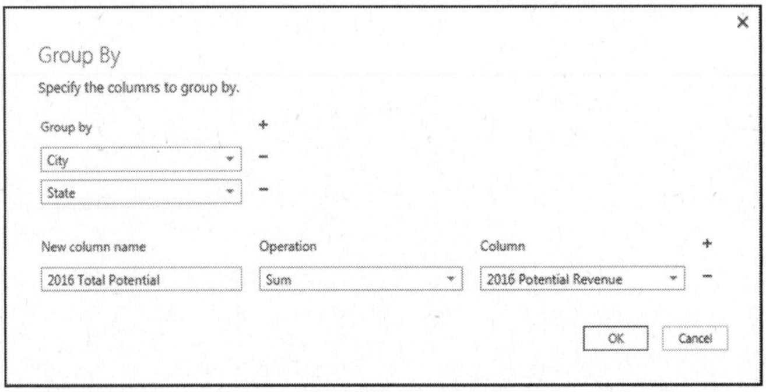

Figure 10-32: Using the Group By dialog box to create a view of 2016 Total Potential by State and City.

> Group By
>
> Specify the columns to group by.
>
> Group by   +
>
> | City | ▾ | − |
> | State | ▾ | − |
>
> | New column name | Operation | Column | + |
> | 2016 Total Potential | Sum ▾ | 2016 Potential Revenue ▾ | − |
>
> OK   Cancel

3. **Use the New Column Name input box to give the new aggregate column a name (for example, 2016 Total Potential).**

4. **From the Operation drop-down list, select the kind of aggregation you want to apply (Sum, Count, Avg, Min, Max, and so on).**

5. Use the Column drop-down list to choose the column that will be aggregated (for example, 2016 Potential Revenue).

6. Click the OK button to confirm and apply your changes.

   Figure 10-33 illustrates the resulting output.

State	City	2016 Total Potential
ab	airdrie	9792
ab	bonnyville	3689
ab	brooks	3689
ab	calgary	55403
ab	coaldale	8709
ab	edmonton	54368
ab	fort mcmurray	5551
ab	grande prairie	31222
ab	innisfail	2775
ab	leduc	9242
ab	lethbridge	40445
ab	lloydminster	3689
ab	medicine hat	9242
ab	nisku	11745

Figure 10-33: The resulting aggregate view by State and City.

When you apply the Group By feature, Power Query removes all columns that were not used when configuring the Group By dialog box. This leaves you with a clean view of just your grouped data.

Chapter 11

Making Queries Work Together

Data is frequently analyzed in layers, with each layer of analysis using or building on the previous layer. You may not know it, but you already build layers all the time. For instance, when you build a pivot table using the results of a Power Query output, you're layering your analysis. When you build a query based on a table created by a SQL Server view, you're also creating a layered analysis.

Sure, you would probably love to be able to analyze a single data source and call it a day. But that's not how data analysis works. You often find the need to build queries on top of other queries to get the results you're looking for. That's what this chapter is all about. In this chapter, I help you examine a few ways you can advance your data analysis by making your queries work together.

Reusing Query Steps

Data analysts commonly rely on the same main data tables for all kinds of analysis. Even the simple table shown in Figure 11-1 can be used to create different views: sales by employee, sales by business segment, or sales by region, for example.

Of course, you can build separate queries, each performing different grouping and aggregation steps, but that would mean repeating all the data clean-up steps you needed before performing any kind of analysis.

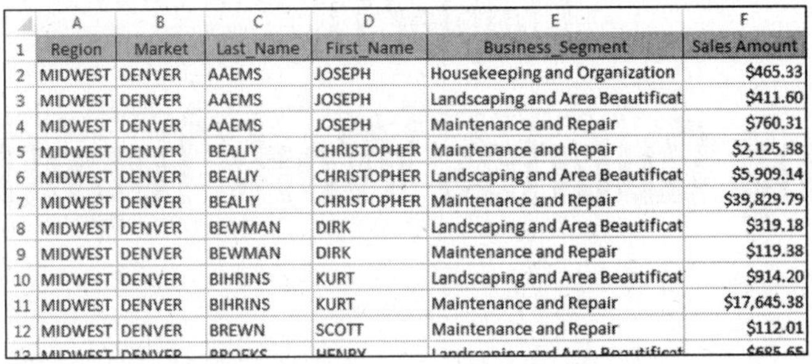

Figure 11-1:
This data
can be used
as the
source for
various
levels of
aggregated
analysis.

	A	B	C	D	E	F
1	Region	Market	Last_Name	First_Name	Business_Segment	Sales Amount
2	MIDWEST	DENVER	AAEMS	JOSEPH	Housekeeping and Organization	$465.33
3	MIDWEST	DENVER	AAEMS	JOSEPH	Landscaping and Area Beautificat	$411.60
4	MIDWEST	DENVER	AAEMS	JOSEPH	Maintenance and Repair	$760.31
5	MIDWEST	DENVER	BEALIY	CHRISTOPHER	Maintenance and Repair	$2,125.38
6	MIDWEST	DENVER	BEALIY	CHRISTOPHER	Landscaping and Area Beautificat	$5,909.14
7	MIDWEST	DENVER	BEALIY	CHRISTOPHER	Maintenance and Repair	$39,829.79
8	MIDWEST	DENVER	BEWMAN	DIRK	Landscaping and Area Beautificat	$319.18
9	MIDWEST	DENVER	BEWMAN	DIRK	Maintenance and Repair	$119.38
10	MIDWEST	DENVER	BIHRINS	KURT	Landscaping and Area Beautificat	$914.20
11	MIDWEST	DENVER	BIHRINS	KURT	Maintenance and Repair	$17,645.38
12	MIDWEST	DENVER	BREWN	SCOTT	Maintenance and Repair	$112.01
13	MIDWEST	DENVER	BROEKS	HENRY	Landscaping and Area Beautificat	$685.65

To get a better understanding of how query steps can help save time, take a moment to follow these steps:

1. **Open the Sales By Employee.xlsx workbook, found in the sample files for this book.**

2. **Place the cursor anywhere inside the table, and then choose Data⇨From Table.**

   Power Query opens the Query Editor.

3. **While in the Query Editor, click the Filter drop-down list for the Market field and filter out the Canada market. (Remove the check mark next to Canada.)**

4. **Select the Last_Name and First_Name fields, and then choose Transform⇨Merge Columns.**

   The Merge Columns dialog box appears.

5. **Create a new Employee field, joining Last_Name and First_Name and separating them by a comma, as shown in Figure 11-2.**

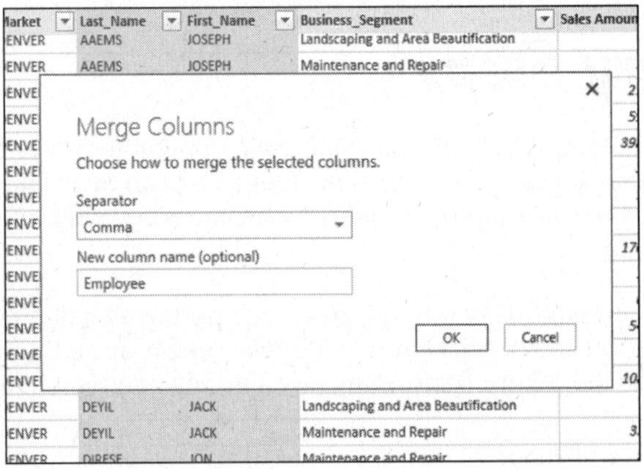

Figure 11-2:
Merge the
Last_Name
and First_
Name
columns to
create a
new
Employee
field.

6. **Click the Group By command on the Transformation tab.**

   The Group By dialog box opens, as shown in Figure 11-3.

7. **The goal is to Group By the Employee field to get the Sum of Sales Amount, as shown in Figure 11-3. Name the new aggregated column Revenue.**

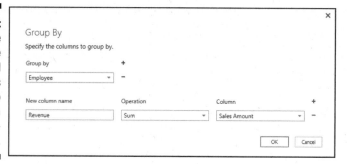

Figure 11-3:
Group the
Employee
field and
Sum Sales
Amount to
create a
new Reve-
nue column.

At this point, you've successfully created a view that shows total revenue by employee. As you can see in Figure 11-4, the query steps include all the preparation work you did before grouping.

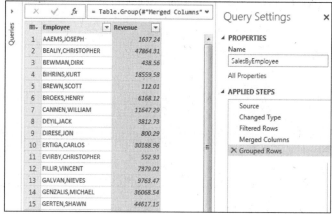

Figure 11-4:
All the query
steps before
Grouped
Rows are
needed
in order to
prepare the
data for
grouping.

What happens if you want to create another analysis using the same data? For instance, what if you want another view that shows Employee sales by business segment?

You could always start from Step 1 and import another copy of the source data, but you'd have to repeat the preparation steps (the steps for Filtered Rows and Merged Columns, in this case).

A better way is to reuse the steps you've already created by extracting them into a new query. The idea is to first decide what steps you want to reuse and then right-click the step immediately below it. In this scenario (refer to Figure 11-4), you keep all query steps until Grouped Rows.

8. **Right-click the Grouped Rows step and select Extract Previous.**

   The Extract Steps dialog box opens.

9. **Name the new query SalesByBusiness, as shown in Figure 11-5. Click the OK button confirm.**

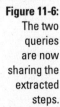

Figure 11-5:
Naming the new query SalesBy-Business.

> ×
>
> Extract Steps
>
> Extract the steps before the selected step into a new query.
>
> New query name
>
> SalesByBusiness
>
> OK   Cancel

After you click OK, Power Query does two things:

✔ Moves all extracted steps to the newly created query

✔ Ties the original query to the new query

That is to say, both queries are sharing the extracted steps. You can see the new SalesByBusiness query in the pane on the left, as shown in Figure 11-6.

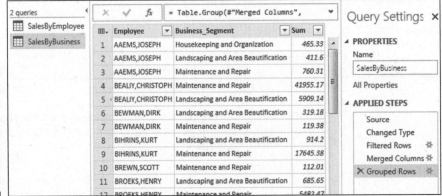

Figure 11-6:
The two queries are now sharing the extracted steps.

You now can click on the SalesByBusiness query and start applying any needed transformations. In Figure 11-6, a Group By step has been added to create a view of sales by employee and by business segment.

This concept of extracting steps can be a bit confusing. The bottom line is that instead of starting from square one with a brand-new query, you're telling Power Query you want to create a new query that uses the steps you've already created.

When two or more queries share extracted steps, the query that contains the extracted steps serves as the data source for the other queries. Because of this link, the query that contains the extracted steps cannot be deleted. You have to first delete all dependent queries before deleting the query that holds the extracted steps.

Understanding the Append Feature

Power Query's Append feature allows you to add the rows generated from one query to the results of another query. In other words, you copy records from one query and add them to the end of another.

The Append feature comes in handy when you need to consolidate multiple identical tables into one table. For example, if you have tables from the North, South, Midwest, and West regions, you can consolidate the data from each region into one table using the Append feature.

To help you better understand the Append feature, I'll walk you through an exercise that consolidates data from four different regions into one table. In this walk-through, I use the region data found on four different tabs in the Appending_Data.xlsx sample file, shown in Figure 11-7.

You can find the Appending_Data.xlsx workbook in the sample files for this book.

Creating the needed base queries

The Append feature works on only existing queries. That is to say, no matter what kind of data sources you have, you need to import them into Power Query before you can append them together. In this case, it means importing all the region tables into queries.

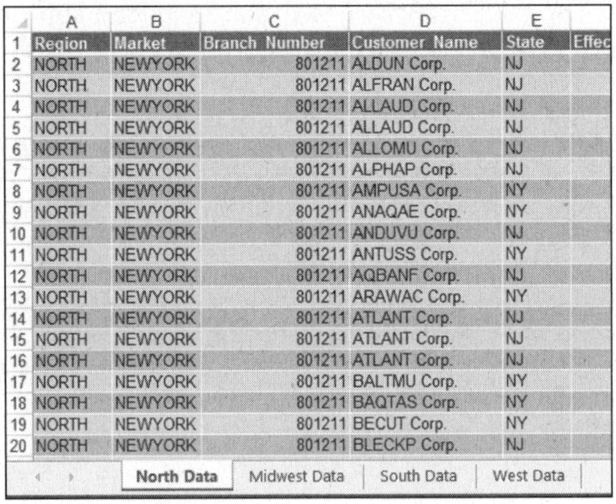

	A	B	C	D	E	
1	Region	Market	Branch Number	Customer Name	State	Effec
2	NORTH	NEWYORK	801211	ALDUN Corp.	NJ	
3	NORTH	NEWYORK	801211	ALFRAN Corp.	NJ	
4	NORTH	NEWYORK	801211	ALLAUD Corp.	NJ	
5	NORTH	NEWYORK	801211	ALLAUD Corp.	NJ	
6	NORTH	NEWYORK	801211	ALLOMU Corp.	NJ	
7	NORTH	NEWYORK	801211	ALPHAP Corp.	NJ	
8	NORTH	NEWYORK	801211	AMPUSA Corp.	NY	
9	NORTH	NEWYORK	801211	ANAQAE Corp.	NY	
10	NORTH	NEWYORK	801211	ANDUVU Corp.	NJ	
11	NORTH	NEWYORK	801211	ANTUSS Corp.	NY	
12	NORTH	NEWYORK	801211	AQBANF Corp.	NJ	
13	NORTH	NEWYORK	801211	ARAWAC Corp.	NY	
14	NORTH	NEWYORK	801211	ATLANT Corp.	NJ	
15	NORTH	NEWYORK	801211	ATLANT Corp.	NJ	
16	NORTH	NEWYORK	801211	ATLANT Corp.	NJ	
17	NORTH	NEWYORK	801211	BALTMU Corp.	NY	
18	NORTH	NEWYORK	801211	BAQTAS Corp.	NY	
19	NORTH	NEWYORK	801211	BECUT Corp.	NY	
20	NORTH	NEWYORK	801211	BLECKP Corp.	NJ	

North Data | Midwest Data | South Data | West Data

Figure 11-7: The data found on each region tab needs to be consolidated into one table.

Follow these steps to import the needed base queries:

1. **Go to the North Data worksheet, place the cursor anywhere inside the table, and then choose Data⇨From Table.**

   The Query Editor activates, showing you the contents of the table you just imported.

   To finalize the creation of the query, you need to close and load the query. Now, because you're creating this query simply for the purpose of appending it to other queries, you don't need to close and load to the workbook. You can choose instead to close and load the data as connection-only.

2. **On the Home tab of the Query Editor, click the drop-down arrow under the Close & Load command and select Close & Load To.**
3. **In the Load To dialog box, choose the option Only Create Connection, and then click the Load button.**
4. **Repeat Steps 1 through 3 for the other worksheets in the workbook.**

After you've created queries for each region, open the Workbook Queries pane (choose Data⇨Show Queries) to see all queries. As you can see in Figure 11-8, each query is a connection-only query.

Now that your data is in queries, you can start appending.

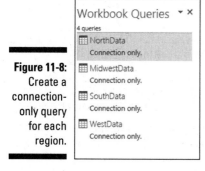

Figure 11-8: Create a connection-only query for each region.

Appending the data

In a perfect world, this section is where you would read about the nifty button that appends all your queries at one time. Unfortunately, Power Query doesn't have a nifty button that lets you append many tables all in one shot. You can append only one table at a time.

To append data, follow these steps:

1. **In the Workbook Queries pane, right-click on the NorthData query and select Edit to open the Query Editor.**

2. **On the Home tab of the Query Editor, click the Append Queries command.**

   The Append dialog box opens.

3. **The drop-down menu contains a list of all queries in the current workbook, as shown in Figure 11-9. The idea is to select the query you want to append to the query you're editing. Select one of the region queries, and then click the OK button.**

Figure 11-9: Select the query that you want appended to the query you're editing.

Append

Select the table to append.

NorthData (Current)
MidwestData
SouthData
WestData

OK   Cancel

4. Repeat Steps 2 and 3 until you've appended the SouthData, MidwestData, and WestData queries.

5. After all queries have been appended, click the Close & Load command to save the data and exit the Query Editor.

At this point, the NorthData query contains the data for all regions. To see the full consolidated table, you need to change the load destination of the NorthData query to the workbook instead of the connection only.

6. In the Workbook Queries pane, right-click the NorthData query and select Load To.

The Load To dialog box opens.

7. Select the option for Table, and then click OK.

Figure 11-10 illustrates the final output. You've successfully created a consolidated table of region data.

Figure 11-10:
The final consolidated table of all region data.

	Region	Market	Branch_Number	Customer_Name	State	
31	MIDWEST	TULSA	401612	JUHNST Corp.	OK	
32	MIDWEST	TULSA	401612	PRANTA Corp.	OK	
33	MIDWEST	TULSA	401612	UKLAFU Corp.	OK	
34	MIDWEST	TULSA	401612	UKLOHU Corp.	OK	
35	SOUTH	NEWORLEANS	601310	ANTUSM Corp.	GA	
36	SOUTH	NEWORLEANS	601310	SUASHU Corp.	GA	
37	SOUTH	NEWORLEANS	601310	TAREPR Corp.	GA	
38	SOUTH	NEWORLEANS	801607	MUDACA Corp.	MS	
39	WEST	PHOENIX	201714	VANCHU Corp.	AZ	
40	WEST	PHOENIX	701708	CUAQTU Corp.	NV	
41	WEST	PHOENIX	701708	EASOTU Corp.	NV	
42	NORTH	NEWYORK	801211	BECUT Corp.	NY	
43	NORTH	NEWYORK	801211	BUYUSB Corp.	NJ	

Note in Figure 11-9 the option for NorthData (Current). You see the term *(Current)* next to the NorthData query because you're editing that query. Be careful not to select any query with (Current) next to it. Otherwise, you'll append the query to itself, effectively duplicating all records within the query. Unless you have some strange requirement where creating exact copies of records is beneficial, avoid appending the current query to itself.

As you append each query, you may be tempted to scroll down to the bottom of the data to see the newly added records. Unfortunately, the data preview in the Query Editor shows only a truncated sample set of records. Even if you scroll to the bottom of the preview, you're unlikely to see the appended data.

Beware of mismatched column labels

When you append one query to another, Power Query first scans the column labels for both queries to capture all column names. It then outputs all distinct column names and consolidates the data from both queries into the appropriate columns. It uses the column labels as a guide to knowing which data should be placed in which column.

If the column labels in your queries don't match, Power Query consolidates data for any match column, leaving null values in any columns that don't match.

Imagine that you have one query with the column labels Region and Revenue, and another query with the column labels Region and SalesAmount. Appending these two records yields a final table with all three columns: Region, Revenue, and SalesAmount. The records from the first query are entered into the Region and Revenue fields. The records from the second query are entered into the Region and SalesAmount fields, essentially leaving gaps in the Revenue and SalesAmount fields.

The bottom line is to make sure the column labels in your queries are identical before appending. As long as the column labels in each query are identical, Power Query can append the data correctly. Even if the columns in each query are positioned in a different sequence, Power Query can use the column labels to get all the data into the correct columns.

Understanding the Merge Feature

In your data adventures, you often find the need to build queries that join the data between two tables. For example, you may want to join an employee table to a transaction table to create a view that contains both transaction details and information on the employees who logged those transactions.

In this section, I describe how you can leverage the Merge feature in Power Query to join data from multiple queries.

Understanding Power Query joins

Similar to VLOOKUP in Excel, the Merge feature joins the records from one query to the records in another by matching on a unique identifier. An example of a unique identifier is Customer ID or Invoice Number.

You can join two datasets in one of several ways. The kind of join you apply is important because it determines which records are returned from each dataset.

Power Query supports six kinds of joins, as described in the following list and shown in Figure 11-11:

- ✔ **Left Outer:** Tells Power Query to return all records from the first query, regardless of matching, *and* only those records from the second query that have matching values in the joined field.

- ✔ **Right Outer:** Tells Power Query to return all records from the second query, regardless of matching, *and* only those records from the first query that have matching values in the joined field.

- ✔ **Full Outer:** Tells Power Query to return all records from both queries, regardless of matching.

- ✔ **Inner:** Tells Power Query to return only those records from both queries that have matching values.

- ✔ **Left Anti:** Tells Power Query to return only those records from the first query that don't match any of the records from the second query.

- ✔ **Right Anti:** Tells Power Query to return only those records from the first query that don't match any of the records from the second query.

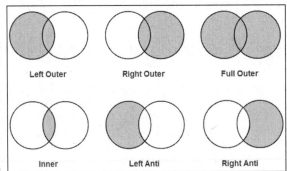

Figure 11-11:
The kinds of joins supported by Power Query.

Left Outer   Right Outer   Full Outer

Inner   Left Anti   Right Anti

Merging queries

To better understand the Merge feature, I'll walk you through an exercise that merges interview questions and answers. In this walk-through, I use the predefined queries found in the Merging_Data.xlsx sample file available online at www.dummies.com/go/excelpowerpivotpowerqueryfd.

As you can see in Figure 11-12, two existing queries are in the Workbook Queries pane: Questions and Answers. These queries represent the questions and answers from the interview. The goal is to merge these two queries to create a new table showing questions and answers side-by-side.

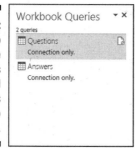

Figure 11-12:
You need to
merge the
Questions
and
Answers
queries into
one table.

The Merge feature can be used only with existing queries. That is to say, no matter what kind of data sources you have, you need to import them into Power Query before you can use them in a merge.

Follow these steps to perform the merge:

1. **Choose Data⇨New Query⇨Combine Queries⇨Merge (see Figure 11-13).**

   This step opens the Merge dialog box.

   In this dialog box, you use the drop-down boxes to select the queries you want to merge and then choose the columns that defined the unique identifier for each record. In this case, the InterviewID and QuestionID/ AnswerID fields make up the unique identifier for each record.

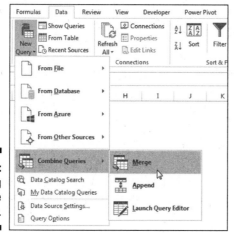

Figure 11-13:
Activating
the Merge
dialog box.

2. **Select the Questions query in the top drop-down box.**

3. **Hold down the Ctrl key on the keyboard, and then click InterviewID and QuestionID — in that order.**

4. **Select the Answers query in the lower drop-down box.**

5. **Hold down the Ctrl key on the keyboard, and then click InterviewID and AnswerID — in that order.**

6. **Use the Join Kind drop-down box to select the kind of join you want Power Query to use. In this case, the default, Left Outer, works.**

7. **Click the OK button to finalize and open the Query Editor.**

   In Figure 11-14, note the small numbers 1 and 2 in the InterviewID and QuestionID fields. These small numbers are assigned based on the order in which you selected them (refer to Steps 3 and 5).

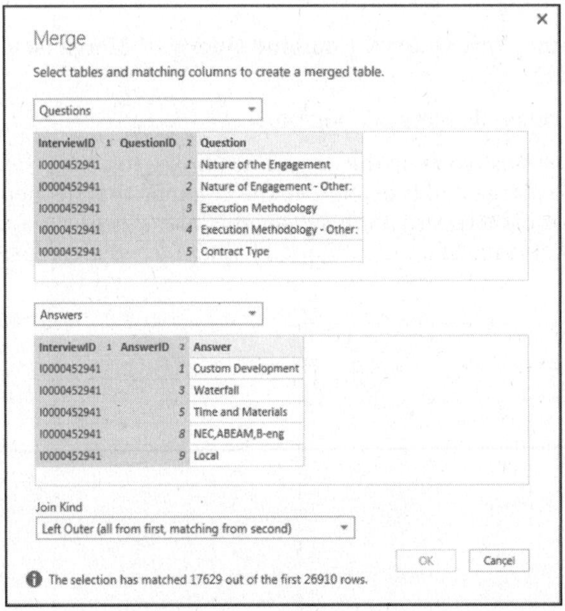

Figure 11-14:
The Merge
dialog box.

The order in which you selected the unique identifiers in each query matters. The two columns tagged with the small number 1 will be joined regardless of column labels. The two columns tagged with the small number 2 will also be joined.

At the bottom of the Merge dialog box, Power Query shows you how many records from the lower query match the top query, based on the unique identifiers you selected. In this case, about 17,600 answer records match the 26,910 question records.

REMEMBER

You don't need a 100 percent match for the merge to be valid. There might be a good reason that the records in the two queries don't all match up. In this case, not all questions were answered in all interviews, so the Answers query has fewer records.

8. **With the new merged query open in the Query Editor, click the Expand icon in the NewColumn field and choose the fields you want included in the final output (as shown in Figure 11-15). In this case, just choose the Answer field.**

Figure 11-15: Expand the NewColumn field and choose the merged fields you want to output.

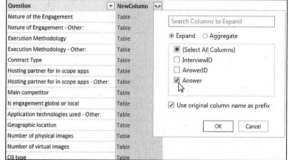

At this point, you can apply more transformations, if needed.

9. **When you're happy with the way things look, click the Close & Load command to output the results to the workbook.**

Figure 11-16 shows the final merged query.

Figure 11-16: The final table with merged questions and answers.

	A	B	C	D
1	InterviewID	QuestionID	Question	Answer
2	I0000452941	1	Nature of the Engagement	Custom Development
3	I0000452941	2	Nature of Engagement - Other:	
4	I0000452941	3	Execution Methodology	Waterfall
5	I0000452941	4	Execution Methodology - Other:	
6	I0000452941	5	Contract Type	Time and Materials
7	I0000452941	6	Hosting partner for in scope apps	
8	I0000452941	7	Hosting partner for in scope apps - Other:	
9	I0000452941	8	Main competitor	NEC,ABEAM,B-eng
10	I0000452941	9	Is engagement global or local	Local
11	I0000452941	10	Application technologies used - Other:	Java

If you need to adjust or correct a merged query, right-click the query in the Workbook Queries pane and select Edit. In the Query Editor, click the Gear icon next to the Source query step, as shown in Figure 11-17. This action opens the Merge dialog box, where the necessary changes can be applied.

Figure 11-17: Click the Gear icon next to the Source query step to reopen the Merge dialog box.

Chapter 12

Extending Power Query with Custom Functions

. . . .

In This Chapter

▶ Making a custom function

▶ Using custom functions in other queries

▶ Creating a parameter query

. . . .

*I*n Chapter 8, you see that Power Query records all actions using its own formula language (known as the *M* language). When you connect to a data source and apply transformations to that data, Power Query diligently saves your actions as M code behind the scenes in query steps. The transformation steps can then be repeated when you refresh the data in your query.

That backstage coding is relatively transparent, and can, for the most part, be ignored for most data processing activities. In this chapter, I show you how to leverage the M language to extend the capabilities of Power Query to create your own custom functions and perform truly heroic data processing.

Creating and Using a Basic Custom Function

When building a custom function for Power Query, you're essentially doing nothing more than creating a query and manipulating its M code to return a desired result. That result can be an array, a data table, or a single value.

To help you gain a sense of the general steps taken to create a custom function, I show you now how to build a basic mathematical function that calculates profit. This function should be able to take a revenue amount and a cost amount and output a profit amount using this basic mathematical operation:

Revenue – Cost = Profit

For basic functions such as this one, you can start with a blank query and simply enter the needed M code from scratch. Follow these steps:

1. **Click the Data tab in Excel and select New Query ⇨ From Other Data Sources ⇨ Blank Query.**

   This step activates the Query Editor window.

2. **On the Query Editor Ribbon, click on the View tab and select the Advanced Editor command.**

3. **When the Advanced Editor window opens, delete the starter syntax you see in the code input box.**

4. **Enter the following code into the code input box:**

```
let Profit = (Revenue, Cost)=>
Revenue-Cost
in Profit
```

   - Line 1 of the code tells Power Query that this is a function called Profit, requiring two parameters. For clarity, the two parameters are named Revenue and Cost, though Power Query doesn't care what you name them as long as the names start with a letter and have no spaces.

   - Line 2 in the code essentially tells Power Query to subtract the Cost parameter from the Revenue parameter.

   - Line 3 of the code tells Power Query to return the result.

Figure 12-1 illustrates what the code looks like in the Advanced Editor window.

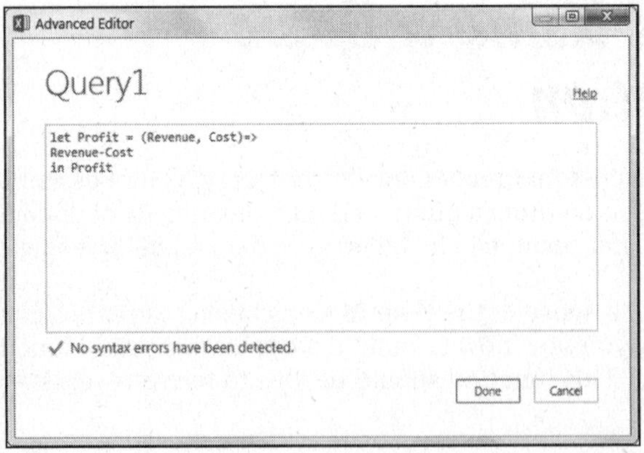

Figure 12-1: Enter your custom code in the Advanced Editor window.

5. **Click the Done button to close the Advanced Editor window.**
6. **In the Query Settings pane, change the name of the query in the Name input box. The goal here is to give your function a reasonably descriptive name, as opposed to Query1. In this case, enter** FunctionProfit **in the Name input box.**
7. **At this point, you can select the Home tab of the Query Editor and click the Close & Load button.**

   As you can see in Figure 12-2, Power Query adds the query to the Workbook Queries pane as a connection-only query. Queries recognized as functions are automatically saved as connection-only.

Figure 12-2: Your function is ready to use.

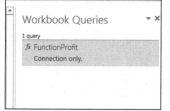

You can now use this function in other queries that contain revenue and cost fields. For example, Figure 12-3 illustrates the contents of the Chapter 12 Sample text file, which you can find in the download files for this book.

Chapter12_Sample.txt - Notepad
File Edit Format View Help

InvoiceNumber	Quantity	UnitCost	UnitPrice
ORDST1022	1	59.29	119.95
ORDST1015	1	3290.55	6589.95
ORDST1016	10	35	34.95
ORDST1017	50	91.59	189.95
ORDST1018	1	59.29	119.95
INV1010	1	674.5	1349.95
INV1011	1	91.25	189.95
INV1012	1	303.85	609.95
ORDST1020	1	59.29	119.95
ORDST1021	1	59.29	119.95
INV1015	1	179.85	359.95
INV1016	1	3.29	9.95
INV1017	1	2998.15	5999.95
BK01001	1	34550	69109.95
BK01003	10	41.98	89.95

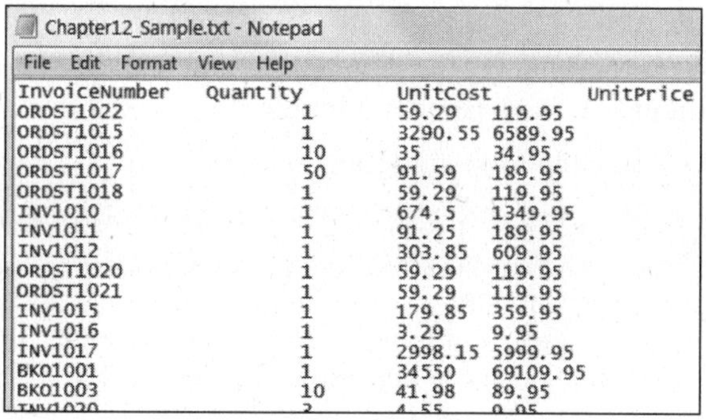

Figure 12-3: A text file containing Invoice details.

This text file contains a table of invoices with the fields Qty, UnitCost, and UnitPrice. Your newly created function can be used to calculate profit using these fields.

To create a new query from this text file, follow these steps:

1. **Click the Data tab in Excel and select New Query ⇨ From File ⇨ From Text.**

   This step opens the Import Data dialog box.

2. **Browse for, and select, the Chapter_12 Sample text file.**

   Power Query opens the text file and opens the Query Editor.

3. **While in the Query Editor, click the Add Column tab and then click the Add Custom Column button, as shown in Figure 12-4.**

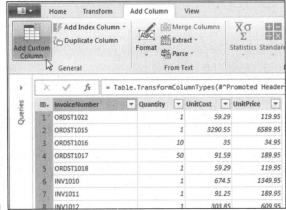

Figure 12-4: Add a custom column.

   The Add Custom Column dialog box opens, and you can call the custom function and pass it the needed parameters.

4. **In this case, enter the following line:**

   ```
   = FunctionProfit([UnitPrice], [UnitCost])*[Quantity]
   ```

   This syntax calls the FunctionProfit custom function and passes the UnitPrice and UnitCost fields as the required parameters. The results are then multiplied by the Quantity field. The Add Custom Column dialog box should look similar to the one shown in Figure 12-5.

5. **Click the OK button to apply the custom column.**

   When you confirm the changes, Power Query triggers the function for each row in the data table.

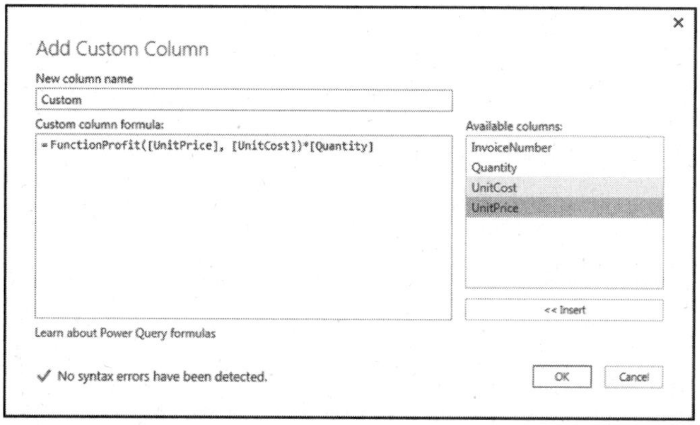

Add Custom Column   ×

New column name

Custom

Custom column formula: Available columns:

= FunctionProfit([UnitPrice], [UnitCost])*[Quantity]   InvoiceNumber
                                                    Quantity
                                                    UnitCost
                                                    UnitPrice

Figure 12-5:
Use the Add
Custom
Column
action to   << Insert
invoke your   Learn about Power Query formulas
function.
                 ✓ No syntax errors have been detected.   OK   Cancel

Although this example is quite basic, it demonstrates that you can define a function that requires parameters and then use the function in other queries. This simple technique is the foundation for creating more useful functions.

Power Query functions are stored in the workbook in which they reside. Unfortunately, there's no easy way to share functions between workbooks. If you start a new workbook, you need to re-create your functions in that new workbook.

Creating a Function to Merge Data from Multiple Excel Files

When building a basic function, such as the profit function you create in the earlier section "Creating and Using a Basic Custom Function," it's no big deal to start from a blank query and enter all the code from scratch. But for more complex functions, it's generally smarter to build a starter query via Query Editor and then manipulate the M code to accomplish what you need.

Imagine that you have a set of Excel files in a folder (see Figure 12-6). These files all contain a worksheet named MySheet that holds a table of data. The tables in each file have the same structure, but need to be combined into one file. This is a common task/nightmare that most Excel analysts have faced at one time or another. If you don't have a solid knowledge of Excel VBA programming, this task typically entails opening each file, copying the data on the MySheet tab, and then pasting the data into a single workbook.

Figure 12-6:
You need to
merge into
one table
the data in
all the Excel
files in this
folder.

Power Query has the ability to make short work of this task, but it requires a bit of direction via a custom function. Now, it would be difficult for most anyone to start from a blank query and type out the M code for the relatively complex function needed for this endeavor. Instead, you could build a starter query via Query Editor and then wrap the query in a function.

To help you understand this concept, I present the following steps:

1. **On the Excel Data tab, select New Query ➪ From File ➪ From Workbook.**

2. **Browse to the folder that contains all the Excel files, and choose only one of them.**

3. **In the Navigator pane (shown in Figure 12-7), choose the sheet that holds the data that needs to be consolidated, and then click the Edit button to open the Query Editor.**

Figure 12-7:
Connect to
one of the
Excel files in
the target
folder, and
navigate to
the sheet
holding the
data that
needs to be
consolidated.

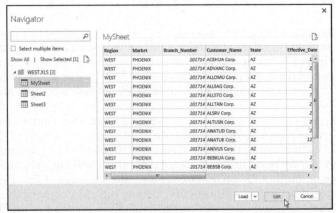

4. Use the Query Editor to apply some basic transformation actions.

For example, in the Applied Steps shown in Figure 12-8, you see that First Row step was promoted to column headers and a few unneeded columns were removed.

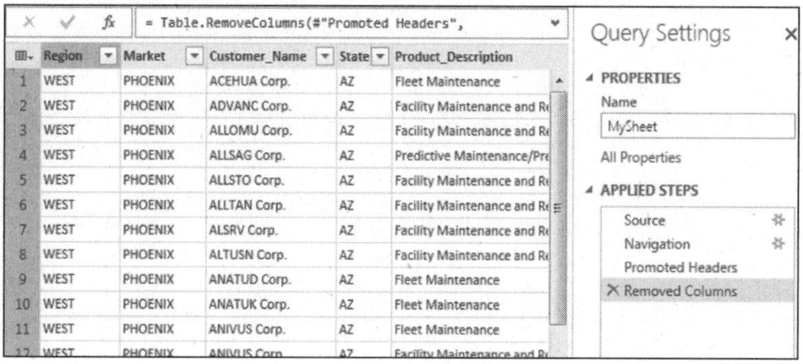

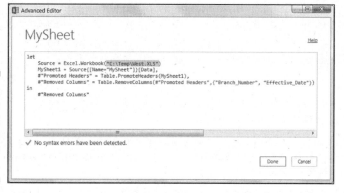

Figure 12-8:
Use the Query Editor to apply any necessary transformation actions.

5. When all the needed transformations are complete, open the Advanced Editor window by clicking the View tab and selecting the Advanced Editor command.

Figure 12-9 demonstrates that as you build out the starter template, Power Query diligently creates the bulk of the code for your function. Note in the portion of the code that's highlighted in gray (for illustration), Power Query has hard-coded the file path and filename of the Excel file that was originally selected. The idea is to wrap this starter code in a function that passes a dynamic file path and filename.

Figure 12-9:
Open the Advanced Editor to see the starter code.

6. **Wrap the entire block of code with function tags, specifying that this function requires two parameters: FilePath and FileName. Also replace the hard-coded file path and filename with each respective parameter.**

Here's the syntax shown in Figure 12-10:

```
let GetMyFiles=(FilePath, FileName) =>

let
    Source =
        Excel.Workbook(File.Contents(FilePath&FileName)),
    MySheet1 = Source{[Name="MySheet"]}[Data],
    #"Promoted Headers" =
        Table.PromoteHeaders(MySheet1),
    #"Removed Columns" =
Table.RemoveColumns(#"Promoted
        Headers",{"Branch_Number", "Effective_Date"})
in
    #"Removed Columns"

in GetMyFiles"
```

Figure 12-10:
Wrapping the starter code with function tags and replacing the hard-coded names with your dynamic parameters.

7. **Close the Advanced Editor.**

8. **In the Query Settings pane, change the name of the query in the Name input box. Give the function a reasonably descriptive name, such as (in this scenario) fnGetMyFiles.**

9. **Click the Home tab of the Query Editor and click the Close & Load button.**

At this point, the custom function is ready to be used on all files in the target folder.

10. **Click the Data tab in Excel and select New Query⇨From File⇨From Folder to start a connection to the folder that contains all the Excel files.**

11. **In the From Folder dialog box, provide Power Query with the file path of the target folder.**

    The Query Editor window activates to show you a table similar to the one shown in Figure 12-11. This table contains a record for each file in the chosen folder. The columns you're interested in are Folder Path and Name, which provide the function with the needed FilePath and FileName parameters.

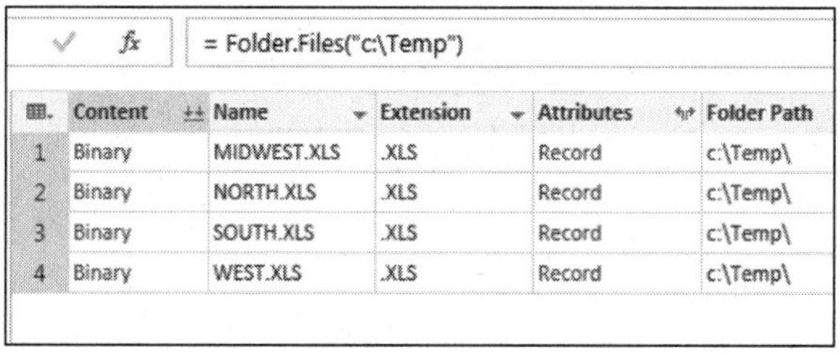
= Folder.Files("c:\Temp")

	Content	Name	Extension	Attributes	Folder Path
1	Binary	MIDWEST.XLS	.XLS	Record	c:\Temp\
2	Binary	NORTH.XLS	.XLS	Record	c:\Temp\
3	Binary	SOUTH.XLS	.XLS	Record	c:\Temp\
4	Binary	WEST.XLS	.XLS	Record	c:\Temp\

Figure 12-11: Create a new query using the From Folder connection type to retrieve a table of all files in the target folder.

12. **Click the Add Column tab, and then click the Add Custom Column command.**

    The Add Custom Column dialog box opens.

13. **Invoke the function and pass the Folder Path and Name fields as parameters separated by commas (see Figure 12-12).**

    When you confirm your changes, Power Query triggers the function for each row in the data table. The function itself grabs the data from each file and returns a table array. Figure 12-13 shows the newly created custom column with a returned table array for each file (specified by a green Table hyperlink).

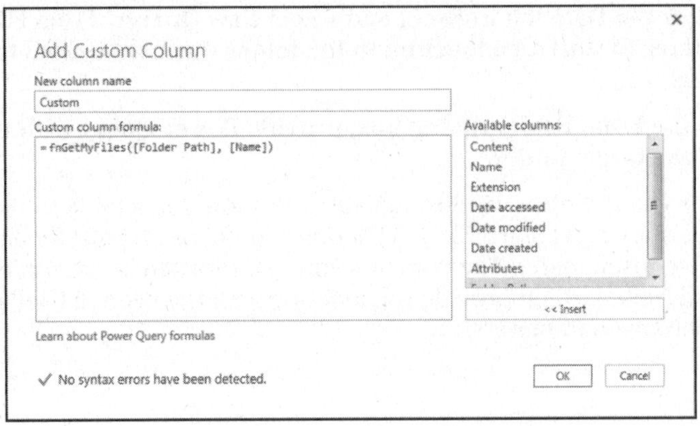

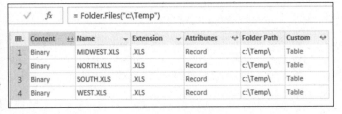

Figure 12-12:
Use the Add
Custom Col-
umn action
to invoke
the function.

Figure 12-13:
Power
Query trig-
gers the
function and
returns a
table array
for each file
in the folder.

14. **Click the Expand icon for your new custom column.**

    You see a list of fields included in each table array, as shown in
    Figure 12-14.

15. **Choose which fields in the table array to show, click the Expand radio
    button, and then click the OK button.**

    With each table array expanded, Power Query exposes the columns
    pulled from each Excel file and adds the detailed records to the data
    preview. Figure 12-15 illustrates the data preview for the final com-
    bined table.

16. **At this point, you can remove unneeded columns and then click the
    Close & Load command to output the combined table.**

As you look at the final combined view, don't lose track of the fact that this
relatively complex task was facilitated by a simple custom function. For all
the steps required to accomplish this task, you expend very little effort on
creating the code for the function. Power Query writes the code for the core
functionality, and you simply wrap that code into a function.

Figure 12-14:
Click the Custom column header to expand the table arrays.

Figure 12-15:
Power Query exposes the columns pulled from each Excel file and adds the detailed records to create the final combined view.

Folder Path	Custom.Region	Custom.Market	Custom.Branch_Num...	Custom.Product_Description
c:\Temp\	NORTH	NEWYORK	801211	Fleet Maintenance
c:\Temp\	NORTH	NEWYORK	804211	Facility Maintenance and Repair
c:\Temp\	SOUTH	NEWORLEANS	801607	Facility Maintenance and Repair
c:\Temp\	WEST	PHOENIX	201714	Fleet Maintenance
c:\Temp\	NORTH	NEWYORK	804211	Green Plants and Foliage Care
c:\Temp\	WEST	PHOENIX	201714	Facility Maintenance and Repair
c:\Temp\	SOUTH	NEWORLEANS	801607	Fleet Maintenance
c:\Temp\	SOUTH	NEWORLEANS	601310	Green Plants and Foliage Care
c:\Temp\	WEST	PHOENIX	201714	Green Plants and Foliage Care

The takeaway here is that you don't have to be an expert on Power Query's M language to pull together effective and useful custom functions. You can leverage the Query Editor to create some base code and then adjust from there.

Creating Parameter Queries

A parameter query is a kind of query that relies on one or more parameters to run. Although that sounds suspiciously like the custom functions covered earlier in this chapter (after all, they ran on parameters), there is a subtle difference.

A *parameter* query is one where *you* provide the parameters. So rather than have the parameters come from a predefined query, you enter the parameters. This comes in handy when creating interactive reporting for others to consume.

In this section, I walk you through creating your first parameter query.

Preparing for a parameter query

To create a proper parameter query, you first have to understand the parameters necessary to make your reporting interactive. The best way to gain this understanding is to explore the target data source.

In this scenario, I'll tell you how to build an interactive view of the top-grossing films for any given year and month. To accomplish this task, leverage the Box Office Mojo website. Box Office Mojo provides an array of box office reporting tools, including a monthly index of top-grossing films.

The URL for the monthly index includes a yr parameter and a month parameter. Enter this URL into any browser and you see a list of the top-grossing films of December 2015:

```
www.boxofficemojo.com/monthly/?yr=2015&month=12
```

A look at the website (shown in Figure 12-16) confirms that the URL opens a web page that contains the table you would expect to see: an index of movies for December 2015 box office. The parameters in the URL are working as expected.

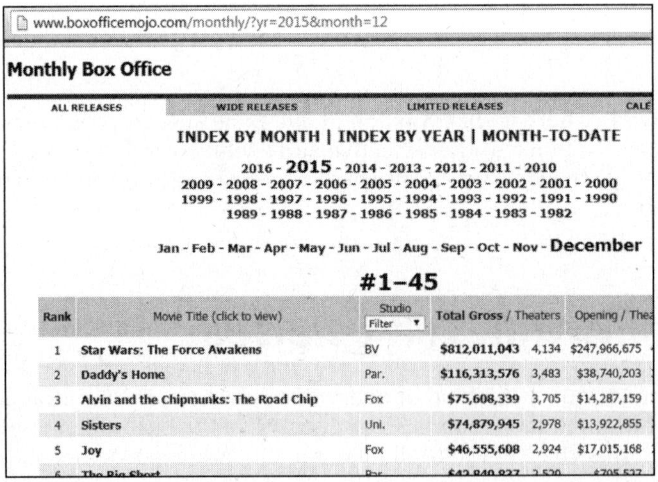

Figure 12-16: Confirming that the parameters in the URL actually work.

Now that you know the year and month number are the parameters, you can get started.

Creating the base query

The best place to start is to create the base query. The *base* query is essentially the one that will pull the data you're working toward. In this scenario, you create a query that pulls the table shown in Figure 12-16 from the Box Office Mojo website.

Follow these steps:

1. **Open a new Excel workbook, and then select Data ⇨ New Query ⇨ From Other Sources ⇨ From Web.**

2. **Enter a starting URL and then click OK. You can use the following URL:**

   www.boxofficemojo.com/monthly/?yr=2015&month=12

3. **Use the Navigator pane to select the correct web table, and then click the Edit button to open the Query Editor.**

4. **Use the Query Editor to rename columns and apply any transformations that are needed to clean the web data.**

   Figure 12-17 illustrates a clean table that makes up the base query.

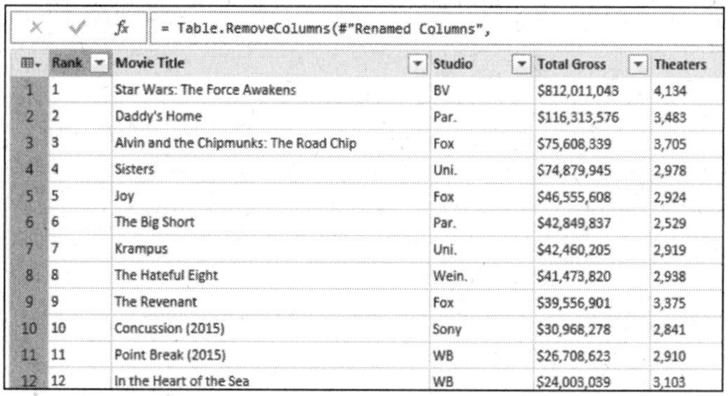

⊞▾	Rank ▾	Movie Title	▾	Studio ▾	Total Gross ▾	Theaters
1	1	Star Wars: The Force Awakens		BV	$812,011,043	4,134
2	2	Daddy's Home		Par.	$116,313,576	3,483
3	3	Alvin and the Chipmunks: The Road Chip		Fox	$75,608,339	3,705
4	4	Sisters		Uni.	$74,879,945	2,978
5	5	Joy		Fox	$46,555,608	2,924
6	6	The Big Short		Par.	$42,849,837	2,529
7	7	Krampus		Uni.	$42,460,205	2,919
8	8	The Hateful Eight		Wein.	$41,473,820	2,938
9	9	The Revenant		Fox	$39,556,901	3,375
10	10	Concussion (2015)		Sony	$30,968,278	2,841
11	11	Point Break (2015)		WB	$26,708,623	2,910
12	12	In the Heart of the Sea		WB	$24,003,039	3,103

fx `= Table.RemoveColumns(#"Renamed Columns",`

Figure 12-17: The clean base query.

5. **After all needed transformations are complete, open the Advanced Editor window by clicking the View tab and selecting the Advanced Editor command.**

6. **Wrap the entire block of code with function tags, specifying that this function requires two parameters: YearNum and MonthNum. Also replace the hard-coded year and month in the URL with each respective parameter.**

Here's the final syntax shown in Figure 12-18:

```
let TopMovies=(YearNum, MonthNum) =>
let
    Source = Web.Page(Web.Contents(
    "http://www.boxofficemojo.com/monthly/?yr=" &
    Number.ToText(YearNum) & "&month=" &
    Number.ToText(MonthNum))),

    Data0 = Source{0}[Data],

#"Renamed Columns" =

    Table.RenameColumns(Data0,{
    {"Movie Title (click to view)", "Movie Title"},
    {"Total Gross /Theaters", "Total Gross"},
    {"Total Gross /Theaters2", "Theaters"}}),

#"Removed Columns" =
    Table.RemoveColumns(#"Renamed Columns",
    {"Opening /Theaters",
    "Opening /Theaters2", "Open", "Close"})
in
    #"Removed Columns"
in
    TopMovies
```

Figure 12-18:
Wrapping
the starter
code with
function
tags and
specifying a
YearNum
parameter
and a
MonthNum
parameter.

```
let TopMovies=(YearNum, MonthNum) =>
let
    Source = Web.Page(Web.Contents(
    "http://www.boxofficemojo.com/monthly/?yr=" & Number.ToText(YearNum) & "&month=" & Number.ToText(MonthNum))),

    Data0 = Source{0}[Data],

#"Renamed Columns" =

    Table.RenameColumns(Data0,{
    {"Movie Title (click to view)", "Movie Title"},
    {"Total Gross /Theaters", "Total Gross"},
    {"Total Gross /Theaters2", "Theaters"}}),

#"Removed Columns" =
    Table.RemoveColumns(#"Renamed Columns",
    {"Opening /Theaters",
    "Opening /Theaters2", "Open", "Close"})
in
    #"Removed Columns"
in
    TopMovies
```

7. **Close the Advanced Editor.**

8. **In the Query Settings pane, change the name of the query in the Name input box. In this scenario, it's fnGetTopMovies.**

9. **Click the Home tab of the Query Editor and click the Close & Load button.**

You now have a fnGetTopMovies function, which can be used to pull web data from a custom function, and it's ready to be used on all files in the target folder.

Creating the parameter query

The final step is to create the parameter query. To do so, you need a simple table that will serve as the feeder for your dynamic parameters.

Staying in the same workbook where you created fnGetTopMovies, create a table similar to the one shown in Figure 12-19.

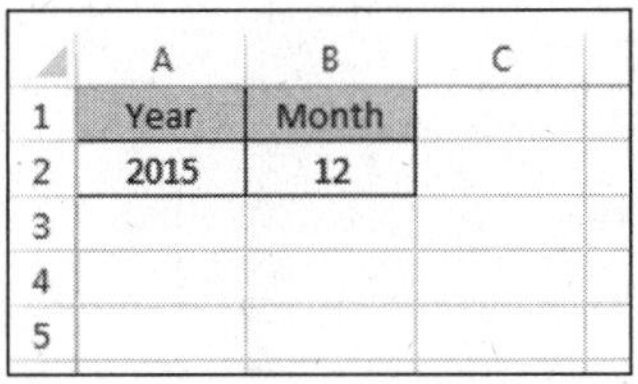

Figure 12-19: Create a simple parameter table.

From here, follow these steps:

1. **Place the cursor in the parameter table, and then select Data ⇨ New Query ⇨ From Table.**

   The Create Table dialog box opens.

2. **Click OK to continue.**

   The Query Editor opens with the parameter table.

3. **Click the Add Column tab, and then click the Add Custom Column command.**

4. **In the Add Custom Column dialog box, invoke the fnGetTopMovies function, passing the year and month fields as parameters (see Figure 12-20).**

Because you're mixing data from the web with data from Excel (though the parameter table can hardly be considered data), Power Query initiates a few data-privacy precautionary measures.

5. **Click Continue.**

The Privacy Levels dialog box opens, as shown in Figure 12-21.

6. **Select Public for both the Current Workbook option and the website. Click the Save button to confirm and save the privacy levels.**

Power Query, at this point, imports data from the website based on the year and month in the parameter table.

7. **The data imports as a table array, so click the green Table hyperlink.**

   Alternatively, you can click the Expand icon.

   Now that you're basically done, it's time to think about where the query should be loaded. If you simply click the Close & Load button, Power Query outputs the final parameter query in its own worksheet. However, it would be more practical to have the parameter table and query results on the same worksheet. This way, you can edit the parameters and see the results without having to flip between worksheets.

8. **Rather than click the Close & Load command button, click the drop-down arrow beneath the button (as shown in Figure 12-22) and select the Close & Load To option.**

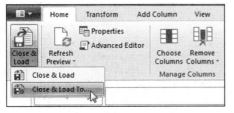

Figure 12-22: Selecting the Close & Load To option.

9. **In the Load To dialog box, choose the Existing Worksheet option, ensuring that you select a cell beneath the parameter table. (See Figure 12-23.)**

10. **Click the Load button to finalize the query (see Figure 12-23).**

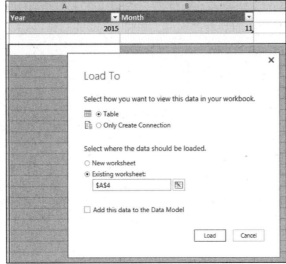

Figure 12-23: Choose to load the final query results under the parameters table.

Figure 12-24 illustrates the final parameter query. Take a moment to think about what's happening here. With this parameter query, you enter a year and a month and click Refresh (or press Ctrl+Alt+F5). Power Query then dynamically imports data back from the Internet based on the parameters you entered — all without your having to enter more than three lines of M language syntax. Truly amazing.

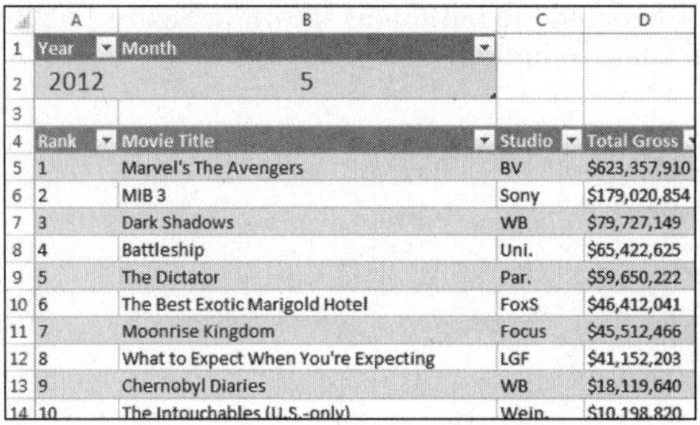

Figure 12-24:
The final parameter query provides an interactive mechanism to flexibly pull data based on dynamic parameters, all with virtually no coding.

	A	B	C	D
1	Year	Month		
2	2012	5		
3				
4	Rank	Movie Title	Studio	Total Gross
5	1	Marvel's The Avengers	BV	$623,357,910
6	2	MIB 3	Sony	$179,020,854
7	3	Dark Shadows	WB	$79,727,149
8	4	Battleship	Uni.	$65,422,625
9	5	The Dictator	Par.	$59,650,222
10	6	The Best Exotic Marigold Hotel	FoxS	$46,412,041
11	7	Moonrise Kingdom	Focus	$45,512,466
12	8	What to Expect When You're Expecting	LGF	$41,152,203
13	9	Chernobyl Diaries	WB	$18,119,640
14	10	The Intouchables (U.S.-only)	Wein.	$10,198,820

Part III
The Part of Tens

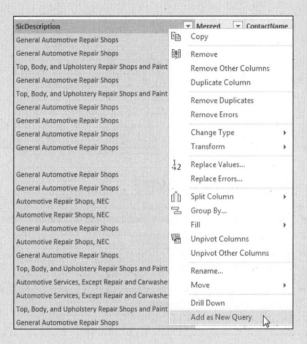

In this part . . .

- ✔ Explore some best practices that can help you avoid Power Pivot performance issues.

- ✔ Examine a few tips and tricks that can save you time when working with Power Query.

- ✔ Uncover Power Query options that disable annoying default settings and improve performance.

Chapter 13

Ten Ways to Improve Power Pivot Performance

*W*hen you publish Power Pivot reports to the web, you intend to give your audience the best experience possible. A large part of that experience is ensuring that performance is good.

The word *performance* (as it relates to applications and reporting) is typically synonymous with speed — or how quickly an application performs certain actions such as opening within the browser, running queries, or filtering.

Because Power Pivot inherently paves the way for large amounts of data with fairly liberal restrictions, it isn't uncommon to produce reporting solutions that work but are unbearably slow. And nothing will turn your intended audience away from your slick new reports faster than painfully sluggish performance.

This chapter offers ten actions you can take to optimize the performance of your Power Pivot reports.

Limit the Number of Rows and Columns in Your Data Model Tables

One huge influence on Power Pivot performance is the number of columns you bring, or *import,* into the data model. Every column you import is one more dimension that Power Pivot has to process when loading a workbook. Don't import extra columns "just in case" — if you're not certain you will use certain columns, just don't bring them in. These columns are easy enough to add later if you find that you need them.

More rows mean more data to load, more data to filter, and more data to calculate. Avoid selecting an entire table if you don't have to. Use a query or a view at the source database to filter for only the rows you need to import. After all, why import 400,000 rows of data when you can use a simple WHERE clause and import only 100,000?

Use Views Instead of Tables

Speaking of views, for best practice, use views whenever possible.

Though tables are more transparent than views — allowing you to see all the raw, unfiltered data — they come supplied with all available columns and rows, whether you need them or not. To keep your Power Pivot data model to a manageable size, you're often forced to take the extra step of explicitly filtering out the columns you don't need.

Views can not only provide cleaner, more user-friendly data but also help streamline your Power Pivot data model by limiting the amount of data you import.

Avoid Multi-Level Relationships

Both the number of relationships and the number of relationship layers have an impact on the performance of your Power Pivot reports. When building your model, follow best practice and have a single fact table containing primarily quantitative numerical data (facts) and dimension tables that relate to the facts directly. In the database world, this configuration is a *star schema,* as shown in Figure 13-1.

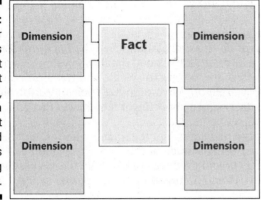

Figure 13-1:
A star
schema is
the most
efficient
data model,
with a
single fact
table and
dimensions
relating
directly to it.

Avoid building models where dimension tables relate to other dimension tables. Figure 13-2 illustrates this configuration, also known as a *snowflake schema*. This configuration forces Power Pivot to perform relationship lookups across several dimension levels, which can be particularly inefficient, depending on the volume of data in the model.

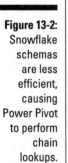 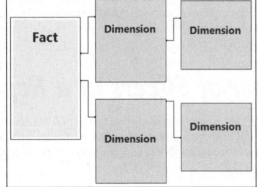

Figure 13-2:
Snowflake
schemas
are less
efficient,
causing
Power Pivot
to perform
chain
lookups.

Let the Back-End Database Servers Do the Crunching

Most Excel analysts who are new to Power Pivot tend to pull raw data directly from the tables on their external database servers. After the raw data is in Power Pivot, they build calculated columns and measures to transform and aggregate the data as needed. For example, users commonly pull revenue and cost data and then create a calculated column in Power Pivot to compute profit.

So why make Power Pivot do this calculation when the back-end server could have handled it? The reality is that back-end database systems such as SQL Server have the ability to shape, aggregate, clean, and transform data much more efficiently than Power Pivot. Why not utilize their powerful capabilities to massage and shape data before importing it into Power Pivot?

Rather than pull raw table data, consider leveraging queries, views, and stored procedures to perform as much of the data aggregation and crunching work as possible. This leveraging reduces the amount of processing that Power Pivot will have to do and naturally improves performance.

Beware of Columns with Non-Distinct Values

Columns that have a high number of unique values are particularly hard on Power Pivot performance. Columns such as Transaction ID, Order ID, and Invoice Number are often unnecessary in high-level Power Pivot reports and dashboards. So unless they are needed to establish relationships to other tables, leave them out of your model.

Limit the Number of Slicers in a Report

The slicer is one of the best new business intelligence (BI) features of Excel in recent years. Using slicers, you can provide your audience with an intuitive interface that allows for interactive filtering of your Excel reports and dashboards.

One of the more useful benefits of the slicer is that it responds to other slicers, providing a cascading filter effect. For example, Figure 13-3 illustrates not only that clicking on Midwest in the Region slicer filters the pivot table but that the Market slicer also responds, by highlighting the markets that belong to the Midwest region. Microsoft calls this behavior *cross-filtering*.

As useful as the slicer is, it is, unfortunately, extremely bad for Power Pivot performance. Every time a slicer is changed, Power Pivot must recalculate all values and measures in the pivot table. To do that, Power Pivot must evaluate every tile in the selected slicer and process the appropriate calculations based on the selection.

Ship Date	▼	Revenue		Region	🍾		Market	🍾
Jan		136,939		Canada			Chicago	
Feb		488,700						
Mar		223,268		Midwest			Kansas City	
Apr		319,675		North			Omaha	
May		645,427						
Jun		291,476		Northeast			Tulsa	
Jul		224,076		South			Baltimore	
Aug		522,541						
Sep		613,202		Southeast			Buffalo	
Oct		246,529		Southwest			California	
Nov		475,655						
Dec		557,068		West			Canada	
Grand Total		**4,744,556**						

Figure 13-3: Slicers work together to show relevant data items based on a selection.

Take this process a step further and imagine adding a second slicer: Because slicers cross-filter, each time you click one slicer, the other one changes also, so it's almost as though you clicked both of them. Power Pivot must now respond to both slicers, evaluating every tile in both slicers for each calculated measure in the pivot. Adding a second slicer effectively doubles the processing time. Add a third slicer, and you triple the processing time.

In short, a slicer is generally bad for Power Pivot performance. However, as mentioned at the beginning of this section, the functionality that the slicer brings to Excel BI solutions is too good to give up completely.

You can help to mitigate performance issues by limiting the number of slicers in your Power Pivot reports. Remove slicers one at a time, testing the performance of the Power Pivot report after each removal. You'll find that removing a single slicer is often enough to correct performance issues.

Remove slicers that have low click rates. Some slicers hold filter values that, frankly, may never be utilized by your audience. For example, if a slicer allows your audience to filter by the current year or by last year, and the last year view is not often called up, consider removing the slicer or using the Pivot Table Filter drop-down list instead.

Create Slicers Only on Dimension Fields

Slicers tied to columns that contain lots of unique values will often cause a larger performance hit than columns containing only a handful of values. If a slicer contains a large number of tiles, consider using a Pivot Table Filter drop-down list instead.

On a similar note, be sure to right-size column data types. A column with few distinct values is lighter than a column with a high number of distinct values. If you're storing the results of a calculation from a source database, reduce the number of digits (after the decimal) to be imported. This reduces the size of the dictionary and, possibly, the number of distinct values.

Disable the Cross-Filter Behavior for Certain Slicers

Disabling the cross-filter behavior of a slicer essentially prevents that slicer from changing selections when other slicers are clicked. This prevents the need for Power Pivot to evaluate the titles in the disabled slicer, thus reducing processing cycles. To disable the cross-filter behavior of a slicer, select Slicer Settings to open the Slicer Settings dialog box, shown in Figure 13-4. Then simply deselect the Visually Indicate Items with No Data option.

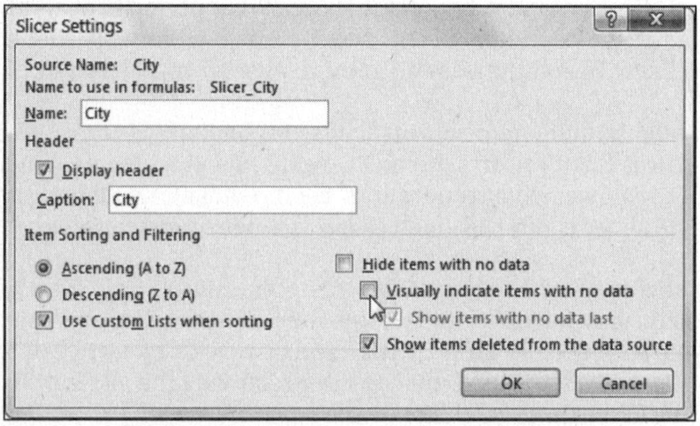

Figure 13-4: Deselecting the Visually Indicate Items option with No Data disables the slicer's cross-filter behavior.

Use Calculated Measures Instead of Calculated Columns

Use calculated measures instead of calculated columns, if possible. Calculated columns are stored as imported columns. Because calculated columns inherently interact with other columns in the model, they calculate every time the pivot table updates, whether they are being used or not. Calculated measures, on the other hand, calculate only at query time.

Calculated columns resemble regular columns in that they both take up space in the model. In contrast, calculated measures are calculated on the fly and do not take space.

Upgrade to 64-Bit Excel

The suggestion in this section is somewhat obvious. If you continue to run into performance issues with your Power Pivot reports, you can always buy a better PC — in this case, by upgrading to a 64-bit PC with 64-bit Excel installed.

Power Pivot loads the entire data model into RAM whenever you work with it. The more RAM your computer has, the fewer performance issues you see. The 64-bit version of Excel can access more of your PC's RAM, ensuring that it has the system resources needed to crunch through bigger data models. In fact, Microsoft recommends 64-bit Excel for anyone working with models made up of millions of rows.

But before you hurriedly start installing 64-bit Excel, you need to answer these questions:

- **Do you already have 64-bit Excel installed?** In Excel 2016 and 2013, choose File ⇨ Account ⇨ About Excel. A dialog box opens, specifying either 32-bit or 64-bit at the top. In Excel 2010, choose File ⇨ Help instead. The text About Excel pops up on the right side of the screen along with the version number and the 32-bit or 64-bit designation.

- **Are your data models large enough?** Unless you're working with large data models, the move to 64-bit may not produce a noticeable difference in your work. How large is large? A Power Pivot workbook with a file size upward of 40 megabytes is considered large. If your workbook is 50 or more megabytes, you would definitely benefit from an upgrade.

- **Do you have a 64-bit operating system installed on your PC?** The 64-bit version of Excel will not install on a 32-bit operating system. You can find out whether you're running a 64-bit operating system by searching for the text *My PC 64-bit or 32-bit* at your favorite search engine. You'll see loads of sites that can walk you through the steps to determine your version.

- **Will your other add-ins stop working?** If you're using other add-ins, be aware that some of them may not be compatible with 64-bit Excel. You wouldn't want to install 64-bit Excel just to find that your trusted add-ins no longer work. Contact your add-in providers to ensure that they are 64-bit compatible. By the way, this advice includes add-ins for all Office products — not just Excel. When you upgrade Excel to 64-bit, you also have to upgrade the entire Office suite.

Chapter 14

Ten Tips for Working with Power Query

*O*ver the past few years, Microsoft has added countless features to Power Query. It has truly become a rich tool set with multiple ways to perform virtually any action you can think of. This growth in functionality has paved the way to a good number of tips and tricks that can help you work more efficiently with your Power Query models.

This chapter presents ten of the more useful tips and tricks you can leverage to get the most out of Power Query.

Getting Quick Information from the Workbook Queries Pane

All the Power Query queries that live in a particular workbook can be views in the Workbook Queries pane. Choose Data ➪ Show Queries to activate the Workbook Queries pane.

In this pane, you can see some quick information about a query by simply hovering the cursor over it. You can see the data source for the query, the last time the query was refreshed, and a sneak peek of the data within the query. You can even click on column hyperlinks to peek at a particular column (see Figure 14-1).

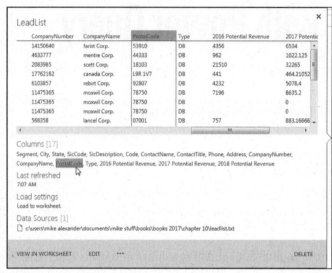

Figure 14-1: Hover the cursor over a query to get quick information, including sneak peeks of column contents.

Organizing Queries in Groups

As you add queries to your workbook, your Workbook Queries pane may start to feel cluttered and disorganized. Do yourself a favor and organize your queries into groups.

Figure 14-2 illustrates the kinds of groups you can create. You can create a group only for custom functions or a group for queries sourced from external databases. You could even create a group where you store small reference tables. Each group is collapsible, so you can neatly pack away queries that you aren't working with.

You can create a group by right-clicking a query in the Workbook Queries pane and selecting Move To Group ➪ New Group. As you can see in Figure 14-3, if you've already created a few groups, you also have the option of moving the selected query to an existing group.

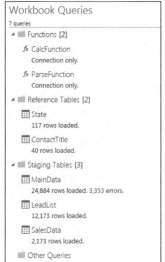

Figure 14-2:
Queries can be orga-
nized into
groups.

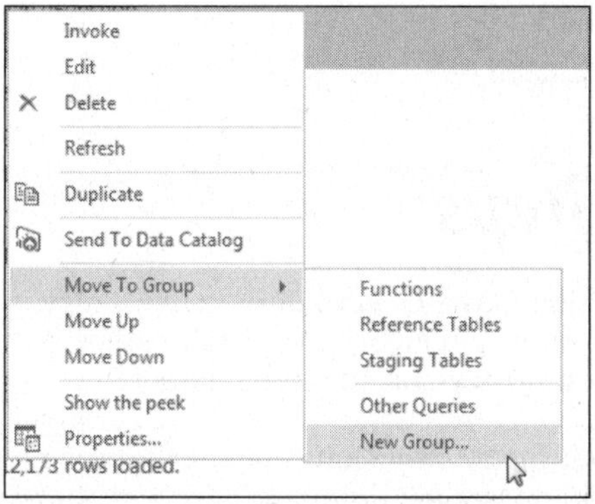

Figure 14-3:
Creating a
new group.

Selecting Columns in Queries Faster

When dealing with a large table with dozens of columns in the Query Editor, it can be a pain to find and select the right columns to work with. You can avoid all that scrolling back and forth by choosing the Choose Columns command on the Home tab.

The dialog box shown in Figure 14-4 opens, showing you all available columns (including custom columns you may have added). You can easily find and select the columns you need.

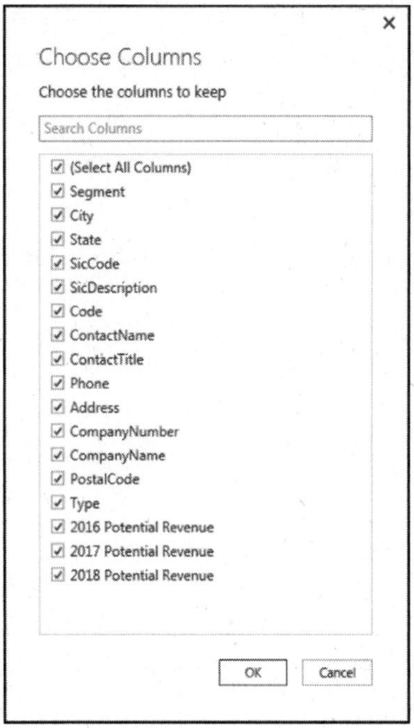

**× **

Choose Columns

Choose the columns to keep

Search Columns

☑ (Select All Columns)
☑ Segment
☑ City
☑ State
☑ SicCode
☑ SicDescription
☑ Code
☑ ContactName
☑ ContactTitle
☑ Phone
☑ Address
☑ CompanyNumber
☑ CompanyName
☑ PostalCode
☑ Type
☑ 2016 Potential Revenue
☑ 2017 Potential Revenue
☑ 2018 Potential Revenue

OK   Cancel

Figure 14-4:
Use the
Choose
Columns
command to
find and
select col-
umns faster.

Renaming Query Steps

Every time you apply an action in the Query Editor, a new entry is made in the Query Settings pane, as shown in Figure 14-5. Query steps serve as a kind of audit trail for all the actions you've taken on the data.

Why not make sure that your query steps have names that aren't generic names, like Uppercased Text or Merged Columns. Sure, you know what each step does now, but what about in six months? Why not take the time to add some clarity on what each step is doing?

You can rename your steps by right-clicking each step and selecting Rename.

Figure 14-6 shows the same steps renamed, to provide a bit more insight about the purpose of each one.

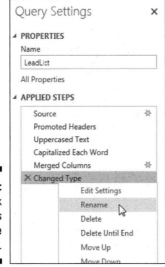

Figure 14-5:
Right-click
query steps
to rename
them.

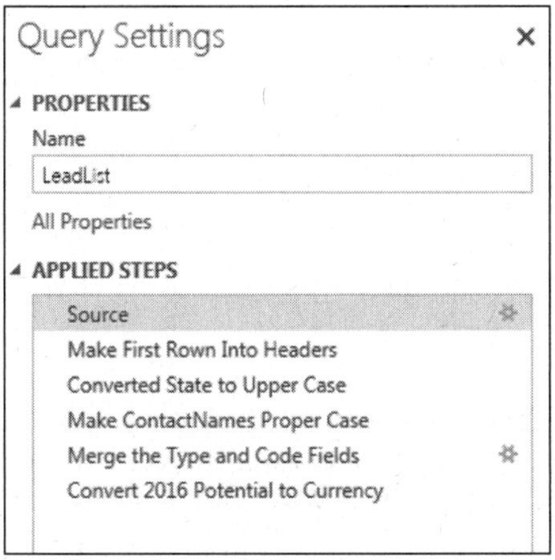

Figure 14-6:
Add clarity
by adding
friendly
names to
query steps.

Quickly Creating Reference Tables

A handful of columns in a dataset always make for fantastic reference tables. For instance, if your dataset contains a column with a list of product categories, it would be useful to create a reference table of all the unique values in that column.

Reference tables are often used to map data, feed menu selectors, serve as lookup values, and much more.

While in the Query Editor, you can right-click the column from which you want to create a reference table and then select Add as New Query, as shown in Figure 14-7.

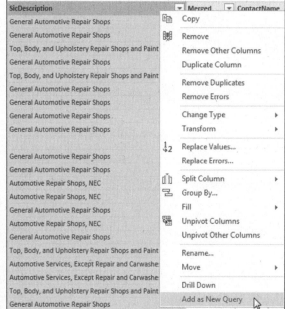

Figure 14-7:
Create a
new query
from an
existing
column.

A new query is created, using the table you just pulled from as the source. The Query Editor jumps into action, showing only the column you selected. From here, you can use the Query Editor to clean up duplicates or remove blanks, for example.

Copying Queries to Save Time

It's always smart to reuse work wherever you can. Why reinvent the wheel when your Workbook Queries pane is full of wheels you've already created?

Save time by duplicating the queries in your workbook. To do so, activate the Workbook Queries pane, right-click on the query you want to copy, and then select Duplicate. As you can see in Figure 14-8, you can also duplicate custom functions.

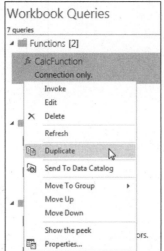

Figure 14-8: Duplicating a query.

Setting a Default Load Behavior

If you're working heavily with Power Pivot and with Power Query, chances are good that you load your Power Query queries to the Internal Data Model a majority of the time.

If you're one of those analysts who always loads to the Data Model, you can tweak the Power Query options to automatically load to the Data Model.

Choose Data ⇨ New Query ⇨ Query Options to open the dialog box shown in Figure 14-9. Select Data Load in the Global section, and then choose to specify a custom default load setting. This enables the options to load to the worksheet or Data Model by default.

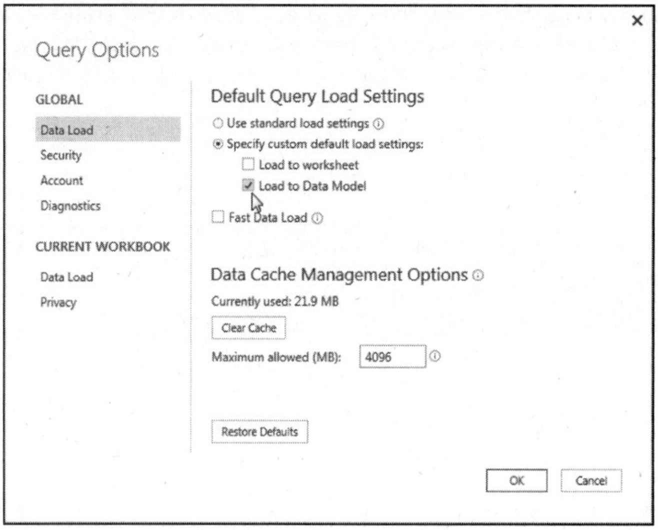

Figure 14-9:
Use the
Global Data
Load
options
to set a
default load
behavior.

Preventing Automatic Data Type Changes

One of the more recent additions to Power Query is the ability to automatically detect data types and to proactively change data types. This type detection is most often applied when new data is introduced to the query.

For instance, Figure 14-10 shows the query steps after importing a text file. Note the Changed Type step, which was automatically performed by Power Query as part of its type detection feature.

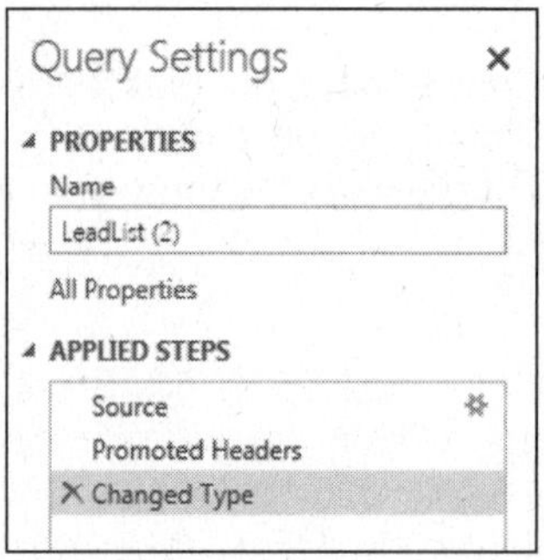

Figure 14-10:
Power
Query auto-
matically
adds a step
to change
data types
when data
is imported.

Although Power Query does a decent job at guessing what data types should be used, applied data type changes can sometimes cause unexpected issues.

Some veterans of Power Query, frankly, find the type detection feature annoying. If data types need to be changed, *they* want to be the ones to make that determination.

If you'd rather handle data type changes without help from Power Query's type detection feature, you can turn it off.

Choose Data⇨New Query⇨Query Options to open the dialog box shown in Figure 14-11. Select Data Load in the Current Workbook section, and then deselect the option to automatically detect column types and headers for unstructured sources.

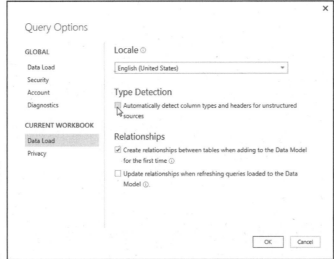

Figure 14-11: Disabling the type detection feature.

Disabling Privacy Settings to Improve Performance

The privacy-level settings in Power Pivot (explored in Chapter 11) are designed to protect organizational data as it gets combined with other sources. When you create a query that uses an external data source with an internal data source, Power Query stops the show to ask how you want to categorize the data privacy levels of each data source.

For a majority of analysts, who deal solely with organizational data, the privacy-level settings do little more than slow down queries and cause confusion.

Fortunately, you have the option to ignore privacy levels.

Choose Data ⇨ New Query ⇨ Query Options to open the dialog box shown in Figure 14-12. Select Privacy in the Current Workbook section, and then choose the option to ignore privacy levels.

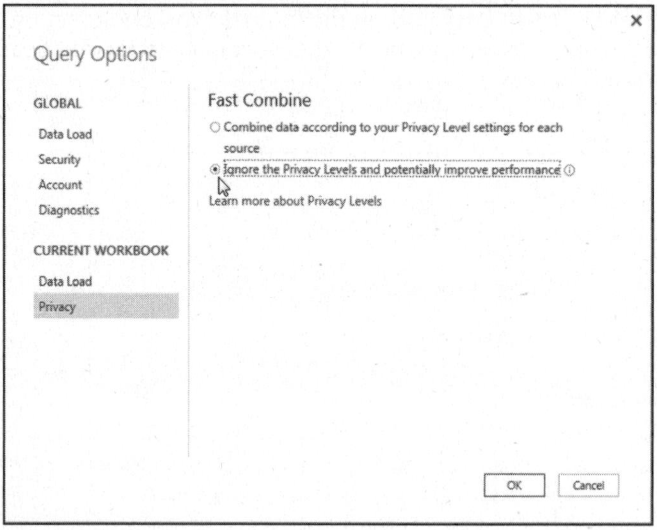

Figure 14-12:
Disabling
the privacy-
level
settings.

Disabling Relationship Detection

When you're building a query and choosing Load to Data Model as the output, Power Query, by default, attempts to detect relationships between queries and creates those relationships within the Internal Data Model. The relationships between queries are primarily driven by the defined query steps. For instance, if you were to merge two queries and then load the result into the Data Model, a relationship would be automatically created.

In larger data models with a dozen or so tables, Power Query's relationship detection can affect performance and increase the time it takes to load the Data Model.

You can avoid this hassle and even gain a performance boost by disabling relationship detection.

Choose Data ⇨ New Query ⇨ Query Options to open the dialog box shown in Figure 14-13. Select Data Load in the Current Workbook section, and then deselect the option to create relationships when adding loading to the Data Model.

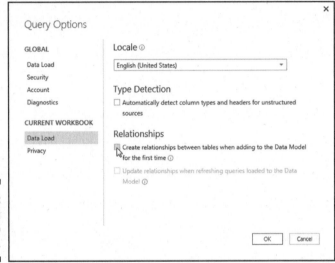

Figure 14-13:
Disabling relationship detection.

Index

About the Author

Michael Alexander is a Microsoft Certified Application Developer (MCAD) with over 15 years experience in consulting and developing office solutions. He is the author of over a dozen books on business analysis using Microsoft Excel and Access. He has been named Microsoft Excel MVP for his contributions to the Excel community. Visit Michael at `DataPigTechnologies.com`, where he offers free Excel and Access training.

Dedication

To my family.

Author's Acknowledgments

My deepest thanks go to the professionals at John Wiley & Sons for all the hours of work put into bringing this book to life. Thanks also to Mike Talley for suggesting numerous improvements to the examples and text in this book. Finally, a special thank-you goes out to Mary, for putting up with all the time I spent locked away on this project.

Publisher's Acknowledgments

Acquisitions Editor: Katie Mohr

Project Editor: Kim Darosett

Technical Editor: Mike Talley

Editorial Assistant: Matt Lowe

Sr. Editorial Assistant: Cherie Case

Production Editor: Antony Sami

Front Cover Image: ©hywards/Shutterstock

Apple & Mac

iPad For Dummies,
6th Edition
978-1-118-72306-7

iPhone For Dummies,
7th Edition
978-1-118-69083-3

Macs All-in-One
For Dummies, 4th Edition
978-1-118-82210-4

OS X Mavericks
For Dummies
978-1-118-69188-5

Blogging & Social Media

Facebook For Dummies,
5th Edition
978-1-118-63312-0

Social Media Engagement
For Dummies
978-1-118-53019-1

WordPress For Dummies,
6th Edition
978-1-118-79161-5

Business

Stock Investing
For Dummies, 4th Edition
978-1-118-37678-2

Investing For Dummies,
6th Edition
978-0-470-90545-6

Personal Finance
For Dummies, 7th Edition
978-1-118-11785-9

QuickBooks 2014
For Dummies
978-1-118-72005-9

Small Business Marketing
Kit For Dummies,
3rd Edition
978-1-118-31183-7

Careers

Job Interviews
For Dummies, 4th Edition
978-1-118-11290-8

Job Searching with Social
Media For Dummies,
2nd Edition
978-1-118-67856-5

Personal Branding
For Dummies
978-1-118-11792-7

Resumes For Dummies,
6th Edition
978-0-470-87361-8

Starting an Etsy Business
For Dummies, 2nd Edition
978-1-118-59024-9

Diet & Nutrition

Belly Fat Diet For Dummies
978-1-118-34585-6

Mediterranean Diet
For Dummies
978-1-118-71525-3

Nutrition For Dummies,
5th Edition
978-0-470-93231-5

Digital Photography

Digital SLR Photography
All-in-One For Dummies,
2nd Edition
978-1-118-59082-9

Digital SLR Video &
Filmmaking For Dummies
978-1-118-36598-4

Photoshop Elements 12
For Dummies
978-1-118-72714-0

Gardening

Herb Gardening
For Dummies, 2nd Edition
978-0-470-61778-6

Gardening with Free-Range
Chickens For Dummies
978-1-118-54754-0

Health

Boosting Your Immunity
For Dummies
978-1-118-40200-9

Diabetes For Dummies,
4th Edition
978-1-118-29447-5

Living Paleo For Dummies
978-1-118-29405-5

Big Data

Big Data For Dummies
978-1-118-50422-2

Data Visualization
For Dummies
978-1-118-50289-1

Hadoop For Dummies
978-1-118-60755-8

Language &
Foreign Language

500 Spanish Verbs
For Dummies
978-1-118-02382-2

English Grammar
For Dummies, 2nd Edition
978-0-470-54664-2

French All-in-One
For Dummies
978-1-118-22815-9

German Essentials
For Dummies
978-1-118-18422-6

Italian For Dummies,
2nd Edition
978-1-118-00465-4

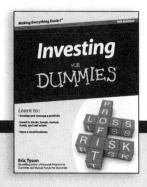
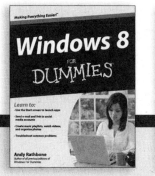

Math & Science

Algebra I For Dummies,
2nd Edition
978-0-470-55964-2

Anatomy and Physiology
For Dummies, 2nd Edition
978-0-470-92326-9

Astronomy For Dummies,
3rd Edition
978-1-118-37697-3

Biology For Dummies,
2nd Edition
978-0-470-59875-7

Chemistry For Dummies,
2nd Edition
978-1-118-00730-3

1001 Algebra II Practice
Problems For Dummies
978-1-118-44662-1

Microsoft Office

Excel 2013 For Dummies
978-1-118-51012-4

Office 2013 All-in-One
For Dummies
978-1-118-51636-2

PowerPoint 2013
For Dummies
978-1-118-50253-2

Word 2013 For Dummies
978-1-118-49123-2

Music

Blues Harmonica
For Dummies
978-1-118-25269-7

Guitar For Dummies,
3rd Edition
978-1-118-11554-1

iPod & iTunes
For Dummies, 10th Edition
978-1-118-50864-0

Programming

Beginning Programming
with C For Dummies
978-1-118-73763-7

Excel VBA Programming
For Dummies, 3rd Edition
978-1-118-49037-2

Java For Dummies,
6th Edition
978-1-118-40780-6

Religion & Inspiration

The Bible For Dummies
978-0-7645-5296-0

Buddhism For Dummies,
2nd Edition
978-1-118-02379-2

Catholicism For Dummies,
2nd Edition
978-1-118-07778-8

Self-Help & Relationships

Beating Sugar Addiction
For Dummies
978-1-118-54645-1

Meditation For Dummies,
3rd Edition
978-1-118-29144-3

Seniors

Laptops For Seniors
For Dummies, 3rd Edition
978-1-118-71105-7

Computers For Seniors
For Dummies, 3rd Edition
978-1-118-11553-4

iPad For Seniors
For Dummies, 6th Edition
978-1-118-72826-0

Social Security
For Dummies
978-1-118-20573-0

Smartphones & Tablets

Android Phones
For Dummies, 2nd Edition
978-1-118-72030-1

Nexus Tablets
For Dummies
978-1-118-77243-0

Samsung Galaxy S 4
For Dummies
978-1-118-64222-1

Samsung Galaxy Tabs
For Dummies
978-1-118-77294-2

Test Prep

ACT For Dummies,
5th Edition
978-1-118-01259-8

ASVAB For Dummies,
3rd Edition
978-0-470-63760-9

GRE For Dummies,
7th Edition
978-0-470-88921-3

Officer Candidate Tests
For Dummies
978-0-470-59876-4

Physician's Assistant Exam
For Dummies
978-1-118-11556-5

Series 7 Exam For Dummies
978-0-470-09932-2

Windows 8

Windows 8.1 All-in-One
For Dummies
978-1-118-82087-2

Windows 8.1 For Dummies
978-1-118-82121-3

Windows 8.1 For Dummies,
Book + DVD Bundle
978-1-118-82107-7

e Available in print and e-book formats.

Take Dummies with you everywhere you go!

Whether you are excited about e-books, want more from the web, must have your mobile apps, or are swept up in social media, Dummies makes everything easier.

Leverage the Power

For Dummies is the global leader in the reference category and one of the most trusted and highly regarded brands in the world. No longer just focused on books, customers now have access to the For Dummies content they need in the format they want. Let us help you develop a solution that will fit your brand and help you connect with your customers.

Advertising & Sponsorships

Connect with an engaged audience on a powerful multimedia site, and position your message alongside expert how-to content.

Targeted ads • Video • Email marketing • Microsites • Sweepstakes sponsorship

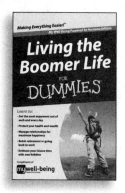

Dummies products make life easier!

- DIY
- Consumer Electronics
- Crafts
- Software
- Cookware
- Hobbies
- Videos
- Music
- Games
- and More!

For more information, go to **Dummies.com** and search the store by category.

For Dummies is a registered trademark of John Wiley & Sons, Inc.

FOR
DUMMIES

A Wiley Bran